# The
# Confident
# Decision
# Maker

# ALSO BY ROGER DAWSON

### BOOKS

*You Can Get Anything You Want—*
*   The Secrets of Power Negotiation*
*Secrets of Power Persuasion*

### AUDIOCASSETTE PROGRAMS

*Secrets of Power Persuasion*
*Secrets of Power Negotiating*
*Secrets of Power Performance*
*Confident Decision Making*
*Beyond Goals*

### VIDEO TRAINING PROGRAMS

*Guide to Everyday Negotiating*
*Guide to Business Negotiating*

# The
# Confident
# Decision
# Maker

How to Make the Right Business
and Personal Decisions Every Time

# Roger Dawson

William Morrow and Company, Inc.
New York

It is the policy of William Morrow and Company, Inc., and its imprints and affiliates, recognizing the importance of preserving what has been written, to print the books we publish on acid-free paper, and we exert our best efforts to that end.

Library of Congress Cataloging-in-Publication Data

Dawson, Roger.
    The confident decision maker : how to make the right business and
personal decisions every time / Roger Dawson.
        p.   cm.
    ISBN 0-688-11564-0
    1. Decision-making—United States.   I. Title.
HD30.23.D373   1993
658.4'03—dc20                                            92-21364
                                                              CIP

Printed in the United States of America

First Edition

1   2   3   4   5   6   7   8   9   10

BOOK DESIGN BY BARBARA COHEN

*Dedicated to:*

Goody. Marrying you was the smartest decision I ever made.

Julia, Dwight, and John. Thanks for believing in me.

Mike Willbond and Jill Schacter. Who first approached me about this project.

Sue Telingator. Who worked so hard and added so much.

# CONTENTS

# The
# Confident
# Decision
# Maker

# CHAPTER ONE

# The Qualities of a Good Decision Maker

James Michael Goldsmith, a millionaire living in Paris in the late 1950s, had everything going for him—he was the head of a successful pharmaceuticals company, Laboratoires Cassene, which in the three years since its inception had become one of France's greatest success stories; he had eloped with the beautiful heiress to a $75 million fortune; and he was only twenty-four years old. A romance novelist couldn't have dreamed of a more amazing character.

But on the morning of July 10, 1957, everything was about to change. Because of some tough and extraordinary decisions James Goldsmith had made, he was on the brink of financial and personal ruin. And without a stroke of luck, coincidence, and some fast thinking, Goldsmith might have been just another go-getter who burned out too fast, too young.

From the time Goldsmith started his company, it expanded at an enormously rapid pace. He bought the rights to sell American pharmaceutical products in France. This was a smart decision—his business grew, and soon he was grossing nearly $3 million a year. Coasting on his good fortune, he commissioned a new property to be built for warehousing pharmaceuticals and re-searching new drugs. Yet, as with many young entrepreneurs who run on the adrenaline of their newfound success, his dreams had grown larger than his bank account.

By the spring of 1957, sales had plummeted. Burdened with the financial and personal pressures of his situation, Goldsmith made a deal with two Italian backers who agreed to buy a 50 percent share of the company. But after three weeks, the backers changed their minds and asked for an 80 percent share for the same money. Goldsmith was dumbfounded. The prospect of giving over that much control of a company he had personally founded was too upsetting. He made a decision based on principle and an enormous amount of confidence—the same confidence that had made him successful in the first place. He refused the deal.

It took a lot of courage for Goldsmith to make his decision. Unfortunately, it seemed the consequences were dismal. By the first week in July, bankruptcy was staring the twenty-four-year-old boy wonder in the face. On the last possible day before his financial ruin, when all his creditors would find out that he couldn't possibly pay them, James Goldsmith went to the corner to buy a newspaper. He expected the headlines to report the demise of Laboratoires Cassene. Instead, they headlined a bank strike that would cripple all of France for at least the next week. It was a dramatic reprieve for Goldsmith. His creditors couldn't collect because the banks were closed; it was all the time this fast-thinker needed to turn his luck around.

The very next morning he was on the phone with his competition, Laboratoires Roussel. By the end of the month, he had managed to sell practically everything, with the exception of the royalties to one pharmaceutical product from which he could support his family. He made over $250,000 (a substantial sum in the 1950s) from the sale and spent the next two months in Spain, recuperating.

Today, young Jimmy Goldsmith is Sir James Goldsmith, the billionaire owner of a huge conglomerate and a master decision maker who has continually relied on his intuitive ability—for better or for worse.

## Decisions Are the Building Blocks of Life.

How important are the decisions we make? As you can see from the story of James Goldsmith, decisions have the power to change your life forever. Some decisions are good, some brilliant, some bad, and some just plain disastrous. Of course, we're conscious of the major decisions we make in our lives because they cause us the most stress. But the major decisions aren't the only ones that affect our future. We make decisions a hundred times a day, and nothing affects our lives more than our ability to make the right decisions. All that you have achieved and all that you have failed to accomplish can be traced to the decisions you've made. More important, all that lies ahead of you—all your hopes, dreams, and goals—depend on your ability to make wise decisions.

Yet the strange thing is, nobody seems to know how to make the best decisions. In my career as a full-time speaker, I travel ten months a year around the country, conducting seminars for corporations and associations. Whenever my schedule permits, I like to have dinner the night before my seminar with the president of the company I'll be addressing, or the top performer in an association, and pick his brains about what made him so successful. As I became more immersed in the topic of decision making, I started focusing my questions on how these successful people made the right decisions. What process did they use? Did they incorporate the opinions of others in their company?

What I found was absolutely fascinating. Almost nobody knows how he or she makes decisions. I spoke with people who built empires and people who dominated their industry. If their market penetration got any better, they'd be a monopoly. These are people who commit $10 million to a project without losing a moment's sleep. Yet in reply to my questions, they just stammered and stuttered. "We don't have a way we make decisions," they'd say. "Something comes up, we kick it around, and if it feels right and we can afford it, we make a move." Isn't that astounding? I wondered how much better they could be at what they do if they would just get a little bit better at decision making.

How's *your* decision-making track record? If you don't think it's very good, you're not alone. A survey by the American Management Association determined that businesspeople only make the right decision 50 percent of the time. Doesn't that say something about the strength of our economy? Businesses that can remain successful even though half the time they are making the wrong decisions are especially impressive. But to me, making the right decision only half of the time is a cop-out. It brings down the acceptable standard of performance in industry.

## Separating the Decision from the Decision-Making Process

There's a better way to make decisions, and in the next few chapters I'm going to show you how you can consistently make the smartest decisions possible. The starting point is to change the way you think about decision making. To become a better decision maker, you have to stop focusing on the decision itself and concentrate on the decision-making process. Once you rely on the process, you will have the confidence that you're making the best choice every time.

For example, consider the following three scenarios. All three concern people making personal decisions that could change the direction of their lives. All three were at a loss as to how to make the best decision for themselves. In the first instance, a man from Italy wrote me that he wanted to move to California. He had a business opportunity waiting there and felt he could be very successful. However, it would mean leaving his wife and two young daughters behind for at least five years. Should he go?

In another situation, a woman phoned me from San Francisco to tell me that her husband transferred to San Diego. He'd be there for at least a year and possibly longer. Then they would promote him again and probably transfer him back to the head office in the San Francisco Bay area. She couldn't decide whether to go through the trauma of selling their home and moving to San Diego, or stay and wait for him to come back. Could I help her choose?

In the third case, a young man approached me at a seminar. He said he and a business acquaintance wanted to start their own printing business, but he hadn't known the man very long and wasn't sure if he trusted him. He wanted to know how to assess such a decision. Should he trust this man?

How would you have advised these people? When I looked at their situations more carefully, I realized that in each scenario, an important decision-making technique was necessary to make the best possible choice. In the instance of the man from Italy who wanted to move to California, he needed the skill to categorize his decision correctly. Instead of making it an either/or proposition, he needed to look for deeper answers that involved some creative thinking. I told him that he'd be crazy to leave his family for five years. He'd miss the chance of seeing his two young daughters grow up and mature into young women. Instead of worrying about whether he should or shouldn't leave his family behind, I told him to concentrate on figuring out a way to move to California and bring his family with him.

As for the dilemma of the woman from San Francisco, I simply told her to take the next plane to San Diego if she cared anything about her marriage. She wasn't thinking through the consequences of her actions. If she let her husband play bachelor for a whole year, there was a chance it could destroy their marriage. Using logical decision-making techniques would have shown her that she had everything to lose and nothing to gain.

Finally, concerning the young man at the seminar who wanted to know if he should go into business with an acquaintance, I told him that going into business for himself was a great idea if he had a burning desire to do it, but not with this person. His problem was that he had clouded two decisions into one decision. Being self-employed and creating something from the ground up can be extremely fulfilling, but if his instincts were telling him that his acquaintance couldn't be trusted, he should listen to those doubts. When he found the right person, I told him, nothing would hold him back, and he probably wouldn't ask a complete stranger for advice.

## The Consequences of Decision Making

In each of these instances, you can see how the inability to make decisions leads us to a standstill. It impedes our faculty to think clearly and to understand our true feelings. And most of all, it frustrates our capacity to better understand ourselves. An important thing happens every time we make a decision—we come closer to knowing who we really are. That's because we pour our ethics, priorities, and values into every decision. We become, in essence, the sum total of all the decisions we make in our life. And our decisions can have an effect on the people around us, as well. As an employer or as a parent, you mold the people around you. The decisions you make affect everyone with whom you come in contact.

Think of the three most critical decisions you've made in your life. How would your life have been different if you'd gone in a different direction? What if you'd decided to go into the work force after high school instead of going to college? What if you'd married the first person with whom you were infatuated? What if you'd accepted that job offer you turned down? How might your life have played out differently if you had chosen the road not taken?

Of course, looking back on your choices, you might very easily defend every decision you've made. Then again, you might decide there was an opportunity you'd missed along the way. Maybe you've made the right decisions career-wise and fallen short in your personal life. Or maybe you said "no" to that business opportunity that might have led you to another opportunity of which you've always dreamed.

## Assessing Your Decision-Making Ability

Below is a list of some of the different decisions we come up against on a daily basis. Rate them on a scale of 1 to 10, with 10 being the highest, as to how well you are able to make a good decision in each of these areas of your life.

| Type of Decision | Score |
|---|---|
| Business decision making | |
| Decisions involving how to spend money | |
| Decisions involving personal relationships | |
| Decisions about career moves | |
| Decisions involving your children | |
| Investment decisions | |
| Decisions involving your parents | |
| **Total Score** | |

Keep your answers to this self-exam handy. At the end of this book, take this test again. After learning the various techniques I'll explain to you in the next few chapters, you will be surprised at how much your score has improved.

## Sometimes We Make Obvious Decision Errors.

Do you ever wonder what went wrong when businesses make decisions anybody could foresee as disastrous? There's a restaurant near me that has opened and closed under six different owners in the last two years. I'm so sympathetic, I've tried to get there at least once before it goes under, even if it's only for lunch. But the last time they had a grand opening, I was on a speaking tour; and the lease sign was up before I got back. The simplest research would have told them it was a poor location for a restaurant. Most of the people in the area are retired, and restaurants always do better with younger people who have highly disposable incomes. Also, it's located on a divided street that requires a tricky U-turn at a busy intersection to get to its parking lot.

Or consider the director's blunder during the television broadcast of the football game between the New York Jets and the Oakland Raiders. With two minutes to go and the Jets ahead 32 to 29, the network switched to its planned broadcast of the movie *Heidi*. In the last two minutes, Oakland scored twice and won the game 43 to 32. There are station managers all over the country who developed a permanent twitch over that one. How could anyone make such a bad mistake?

Or take a look at the city of Los Angeles. When I first visited L.A. in 1960, the twenty-eight-story city hall building was three times taller than the next highest one in town. Today, there are twenty-three taller ones. In the last five years alone, the entire skyline of Los Angeles has changed. There's been an explosion of huge high-rise buildings. Developers created thousands and thousands of new office spaces without giving any thought to how people were going to get to work. There isn't a single new freeway or public-transportation system to get people there. In the last two years, the average commute time in Los Angeles has gone from forty-five minutes to seventy-five minutes each way. How on earth could the city have approved those new buildings without giving any thought to how people were going to get to work?

## Good Timing Is Characteristic of Confident Decision Makers.

Although there's no one right way to make a decision, there are some characteristics that all confident decision makers share. First, they have an uncanny sense of timing. They know when to make the decision. Last spring, I had dinner in New England with a very successful man. He'd really lived the American dream. Not knowing what he was going to do when he got out of the service, he borrowed five hundred dollars from his grandmother and went into the business of repairing copier machines. He expanded this to include buying broken-down copy machines, fixing them, and then reselling them in his little store.

In the mid 1960s, Canon, a Japanese company, had made a decision to go into the copy-machine business. It wanted to see if it could take away a chunk of business from Xerox, which then had a virtual stranglehold on the market. Canon needed distributors and approached my dinner companion about becoming a distributor for its products in New England. He jumped at the opportunity and eventually became the largest Canon copier distributor in the nation, and by far the largest retailer of copy machines anywhere in New England. He sold his company to a conglomerate for a huge amount of money and invested the money in a series of auto dealerships. He had flown to our meeting in his private six-passenger helicopter, from his 130-foot yacht in Boston Harbor. Would you like to know what he told me about being successful in America?

He said, "Roger, it's true. I was in the right place at the right time, and that's very important. Yet there's something even more important than that: It's *knowing* you're in the right place at the right time. Most people," he told me, "make a decision based on how they feel about it. Then, later, they either say to themselves, Well, wasn't that great, I was in the right place at the right time, or they decide not to go ahead. If they don't seize the opportunity, then later they might say, I wish I'd known then what I know now. I was in the right place at the right time, and I didn't realize it. The key to success is knowing that you're in the right place at the right time."

Confident Decision Makers know how to make decisions effectively. So they're much better at knowing when they're in the right place at the right time. Whether you feel compelled to make a decision or decide to hold back on an opportunity depends on your personality style. For example, if you are an impulsive, take-charge type of person, you probably make decisions quickly—very often too quickly. I'll teach you why, in some instances, making a decision quickly can be a big mistake. That may not sound like good news to you, but like a golfer learning to slow down his backswing, you'll see a dramatic improvement in your score.

If you're a more analytical, laid-back kind of person, you probably make decisions too slowly. I'll give you a process that'll take you right to the heart of the problem quickly. You'll not only be making the right decision faster, but you'll also be removing most of the stress you feel when you're forced to decide.

# Delegating: The Art of Training People to Make Good Decisions

The second characteristic common to Confident Decision Makers is the courage to delegate. They know when to let someone else make the decision. You can't delegate power unless you know how to train your people to make good decisions. Many managers can make good decisions, but they do it so instinctively, they don't know how they're doing it.

In this book, you'll learn not only how to be a Confident Decision Maker, but also how to train your people to make decisions with confidence. When you have greater confidence in their ability to make decisions, it'll be much easier to delegate decisions down to the lowest effective level. Empowerment is an industry buzzword, describing the policy of letting the person closest to the problem make the decision. If you have a good system for making decisions, you can train your people to make intelligent choices, rather than always having them come to you. That's just smart business.

# Accepting Ambiguity Is an Important Part of Decision Making.

The third characteristic a confident decision maker possesses is the ability to live with ambiguity. You might not see the importance of this until I describe the worst decision maker in the world. Think for a moment of people you know who have a very analytical personality style. They've always lived in a very rigid world. All their life, everything's been okay as long as it has been buttoned down, nailed down, and in its proper place. It's when things start to move around and get sloppy—from the viewpoint of analytical people—that they've always run into trouble. They can't stand ambiguity. They want to know precisely where everything is and precisely what's going on.

These people are the worst decision makers in the world. In fact, it's almost impossible to get them to make a decision at all. You just can't feed them enough information to help them make a good decision. In fact, these people might be more comfortable in fields that require specificity. A field that consists of highly specialized workers such as lab technicians, engineers, or data processors, that allows for more quantifiable answers and fewer unknown factors, would suit this type of person very well.

Confident decision makers don't have to have every *t* crossed and every *i* dotted. They can move quickly in an environment that contains ambiguity. In fact, your ability to make good decisions is directly related to your ability to handle ambiguity. People who can tolerate the stress of not knowing what the future holds are the kind of people who can successfully navigate their way through a lifetime of opportunities and risks.

## The Right Decision Requires the Courage to Act.

As illustrated in the story of James Goldsmith, the courage to make a decision is ultimately the most valuable characteristic of any decision maker. If you know you've made the right decision, you'll have the courage to act. It's when you're only hoping you've made the right decision that you hesitate. Is there something in your life you've always dreamed of doing but never had the courage to make happen? As Mark Twain said, "Even if you're on the right track, you'll get run over if you stand there long enough." If you know you've made the right decision, you won't hesitate to move ahead.

However, these days it's a lot harder to know if the decision you're making is the correct one. Since the dawn of the computer age, a great shift has taken place in the way we make decisions in this country. We've moved from intuitive decision making to logical decision making. Until the latter part of this century, America roared toward becoming a superpower, and several visionaries were making their decisions based on their intuition. The Wright brothers only *felt* that their airplane would fly; Charles Lindberg's belief he could cross the Atlantic was stronger than the popular notion that it could not be done; Henry Ford had a hunch that assembly lines would be the answer; Ray Kroc's belief in franchising and Thomas H. Watson's belief in computers were far stronger than any Wall Street analyst could justify.

Today we make decisions differently. We've replaced the intuition of the past with a deluge of computer-generated analyses that stifle our intuition and narrow our focus. Marconi insisted wireless signals could cross the Atlantic, even though the laws of physics at the time proved it to be impossible. Scientists then believed that the curvature of the earth would send the signals off into space. Marconi didn't know the ionosphere would bend the waves, but he instinctively felt his idea would work. If Marconi had a mainframe, he probably would have bred the perfect carrier pigeon instead of inventing radio. Similarly, if Edison had been a CEO of a conglomerate, he probably would have insisted upon the invention of the world's best oil lantern instead of inventing the light bulb. Think of Alexander Graham Bell, who left Edinburgh High School when he was fourteen. With an MBA, he probably would have invented the perfect cablegram system instead of pursuing a flight of fancy that gave us the telephone.

The shift from intuition to logic has created two major problems—first, a suffocation of creative thought; and second, a dangerous assumption that the more detailed information we have, the more accurate our decisions will be. Confident decision making is a blend of logic and intuition. By harnessing the power of logic and fusing it with the genius of intuition, we can sometimes produce explosive creativity.

# Are You Logic-Minded or Intuition-Inspired?

When making decisions, do you tend to depend more on facts or hunches? Take the following short quiz, answering each question as quickly as possible.

---

*1. The company you work for is faltering. The rumor mill is saying profits are down 25 percent. You have a performance review coming up, and you sense you might be the next person to go. You get a call from an executive recruiter who might have a position in which you'd be interested. It would be a lateral move with the same pay, benefits, etc. The problem is, the interview requires you to take a few days off to visit the company and talk with several executives. You're afraid the extra time off might look bad to your boss. But things don't look good for your future, and you have a family to support. Do you:*

a. Lay low. Another opportunity is bound to come along, and besides, if you were about to be axed, you'd have gotten some signals by now.

b. Listen to your suspicions. The position looks as though it might be right for you, and with the economy so bad, you never know when another chance like this will come along.

*2. You have to do a staff layoff. You are down to the final two candidates who hold similar positions in the company. One person does consistently good work, but you sense he is a little too ambitious, and down the road might easily sacrifice company loyalty for the best offer he can get. The other person has a work record that is more uneven, but after talking to him, you get the feeling he is very loyal to the business. Do you:*

a. Choose to keep the person who has a sterling record—after all, it's all there in black-and-white.

b. Trust your instincts. Keep the person who might be a little less productive and hope that extra training will smooth out the wrinkles.

*3. You meet a salesperson from Company Z at a Christmas party. He asks to stop by your office and show you some products in which he thinks your company might be interested. The next week he stops by and leaves you some samples. The vice president has been on your back to develop new ideas. After taking a look at the products, you have a feeling they won't last. Yet the literature you have contains strong testimonials from credible firms and detailed examples of how the product works. The salesperson calls the next day to get an order. Do you:*

a. Take a chance. Try out the products based on the information you have.

b. Take a deep breath and back off from the sale. Assure your vice president you're on top of things and will have something soon.

---

If you have more "a" answers than "b" answers, you prefer to trust logical facts over intuitive feelings. Neither one is better than the other. But it is important to know where your preferences lie. The next time you make a decision, rely on your normal process, then step back for a moment and try looking at the problem using the opposite approach, whether based on logic or intuition. You might find that a more balanced decision-making technique will improve your ability to make the right choice.

## A Few Examples of Some Bad Decisions

We've all made bad decisions in the past. Yet it might comfort you to know that even the worst decisions you've made don't measure up to the real blunders made by some of the more well-known figures and companies in history. Just for fun, let's look at some examples of bad decisions.

For starters, take Manuel Noriega's decision to announce that, as far as he was concerned, Panama was at war with the United States. We invaded at midnight, and he lost his country before breakfast. His demise takes second place only to the British invasion of Zanzibar in 1896, which was all over in thirty-eight minutes. To add insult to injury, the British asked local residents to reimburse them for the cost of ammunition used to destroy the sultan's palace.

What about the time Coca-Cola could have bought Pepsi Cola for one thousand dollars? Pepsi's owner, Charles Guth of Loft, Inc., was willing to let its subsidiary go for that. But Coca-Cola was so sure it controlled the market, it turned down the offer.

Then there's the millions of dollars General Motors spent trying to promote its Nova compact car in Latin America, before somebody realized that *"no va"* means "won't go" in Spanish.

Finally, this gem comes from some time at the turn of the century, when an English cigar maker, John Player, came up with the idea of wrapping finely chopped tobacco in small tubes of paper. He called them cigar-ettes. He offered one of his competitors half interest in the project, but E. G. Alton turned it down, saying, "They'll never become popular, old boy, never."

# My Favorite Example of a Good Decision

On the other hand, a few smart decisions have the power to make people enormously successful. For my favorite "good decision" story, we have to go back to 1919, when the army discharged Conrad Hilton. He wanted to get back into his former profession as a banker, so he went to Cisco, Texas, to buy a bank. The owners wanted seventy-five thousand dollars for it, and Conrad could see it was a good buy. He quickly wired a full-price offer to the owners in Kansas City. After receiving his offer, they figured that if he was that eager to pay seventy-five thousand dollars, he'd surely pay eighty thousand dollars. They wired him back, "PRICE UP TO $80,000 AND SKIP THE HAGGLING." Conrad could afford the extra five thousand dollars but he decided to sleep on it at the hotel across the street. At the Mobley Hotel, a tired Conrad Hilton was denied a hotel room. The desk clerk told him the hotel didn't have a room available at the moment, but if Hilton could wait until later, a room would be available for eight hours.

"Why only eight hours?" he asked.

The clerk said there was an oil boom going on, and the hotel could rent out its rooms three times a day. "It was a cross between a flophouse and a gold mine," Hilton said later. Suddenly, he lost all interest in banking and bought the hotel the next day for forty thousand dollars. It was the start of the Hilton Hotel empire.

Conrad Hilton possessed all the qualities of a good decision maker. An uncanny sense of timing, the ability to make a decision effectively, the courage to make a decision, and the facility to live with ambiguity—all were necessary for Hilton to make his first move. What about the ability to delegate? Much of Hilton's success in management can be traced to that very skill. While possessing good decision-making qualities is important, it is still only one small piece of the puzzle. Now let's explore how the ability to look at a decision and categorize it correctly helps to facilitate the decision-making process.

# CHAPTER TWO

# Categorizing the Decision

## How We Make Our Major Decisions

Many times we make all our decisions using the same techniques. But not all are equal in importance. When your most important decisions didn't work out, did you ever try to assess why not? Think about your major life decisions, such as schooling or training, vocation, career moves, marriage, where you live, where you've relocated or what investments you've made. Pick five, and as you write them down, indicate whether each decision worked for you or didn't. Try to choose a combination of successful and unsuccessful decisions.

### Five Major Decisions I've Made

1. _____

2. _____

3. _____

4. _____

5. _____

Now try analyzing the decisions to discover the common elements that went into each decision. Do you remember the circumstances surrounding each decision? Can you categorize your decisions by the methods you used to reach a conclusion? Were they intuitive decisions or logical ones? As I've mentioned before, when it comes to making a decision, the problem usually doesn't begin with the decision itself; it starts with defining the decision you want to make. When faced with a decision, most people flounder in the dark, searching for an answer—and that's when all the trouble starts. When you aren't really sure of your decisions, you're liable to take drastic steps that can sometimes transform a manageable problem into an impossible one.

## The Five Categories of Decision Making

The Confident Decision Maker takes the middle ground, weighing the various aspects of a decision before arriving at a sensible conclusion. And how do you determine the best solution? One way is through Categorizing. When you examine a decision closely, you'll notice that there are different ways to categorize or define it. Once you determine how to define it, you can decide on the best method to use for reaching a conclusion. Most decisions will fall into one of the following categories:

The first category is *parameters*. Your least important decisions should take up the least amount of time. For these kinds of decisions, establish minimum standards and accept the first alternative that meets those standards. The most important thing to remember is that one choice is not much better than another. The object is to pick the first choice and free yourself to decide other things. Many decisions go here, and learning to maximize the use of this category can increase your decision-making ability.

The second category is *policy decisions*. This category is for your most significant decisions. They should be based upon your "mission statement" or "policy manual" and your values. Does the decision support this criteria? Also, do you need to create a new policy, or should you just amend an old one?

The third category is decisions requiring *analysis*. This category is where you analyze what might work and what definitely doesn't work. This is the best category for decisions that call for a right or wrong answer.

Fourth come decisions demanding *judgment*. Sometimes several choices are available to you, and you have to determine the best one. Decisions like this call for a judgment, using logical decision-making skills to make a choice.

And finally, decisions involving *synthesis*. When many factors must be brought together to develop a new solution, they belong in this category. This is where you bring your problem when none of the solutions you've come up with seems like the right decision. Decisions in this category are usually creative and unique.

## Choosing a Decision-Making Process

Once you've established under which category a problem falls, the decision-making process becomes automatic. But how do you know which category to choose?

Consider the following questions:

1. Does the problem require a complex decision?

2. Is it a problem or an opportunity?

3. Are there existing guidelines to follow?

4. Into which pigeonhole will it fit?

5. Is the problem real or imagined?

6. Is it a money problem or a people problem?

7. What would happen if you do nothing about the decision?

8. Is the problem unique?

By asking yourself these questions before you attempt to make a decision, you can hone in on the real issues you are examining. Then all you have to do is pick a category. To show you what I mean, let's take a closer look at each question.

## DOES THE PROBLEM REQUIRE A COMPLEX DECISION?

We all waste a lot of time by trying to make a decision about something that doesn't deserve the effort. Let's say you're on a business trip, traveling from Dallas to Houston. You were planning to spend the night at a hotel near the International Airport in Houston, but you still have ninety miles to go, and you're starting to fall asleep at the wheel. You decide to stop at a motel along the way instead. You see a motel that looks decent, and you're about to pull off the road when suddenly you see another place down the road. You decide to keep going. Once again, you're about to pull off when you see another motel about one hundred yards farther down. Do you see the problem here? Because you are constantly looking for something better, you are never able to decide. Yet when you think about it, this decision isn't important enough to prolong it as much as you do.

When a decision is relatively unimportant, a problem doesn't require a complex decision, and it falls into the *parameters* category mentioned above. When you are faced with a situation where the choice you make answers an immediate need and doesn't have any long-term consequences, such as trying to decide which magazine to buy for a plane trip, then the best way to reach a decision quickly is by establishing parameters. Give yourself a set of criteria, then grab the first choice that meets the criteria you've established. In the case of the motel, for example, by establishing that you want a room that doesn't cost more than fifty dollars, that has a private bathroom, and that is clean, you will be able to stop at the first place that meets those standards.

The first step when making a decision is to ask yourself, How important are the long-term consequences? If they're not that important, use parameters to make a decision.

## IS IT A PROBLEM OR AN OPPORTUNITY?

In sports, football is a problem-solving game, whereas basketball is an opportunity game. When you are playing offense in football, you must solve the problem of breaking through the other team's defense. When you are playing defense, you must solve the problem by anticipating the other team's move. Basketball is essentially different because the ball changes sides so frequently. It is a game of opportunity as each side waits for the slightest error by the other team. When it happens, a player must move quickly to take advantage. The end result is the same for both—you want to score—but the approach is different. Take a look at the decision you have to make. Does something need to be fixed, or is there an opportunity to seize that might really pay off? Once you separate a problem from an opportunity, then you can figure out which decision-making techniques to use and how fast to use them.

For example, with problems, if you attack them too quickly, you might panic prematurely and think a problem is bigger than it really is. And, if you move too slowly, you can become paralyzed and spend too much time analyzing the problem, which can make the situation worse. And with opportunities, if you grab them too quickly, you might find yourself responsible for expensive start-up costs while your competitor stands ready to grab the idea after you've paid for a series of false starts. And if you go too slowly, your competition could pass you up.

That's what happened to the makers of the Swatch watch. For a long time, the Swiss dominated the watchmaking industry, from top-of-the-line products on down. Then, in the 1970s, a peculiar thing happened. The Japanese, who have long been known for their electronic prowess, invented a watch that challenged the Swiss both in terms of design and price. The quartz watch had originally been invented by the Swiss, but they had never run with it because of their dominance in high-priced watches. The Japanese adapted quartz technology to produce a watch that was just as accurate as Swiss watches costing ten times as much. It nearly destroyed the Swiss watch industry.

How could the Swiss have allowed this to happen? Somewhere along the way, someone made the wrong decision—the decision to maintain a traditional watch design rather than forge ahead with a new opportunity for innovation. And, to make matters worse, while the Swiss pondered their increasing slip in the marketplace, the Japanese moved even further ahead in their attempts to capture the marketplace, this time improving on top-of-the-line Swiss watch designs by creating the slimmest watch ever—only 2.5 millimeters thick.

This last tactic was what motivated the Swiss to counterattack. Turning their problems into opportunities, they rethought the design of their own products, creating a watch that was just under a millimeter thick. Then they reassessed their marketplace, choosing to appeal to the mass market with a product that maintained their high standards of design and electronic ingenuity and a price affordable to a broad consumer base. Finally, in a brilliant marketing maneuver, they designed the watch to be manufactured in a myriad of colors and styles, and the Swatch—short for Swiss watch—was born. By the late 1980s, 30 million Swatches had saturated the industry, and the Swiss watch industry was saved.

Sometimes you have very little control when it comes to timing your decision. That's when luck can play an important role. In his book *The World Is My Home*, James Michener tells the story of how his good luck catapulted his first book, *Tales of the South Pacific*, into a major success. At the end of 1946, while final touches were being made on his manuscript prior to publication by Macmillan, *The Saturday Evening Post* asked to publish two stories from the collection in its magazine. The *Post*'s problem was that it would be unable to print the stories until early 1947, after the book's release. Michener needed to make a decision quickly. If he wanted to take advantage of this opportunity, he would have to convince his publisher to hold off publication until the early part of 1947.

Michener decided to grab the *Post* opportunity and delay his publishing opportunity—a fortuitous decision for him. Pulitzer Prizes are usually awarded to books released during the previous year. In 1946, the Pulitzer went to Robert Penn Warren's *All the King's Men*. In 1947, the award went to *Tales of the South Pacific*. If Michener's book had come out at the end of 1946 as planned, by his assessment he surely would have lost to Robert Penn Warren's masterpiece. As he saw it, the publishing field in 1947 was less competitive, and his book had its greatest chance to succeed that year.

That's why making smart and efficient decisions is so important when it comes to both problems and opportunities. First decide which of the two you face, then make sure you categorize it within an appropriate time frame.


## ARE THERE EXISTING GUIDELINES TO FOLLOW?

One of the key things to look for in decision making is an existing precedent that tells you whether you should or shouldn't go ahead. Let's say you've got a salesperson who's been selling $300,000 worth of snowblowers in the Northeast region for the past five years. This year it's down to $250,000. There's obviously been a deviation from past performance. Should you fire this person or give him another chance?

Instead of tossing and turning in your sleep, worrying about looking like the bad guy, the best thing to do is consult the existing company policy. What have you done in the past in similar situations? How much leeway do you give to your employees? Is this problem always handled by the sales manager? If you've handled this kind of problem in a certain way in the past but have never made it company policy, consider making it policy now, and save yourself from future uncertainty.

What about an opportunity with which you are faced? Imagine that you run a company in Seattle that distributes garden tools and equipment. One of your buyers told you about a container of ten-speed bikes that's on the water, only five days out from port. The chain of stores that had ordered them declared bankruptcy, and you can pick them up for twenty-five cents on the dollar. It sounds like easy money, but you can't decide.

Again, it's important to take a look at existing policy. If you're in the gardening-equipment business, your corporate-mission statement probably doesn't say anything about the bicycle business. So no matter how much money you could make, you should stay within your mission statement unless you're willing to change the mission. Roy Disney used to say that decision making is easy when your values are clear. If something comes up that violates your values, morals, or the goals of your company, don't do it regardless of the temptation.

One of the reasons Nordstrom department stores are so successful is their policy manual. It's one page long. It says, "Welcome to Nordstrom. We're glad to have you with our company. Our number one goal is to provide outstanding customer service. Set both your personal and professional goals high. We have great confidence in your ability to achieve them. Nordstrom's rules: Rule 1: Use your good judgment in all situations. There will be no additional rules.''

The most successful dairy store in the country, Stew Leonard's in Connecticut, has its policy manual engraved in a rock outside the front door. It's two sentences long and reads, ''Rule One: The customer is always right. Rule Two: If the customer is ever wrong, reread Rule One.'' Isn't that a great policy? If you want to go into a business where the customer is always wrong, become a policeman, not a store owner. Imagine how many times a day an employee at Nordstrom or Stew Leonard's wonders whether she should or shouldn't do something. Then she thinks of the company policy and knows what to do.

So the third factor in Categorizing a decision is to apply it to your corporate and personal policies, and see if it fits. If it does, either follow policy or consider changing policy. However, don't make random exceptions to the policy. If you set up a policy, all future responses can be programmed. Then, when the problem recurs, it doesn't require another decision. Also, if you make a decision for a problem that previously didn't have a policy, write one down based on the decision you made. That way you'll have it available to shape the future of your company.

## INTO WHICH PIGEONHOLE WILL IT FIT?

Another way to look at decisions is to try to figure out what kind of answer you are looking for. There are at least four potential types of answers that a decision can require:

- *A right answer and a wrong answer.* This applies mostly to a decision that involves concrete principles.

- *An answer from a variety of choices.* This is where you are forced to choose the best answer.

- *No answer.* This means you don't see any solution to the problem.

- *The "go or no go" decision.* Not the same as the "right or wrong" answer, this decision doesn't require a judgment, just an action: Should you do it, or shouldn't you?

Right and wrong answers fall under the *analysis* category, where you can determine what works and what doesn't by looking at concrete principles. Let's say you are trying to figure out a solution to the energy problem. You think that a great energy-saving idea would be to devise a system that transmits electricity to automobiles through the air, the same way radio waves and television signals are transmitted. Analysis forces you to look at the concrete principles involved, and when you do, you discover that certain laws of physics prevent this solution from ever becoming a reality. Therefore, you determine that your idea to transmit electricity through the air is definitely a wrong answer.

How about a multiple-choice decision? In the winter of 1991, President Bush had to decide which advisers he was going to take with him on his trade mission to Japan. He could choose business leaders, labor leaders—even his former secretary of state was a potential candidate. Decisions like this require logical decision-making skills and judgment to determine a viable solution. Later on, I will teach you several ways to resolve complex decisions more accurately. For now, it's important to note that decisions with many options fall under the *judgment* category.

What happens when you search for the right answer, and nothing seems like a possibility? The kind of day when your twin forgets your birthday and your income-tax refund check bounces. Seemingly impossible decisions often rely on creativity for a solution—to invent a possibility where none existed previously. This is where *synthesis* comes into play. For example, I'm sure you've heard the story of the hotel in San Diego that had no space for elevators. A group of expensive engineering consultants stood in the lobby overwhelmed by this problem. Finally, a janitor walked up to them and said, "Why don't you just put an elevator on the outside of the building?" The group was shocked. It hadn't even occurred to them! They were too locked into the way they'd always done it before. Fortunately, the engineers were bright enough to consider the janitor's idea, and now we see elevators on the outside of buildings all over the world.

The final option, the *"go or no go"* decision, is perhaps the simplest problem to attack. Questions under this category might include: "Do I or don't I want to go skiing?" or "Do I or don't I want to have lunch today with my accountant?" While these are the simplest decisions to make, they aren't the easiest. There are only two options to choose from, but from either option arises several consequences. Later on, I will teach you more ways to find solutions to these sometimes difficult dilemmas.

Before we go any further, take a look at the following flow chart. If you start in the left-hand corner and follow the arrows, you'll get a better sense of how answering the questions I've given you can help you to categorize your decisions.

Once you have pigeonholed your problem, then you can use the methods I will detail in the next few chapters to help you make decisions. However, before you choose which method to use, there are four more questions you need to ask yourself. Answering these questions might categorize your problem even further, and help you shortcut your decision-making process.

## IS THE PROBLEM REAL OR IMAGINED?

The next stage of categorizing the decision is a critical one. You must decide whether the problem or opportunity is real or imagined. All too often we overreact and spend time and energy on problems and opportunities that are illusions. This principle is

## Determining a Decision's Complexity

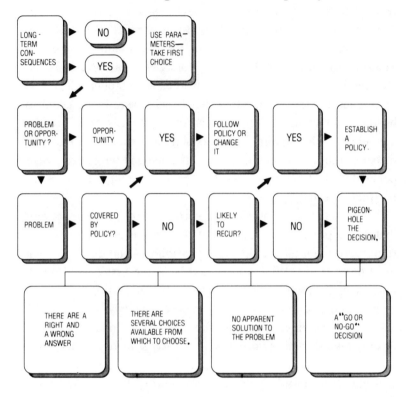

illustrated in many newsrooms where you'll find a big sign that reads: NOTHING IS AS BAD OR AS GOOD AS IT'S FIRST REPORTED. This motto teaches the reporters not to overreact.

Remember in early 1991 when the Iraqis launched the first Scud-missile attack on Tel Aviv? Both CNN and NBC reported the missiles contained chemical warheads, although CBS was more cautious. After reporting that Israelis were being taken to hospitals for treatment of chemical burns, NBC's Tom Brokaw announced, "Retaliation by the Israelis is certain." In fact, the missiles didn't contain chemical warheads, and the Israelis were persuaded not to retaliate. As the sign says, nothing is as bad as it's first reported.

The same thing happens in corporations. There's a rumor that a key person is quitting, and suddenly everyone's mind is running through all the different possibilities and decisions that need to be made. What you should be doing first is confirming or denying the rumor, instead of automatically starting a decision-making process.

The same applies for opportunities—is it a real opportunity or only an apparent opportunity? Let's say somebody tells you a company in your industry is for sale. Would you go directly into a mental decision-making mode—wondering if you could handle the acquisition; how it would affect your employees; what would happen if a competitor snatched it up before you had the opportunity and made a bundle from it?

What you should be doing is finding out if the company is really for sale, and if so, for how much. Can it be bought on a leveraged buyout or in exchange for stock? At this point, you're trying to locate a disqualifier; you continue to gather information unless you find something that rules out the acquisition. It's smart to gather this information well ahead of making a decision. You're really investigating to see if a decision needs to be made, to see if it's a real opportunity or an apparent opportunity. If it's only imagined, quit worrying. Relax and back off—unless you over-react, nothing's going to happen.

## IS IT A MONEY PROBLEM OR A PEOPLE PROBLEM?

The two most important resources in any company are money and people. Unfortunately, that means all problems fall under these two categories as well, or sometimes a problem can involve both. When it comes to decision making, confusion occurs when you can't figure out which of the two categories is causing the problem. Take Bob's case, for example. As he explained:

> I own a chain of sixty-two hamburger stands in New Jersey. I started right out of high school with a thousand bucks I borrowed from my uncle. I built this business with sweat and tears. For three years I worked eighteen hours a day, seven days a week, until I could afford to hire some help. My problem is with my first employee. He's now my execu-tive vice president. I made this guy! I took him off the street, and now he lives in a mansion and drives a Mercedes. Yesterday, he has the gall to tell me that he's quitting and going to work for the competition. How could he do this to me, after all I've done for him? I asked him if he'd stay for more money. He says sure, but he wants fifty thousand dollars more a year! That's blackmail!

This is an example of a person who really has a money problem, not a people problem. If he could only see this clearly, he'd calm down and know how to negotiate a solution to the prob-lem. He should be thinking calmly, Okay, so I can solve this problem for fifty thousand dollars a year. But I can do better than that. Fifty thousand dollars is unreasonable, and he knows it, so he must be upset about something else. We'll talk, I'll butter him up, and we'll work it out. It's probably not going to cost me any more than ten thousand dollars and a new car. Once you define a problem within the proper parameters, the answer is obvious.

## WHAT WOULD HAPPEN IF YOU DO NOTHING ABOUT THE DECISION?

Although it may seem contrary to your instincts, one question you should ask yourself when Categorizing a decision is what would happen if you decide to do nothing? Will the situation improve or deteriorate?

A lot of people call my office if they're involved in a negotiation and don't know which way to go. I'm always happy to help them if I'm there, but sometimes I'm away on a speaking trip and have to return the call when I get back into town. Over the years, I've learned an interesting lesson. If I'm out of town and not able to call them back for a few days, in over half the cases the problem has gone away by the time I reach them. In over half the cases, the best decision was to make no decision at all.

The question to ask yourself is this: If you do nothing, will the situation get worse or better? If it isn't going to get worse, give it some time and see if it goes away.

## IS THE PROBLEM UNIQUE?

The last question to ask yourself when considering a decision is whether the problem is unique. Once you've decided the uniqueness factor, everything else is automatic. You'll know how you should make the decision from that point on. If you're bogged down with a decision, it's probably because you haven't faced it before. Assuming that's true, there are three possibilities:

- Somebody else has faced the same problem.

- Nobody has faced this decision before.

- Underlying causes are exacerbating the problem.

The first possibility is that although you haven't faced the problem before, someone else has. This could be a situation where you have a sick relative, you're having family problems, or even corporate financial problems. When the problem is new to you but not to other people, the solution is to consult an expert such as a doctor, marriage counselor, or accountant. Sometimes you agonize for years over a problem you think is unique. Once you accept that it's only unique to you, you're astounded to find out that there are experts out there who face the same problem dozens of times each week. So, first decide if the problem has been faced by other people. If it has, consult an expert.

The second possibility is that the problem is unique, and no one has faced this decision before. When Johnson & Johnson was confronted with product tampering of Tylenol, the company was left with a crisis that could cripple its business, not to mention hurt a lot of innocent people. This form of sabotage, if handled poorly, not only could cause an enormous amount of damage to consumer confidence in Tylenol, but could leave the drug industry itself extremely vulnerable. Luckily, Johnson & Johnson quickly made the decision to pull its product off the shelves, to hold endless press conferences and, ultimately, to create a tamper-proof capsule. With the right combination of synthesis and analysis, the Johnson & Johnson people were able to assess their problem correctly and to take the actions necessary to save the company's reputation, to protect the public from further harm, and to distinguish themselves as masters in the art of crisis management.

The ultimate example of creative synthesis and analysis is NASA, an organization that faces unique problems in the space program. Nobody has had any past experience in solving them. They work on creating hypotheses using Creative Synthesis, and then they pick the best ones by using Analysis.

The third possibility to consider when a problem is unique to you is that underlying causes might be exacerbating the problem. For example, let's say you own three greeting-card stores, and one of them is always losing money. Should you close it down? Because you have underlying problems involved that may be causing the store to lose money, you need to uncover those problems first. Is there something wrong with the management of the store? How well is the store promoted? What about its location? This type of situation requires analysis and judgment: analysis to sort out the underlying decisions and judgment to help you make the right decision. In the chart "Categorizing the Decision," you can see how these questions have been added to the procedure for categorizing the decision.

## How Would You Categorize Your Own Decisions?

Remember those five decisions I asked you to list at the beginning of the chapter? I want you to look back at your decisions, and using the five possible ways I've mentioned to categorize decisions, place them under appropriate headings in the chart on the facing page.

| Parameter Decisions | Policy Decisions | Analysis Decisions | Judgment Decisions | Synthesis Decisions |
|---|---|---|---|---|
| | | | | |
| | | | | |
| | | | | |

Do you notice any patterns in your decision making? Do you think your decisions might have been different had you used a different category and a different approach to making your decision? What if your decision had been to move to Arizona? Maybe you used certain parameters in making this decision. What if you tried synthesis instead—would your decision have concluded the same way?

By now you should be aware that there are several ways to view decision making. Once you have assessed your problem, asked yourself the right questions, and matched the decision with its proper category—whether it be parameters, policy, analysis, judgment, or synthesis—you have finished with the preliminary steps necessary to help you make a decision. But what happens if you are still unable to make up your mind? Or what if you still can't categorize your decision, even after asking yourself the eight questions I've listed? One problem might be that you still aren't really sure what the decision is that you are trying to make. Framing the decision properly is as important as Categorizing it. The next chapter will tell you how.

# Categorizing the Decision 1

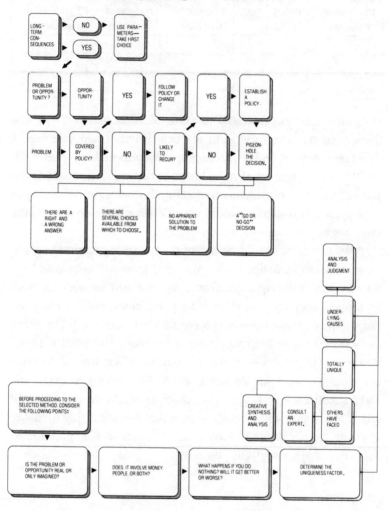

# CHAPTER THREE

# Blueprinting the Decision

## The Importance of Blueprinting

No builder would attempt to build a house until he had a very accurate blueprint from which to build. It is the foundation upon which he builds the foundation. If you don't get the blueprint right, nothing else comes out right. It's the same way with Confident Decision Making.

When I was active as a real estate broker, the company I ran also built houses using standard blueprints. Sometimes we'd discover that a house wouldn't fit on a lot the way the blueprint was drawn. For example, the layout of the house needed to be reversed, with the garage on the left instead of the right. To save the expense of having the plans redrawn, we simply told the builder, "Go ahead and build this, but flip the plans—reverse it." This was not the smartest move we ever made, because it's confusing for the builder. On a couple of occasions, we went out to the site to find that the builder had poured the foundation the way it was drawn in the blueprints. He'd forgotten to reverse it. As Cicero said, "Any man may make a mistake; none but a fool will persist in it." From then on, we went to the expense of drawing new plans, although the change we were making was very simple.

In decision making, it's equally important to blueprint accurately. This means laying out the problem completely, correctly, clearly, and concisely. It's at the heart of Confident Decision Making. It sounds simple, but it isn't.

## Learning to State the Problem Succinctly

Just a few days ago, a man called me and asked me to help him with a problem. I told him that I could only give him five minutes because I had to catch a plane to San Francisco. "Tell me the problem," I said. "If I can't give you an answer right away, I'll think about it on the plane and call you from my hotel." He launched into a long story of how he started his business. I tucked the phone under my ear and kept stuffing things into my briefcase. After two minutes, I said, "I'm sorry, but we're running out of time, and I still don't know your problem."

He said, "I'm getting to that," and kept talking.

After four minutes, I interrupted again, and said, "Please, tell me the problem."

He said, "I'm getting there," and kept talking.

After five minutes, with my assistant tapping her watch to tell me that I was going to miss the plane, I still had no idea why he'd called me. He could be trying to sell me aluminum siding or asking me for a political contribution, or perhaps he really did have a problem. I just couldn't tell. I told him, "Okay, I know your problem now. You don't know what your problem is. Here's my solution: Take a couple of days and work on Blueprinting your problem until you can state it in one short paragraph. Then call me back, and I'll tell you what to do." This guy was so confused, I was afraid to ask him where he was calling from. He probably would have told me, "From a phone booth on the corner of WALK and DON'T WALK."

If there are only five minutes to make a decision, we

shouldn't spend more than one of those five minutes stating the problem. That leaves four to work on finding the right answer. If we have five hours to make a decision, we should spend an hour Blueprinting the situation and four hours finding the right answer. If we have five years to solve a world problem, such as world terrorism, it's a tragedy to spend all five years talking about it without spending any time working on the solution.

So Blueprinting the decision is at the heart of Confident Decision Making. When Picasso said, "Computers are useless, they only give you answers," he wasn't being flippant. Answers aren't useful unless you're asking the right questions. There are some very deep problems involved in accurately Blueprinting the problem.

## How Much Do You Really Know?

As human beings, we all tend to think we know more than we really do. Will Rogers said, "It's not what we don't know that causes trouble, it's what we know that ain't so." Psychologists call it *the optimism factor*. We are usually overly optimistic in our assessments.

Here's a test to prove it. I'm going to ask ten questions that you can answer with a specific number. However, I want you to answer them, not with a specific number, but with a range—a low and a high number. If I ask you how many states there are, instead of saying fifty, you would say between forty-nine and fifty-one, and you would be certain you were right. If I ask you how many miles it is from Los Angeles to New York, you may be less sure, so you would want to give a broader range. You might say, it's between two thousand and three thousand miles, and feel 90 percent sure you were right. You can make the range as broad as you want, but I want you to feel 90 percent certain you're right in your answer.

Again, if you don't know anything about the subject matter, widen the range of your choice until you're 90 percent sure you're right.

1. How many movies did Humphrey Bogart make?

2. What is the height of Mount Everest in feet?

3. How many Oscars did Walt Disney win?

4. What's the length of time the first U.S. satellite stayed in space?

5. How much money would you have if you were to start with a penny and double the amount of money you have every day for thirty days?

6. How old was Martin Luther King, Jr., when he died?

7. How many bones are there in the human body?

8. What's the largest bill currently being printed by the U.S. mint?

9. What was Babe Ruth's salary in 1931?

10. How many different license-plate numbers can you derive from a combination of three letters and three numbers?

The answers are as follows:

1. Humphrey Bogart made 77 movies from *Broadway's Like That* in 1930 to *The Heart of a Fall* in 1976.

2. Mount Everest is 29,028 feet tall.

3. Walt Disney won fifty-one Oscars.

4. The length of time the first U.S. satellite stayed in space was twelve years, from 1958 to 1970.

5. If you doubled a penny every day for thirty days, you'd have $5,368,709.12.

6. Martin Luther King, Jr., was thirty-nine years old when he died.

7. There are 206 bones in the human body.

8. Since 1969, the largest bill printed has been the $100 bill. They used to print bills up to $100,000 but they discontinued them, because of lack of demand.

9. Babe Ruth's salary in 1931 was eighty thousand dollars, which was a record. Most people guess low on that one. His team owner said to him, "Do you realize you made more last year than President Hoover?" He said, "I know—but I had a better year."

10. The number of license plates you can derive from a combination of three letters and three numbers is 17,576,000. That's more than enough to cover every state except California, which has approximately 22 million registered vehicles. The next largest number of state automobile registrations is Texas, with almost 13 million.

So how did you score on the test? If you made the range large enough so that you felt 90 percent sure you were right, you should have had nine right and only one wrong. You probably didn't do nearly that well. In fact, if you got four or more of those right, you're doing very well. The point of this isn't to see how much you know, it's to see how much you think you know. You probably didn't do as well as you felt sure you had. Most people are too optimistic.

When Blueprinting the problem, it's good to be a realist. You probably don't know as much about the problem, or the opportunity, as you think you do. You probably don't have as much information as you really need to make a decision. So be a realist at this stage. Get more information. Once you've made the decision, you can bring optimism into play. Then you can go out and enthusiastically sell it to the troops.

# Do You Have Enough Information to Make a Decision?

The key to accurately Blueprinting the decision is to gather information. First, how much information should you gather? Gathering information is very expensive. You hire an advertising agency to take surveys and do test marketing. You quickly learn you can spend hundreds of thousands of dollars and still not learn very much. So you must balance the cost of gathering information with the necessity of having the right information.

Still, it's really hard to make the right decision when you don't have enough information. Maybe you'll be lucky, but chances are you won't. Any time you're faced with a decision, you should be saying to yourself, "Do I have enough information to make a decision?" If you do, then you should go ahead and make the decision. If you don't, then you're better off calling "time-out" until you get the information you need.

Another point to consider when gathering information is your time constraints. If time is a big consideration, it may limit the amount of information you can gather. When you're marketing a new product, you must balance the need for information with the danger of delaying the decision too long. As I've mentioned before, by waiting too long to make the decision, you may let the competition get the jump on you.

The best tip I can give you on gathering information is to have a system in place that gathers the kind of information that could be useful to you one day. Don't wait until you need to know to start finding the information. For example, if you're going to buy a new car within the next year, subscribe to auto magazines, and clip and file reviews of cars that may interest you. You don't even have to read the reviews, just accumulate them. Clip dealer ads from the classifieds so you build data on pricing. Then, when you get ready to make the decision, you'll already have all the information you need right at your fingertips.

Perhaps you have an idea that one day you'd like to open a restaurant. Maybe it's something vague and far in the future you're considering; but start accumulating information right now. Every time you see an article about a restaurant, clip it out and file it away. When the time eventually comes that you want to make a decision, you'll have a wealth of information to help you make a Confident Decision.

How important is gathering information? Well, obviously information is power. The more information you have, the less likely you are to make a bad decision. Also, information is important, because the more you know, the better your intuition will be. Let me explain why.

## How I Learned to Develop Information Flow

Remember when you were new at something, and you had to concentrate on every detail? Your first day driving a car, you had to make all those separate decisions: putting the turn signal on, shifting down, taking your foot off the gas pedal; putting your left foot on the clutch and your right foot on the brake. Then, as you became more familiar with driving, those things came automatically to you. In one fluid motion, you could go through them, without having to think about them.

My youngest son, John, and I decided to go to Switzerland to do some mountain climbing. We set our sights on two peaks. The first was Mont Blanc, which is about 15,700 feet. The second was the Matterhorn, the mountain on the Paramount Pictures' logo. They are two very different mountains. Mont Blanc is a slow climb where you are roped to the other climbers while wearing crampons. It's a hard and heavy journey to the top. The Matterhorn is different—it's all hand-over-fist rock climbing. Neither one of us had much experience at that kind of ascent.

So we hired a guide at Tahquitz Mountain in Southern California to teach us how to do it. We found out there's a lot to master. You have to learn about carabiners, pitons, and the different strengths of mountain-climbing ropes. You have to learn about gravity, and how you use it as a pressure point against the rock. And you have to know to what extent you can use friction holds on the rocks. You learn not to go out onto a rock face unless you can maintain a three-point hold: That's either two feet and a hand, or two hands and a foot. You also have to learn to climb with your legs and not with your arms. A beginning climber always wants to pull himself up with his arms, which is very tiring. An experienced rock climber knows to maintain holds with the hands but do all the work with the legs. All this is very strange at first. You edge your way up a rock with a clumsy, awkward motion. Then, suddenly, it all comes together and seems to flow. You can anticipate the handholds and the footholds much better, and you just move from one position to another on the rock.

It was on the Matterhorn that I heard the finest motivational talk of my life. At one point, I couldn't see any way to make the next pitch. The rock was perfectly smooth. My French guide was above me, relaying my rope. I could call out to him, but I couldn't see him. "Guy, this isn't going to go," I yelled. "There's no way."

He called back, "Roger, you will find a way to make it go. If you don't, we will 'ave to spend ze night on zis mountain." That's when I really understood motivation for the first time. When the pain of doing nothing exceeds the pain of moving on, you will move on. I swung out onto the rock and somehow made it up.

Confident Decision Making is a lot like learning to climb a mountain. The more information you have, the more you have a framework within which to make decisions. Instead of consciously having to think through every step, you can turn your intuition loose as it flows through the problem.

## Clouding a Decision with Information Drift

As you gather information, try to understand that human beings are very imprecise in the way we collect and analyze information. I call this *Information Drift*. Think of a ship that's leaving San Francisco Harbor sailing out under the Golden Gate Bridge. Its destination is Hong Kong. The navigator has laid out a course of action and knows the route to take. He's probably already adjusted for ocean currents, prevailing winds, and other variables. However, as they proceed on this four-or five-week journey, many things will cause the ship to drift off-course. Many factors will come to bear on it. For each of these factors, the captain of the ship has to compensate.

It's the same way with gathering information. As you gather information about a decision, you need to recognize that many variables cause you to drift off-course. If you don't realize it, you'll make a decision with inaccurate information. There are many types of drifts that can occur.


## AVAILABILITY DRIFT: LOOKING FOR CONVENIENCE

The first type is *Availability Drift.* You tend to give more weight to information that's readily available to you. In simple language, the more you're aware of something, the more you tend to give it emphasis it doesn't deserve. News coverage is often the cause of Availability Drift because newspapers and television news shows don't give equal emphasis to events. Consider the following questions:

Do more people die of stomach cancer or in automobile accidents? You probably thought automobile accidents, because you hear more about automobile accidents than you do about people dying of stomach cancer. In fact, twice as many people die from stomach cancer than in automobile accidents.

Do more people die of pneumonia or murder? You might say murder, because you hear more about it. In fact, three times as many people die of pneumonia.

Is the suicide rate higher in New York or New Mexico? New York has the lowest suicide rate in the nation, about one third of that in states like New Mexico and Arizona, where you'd think life would be much less stressful. If you said New York, you were also a victim of Information Drift in a different way. New York is really a very rural state. We just hear so much more about its urban areas, we tend to think all New Yorkers live in big cities.

Finally, do more people die in shooting accidents or by drowning? Three times as many people drown than die in shooting accidents.

The classic example of Availability Drift is the popular misconception that the Japanese are buying up America. In truth, both the United Kingdom and the Netherlands have made larger investments in the United States than Japan.

## EXPERIENCE DRIFT: INFLUENCED BY PERSONAL PREJUDICE

The second type of Information Drift is the *Experience Drift*. You tend to see things in terms of your personal or professional interest. Let me ask you a question. What's the best-selling size of mattress: twin, full, queen, or king? You probably picked the size you use. Since mine is a king, I was astounded to find out that only 6 percent of beds sold are king size—39 percent are twin, 26 percent are full, and 24 percent are queen.

If you were asked to guess if more people attend basketball games or baseball games, you'd probably pick your favorite sport. You might have trouble believing that auto racing is really the most highly attended spectator sport in the world.

Now you can see how Experience Drift causes you to get off-course. An example of this is the CEO in an automobile company who has come up through the luxury-car division. The competition jumps into the minivan business, but he might pass it off as a fad that won't last because of his background.

## CONFLICT DRIFT: STRUGGLING WITH BELIEFS

The third type of drift is *Conflict Drift*. You tend to reject information that conflicts with your beliefs. If you think watching television is a waste of time, you might have trouble believing the average American watches twenty-eight hours of television a week. Vegetarians have trouble believing the average American consumes more than his weight in meat every year.

## RECALL DRIFT: TRUSTING YOUR MEMORY

The fourth drift is *Recall Drift*. We're not very accurate in our ability to recall information. To illustrate that point, here's a little test. Read these names, and then answer the question that follows: Roseanne Barr, Russell Baker, Anthony Quayle, Irving Stone, Barbara Bush, Jim Backus, Richard Lewis, Leona Helmsley, Andrew Peacock, Diane Sawyer, Margaret Thatcher, and Lucille Ball. The question is, were there more men or more women on that list? You probably answered, "There were more women," although I mentioned six men and six women. The women on the list were more famous than the men. This illustrates that you more easily recall things that are familiar to you.

Here's another question. Do more words start with an *R* or do more words have *R* as the third letter? Chances are, you guessed more words start with an *R*. Although *R* is a very popular letter in a word, there are far more words with *R* as a third letter than words that start with an *R*. But because you have more trouble recalling them, you have trouble believing it's true. You recall things more easily that fit a pattern with which you're familiar. Chess players can quickly recall a game in progress, but have a terrible time trying to recall random placement of pieces on a board.

## SELECTIVITY DRIFT: PICKING YOUR PRIORITIES

The fifth reason for inaccurately analyzing information is *Selectivity Drift*. You can't absorb everything, so you screen out what doesn't interest you. Let's say you run a sporting-goods manufacturing company. You're an avid golfer but have little interest in bowling. Your natural tendency is to be keenly aware of things affecting the golf division, while at the same time to be oblivious to what's going on at the bowling-ball factory. You need to compensate for that. In business, Selectivity Drift can be expensive.

After World War II, Howard Hughes became involved in sophisticated weapons making. He hired two very talented young scientists, Dr. Simon Ramo and Dr. Dean Woolridge, who were former classmates at the California Institute of Technology. Ramo had gone to General Electric and Woolridge to Bell Telephone Laboratories before they began working together again at Hughes Aircraft. Their venture into military electronics went very well indeed. However, it didn't particularly interest Howard Hughes, who was spending more time in Las Vegas courting actress Terry Moore than he was at Hughes Aircraft headquarters in Culver City. Friction broke out among the management, who appealed to Howard Hughes to resolve the problem. Because it didn't interest him as much as his other ventures, he let it slide. It was a disastrous move.

Ramo and Woolridge resigned. After getting financial backing from Thompson products in Cleveland, they went on to form their own company, which they named TRW, after the initials for Thompson, Ramo, and Woolridge. It became a giant of the space and technology industry, even bigger than Hughes Aircraft itself. The moral of the story? Don't let your personal interests affect the way you blueprint the decision.


## ANCHORING DRIFT: WEIGHING ANSWERS TOO HEAVILY

The sixth drift in information analysis is the *Anchoring Drift*. If you have no experience in an area, you tend to anchor to the first number you hear. Harold Geneen, the genius who built ITT into an international conglomerate, was often a victim of Anchoring Drift. I had lunch with the president of one of his companies once. He told me that when he first met Geneen, he was asked for a particular statistic about company production. Not wanting to admit he didn't know the right figure, he made an educated guess. After the meeting, he hurriedly checked the number and found out he was way off. So the next time he met with Harold Geneen, he apologized for it. He gave him the correct number and assured him he'd be more accurate in the future. However, once Harold Geneen had heard the first number, the president couldn't move him off it. Every time the president met him in the future, Geneen always went back to that original number. Geneen assumed it was correct, because his mind had anchored to that particular number.

Real estate agents use anchoring when they present offers to sellers. Before they get the offer out of the briefcase, they might say this to the seller: "Now, Mr. Seller, I'm well aware you're asking two hundred thousand dollars for the property, but please understand that it's very unusual for a full-price offer to come in. In fact, most offers come in at about ten percent below the asking price, which means one hundred eighty thousand dollars is about what we'd expect." This anchors the sellers to the $180,000 amount. Then when the agent presents them the offer of $185,000, it's so much better than the amount to which they anchored, they're more likely to accept it.

I remember driving through the small colonial town of Santa Rosa, Honduras, in Central America looking for a hotel room. My Spanish isn't great, but I could understand the desk clerk, who said the cost of the room was twenty-one lempiras. He also proudly told me that they had a magnificent suite available with carpeting and cable television for seventy-five lempiras. I was aware of the exchange rate. I knew the suite translated to only fourteen dollars a night, which was a real bargain. However, I'd now anchored on the first number he'd given me, which was the twenty-one lempiras. Because of that, the seventy-five lempiras for the suite sounded like a fortune. So I settled on two rooms, one for my son and the other for me, then immediately started kicking myself for being so cheap. What should the clerk have done? He should have told me about the suite first, anchoring me to the seventy-five lempiras. If I didn't agree to that, he could have always come down. What does all this have to do with anything? Time and time again, I've seen salespeople anchor a buyer to the least expensive model because they don't want to scare him or her off. Then they have a terrible time moving the customer up, because they've now anchored him or her to the lower price.

## RECENCY DRIFT: USING YOUR IMMEDIATE PAST

The seventh drift is the *Recency Drift*, where you give more emphasis to what has happened to you recently. That's why the IRS regularly indicts more people in March than in any other month of the year. Surely it was no coincidence that Leona Helmsley had to start serving her prison sentence for tax evasion on April 15. It's why you see a traffic accident and slow down for a few minutes afterward. In business, it's the tendency for salespeople to sell the product that they've been trained on recently. That's why manufacturers' representatives should keep going back to retrain salespeople.

## FAVORABILITY DRIFT: BLINDED BY
YOUR OWN DECISIONS

With the eighth drift, *Favorability Drift*, you tend to look harder for information that supports your beliefs. You need to be disciplined enough to seek information that disregards preconceived notions. Psychologists proved this with a study at a racetrack. They were researching people's attitudes immediately before they placed a bet and immediately after they placed a bet. What they found out was that before placing their bets, people were uptight, anxious, and uncertain they were doing the right thing. Suddenly, once they'd placed the bet, Favorability Drift took over. Their minds worked to support the decision they'd made, and they often went back and doubled the bet before the race started.

The same principle applies, for example, when a business executive makes a decision to invest in a surfboard division. In reality, it's a big mistake. It's a very trendy, highly specialized business that should only be run by people who are fanatical surfers. However, the executive never realizes his mistake because his mind is working to reinforce the decision he made. Have the discipline to look for information that contradicts your beliefs and contradicts the decisions you may have made in the past.

## Recapping Information Drifts

Beware of the Information Drifts I have explained to you. They cause you to make decisions using inaccurate information, and they narrow your field of opportunity. Remember, the eight types of Information Drifts to be aware of are:

**AVAILABILITY DRIFT.** You give more weight to information that's more readily available to you. The more you're aware of something, the more you give it emphasis it doesn't deserve.

**EXPERIENCE DRIFT.** You tend to see things in terms of your personal or professional interest. If you're a horse-racing fan, you tend to think it's the most popular sport in the world.

**CONFLICT DRIFT.** Your natural tendency is to reject information that conflicts with your beliefs.

**RECALL DRIFT.** You more easily recall information about things familiar to you.

**SELECTIVITY DRIFT.** Since you are unable to absorb everything, you screen out information and observations about things that do not interest you.

**ANCHORING DRIFT.** If you lack expertise in a specific area, right or wrong, you latch on to or anchor to the first information you hear.

**RECENCY DRIFT.** You place greater emphasis on what has just happened to you. For instance, a recent traffic ticket will make you much more cautious, even if no police are in sight.

**FAVORABILITY DRIFT.** You are inclined to look harder for information that supports your beliefs rather than input that flies in the face of your preconceived notions.

To work further on information drifts, you can refer back to the five decisions you listed earlier and analyze how an information drift may have been involved in each decision.

## Determining Biased Information

These information drifts come into play when you're gathering or analyzing the information yourself. If other people are giving you information, you have an additional problem. Those people might be biased in the way they present the information to you. If that's the case, go over this checklist in your mind:

1. Does the person giving me this information have a personal stake in this decision? Is he or she consciously or unconsciously trying to sway my opinion?

2. Does the person gathering the information have a reasonable amount of expertise in this area? Observations from nonexperts in an area can be very damaging.

3. Does the person presenting the information have a prejudice of one kind or another? He may not have a personal stake in your decision, but he may have a particular prejudice. For example, he may be more of a risk taker than you'd be. Or less of a risk taker. He may have a prejudice against expanding into different industries, or he may have a prejudice against foreign trade.

4. How much time did this person have to put the data together? If she accumulated the data under too much time pressure, there's a danger of superficial reporting.

## Five Problems to Avoid When Blueprinting

Now, if you've done a good job of gathering information, you're ready to blueprint the decision. There are five problems that can arise in accurately Blueprinting the decision.

First, you're too far from the problem to see it clearly. One of the reasons I love to travel is that I've found out that only by going to a country can you get a true feel for what's really going on.

As soon as the former Soviet Union permitted tourists to visit their country, I took my son John for a two-week visit. I was fascinated finally to be able to visit the superpower that has threatened the world throughout my life. By the time we reached our hotel room in Moscow, we were doubled over in laughter. Superpower? This was a superpower? Nothing works in Russia. The automobiles don't work; the phones don't work; the hotel elevators don't work. This wasn't a superpower—this was a country on the brink of collapse! How could we know, four years before the CIA figured it out, that the Soviet Union was about to collapse? Because we weren't talking to the experts, we were talking to the people. That put us closer to the problem.

Before I spent ten days in Ireland, I had a very simplistic answer to the troubles there: Great Britain should swallow its pride and give Northern Ireland back to Ireland. Once I spent some time talking to people in both the North and the South, I found out that the problem is far more complicated. Hardly anybody in the North wants to be part of the economically depressed South. And hardly anybody in the Republic of Ireland feels that the South could afford to take on the expensive social programs of Northern Ireland.

The second problem is being too familiar with the problem. Try this exercise: Without looking at your watch, can you describe the face? Does it have numbers or strokes or diamonds? Does it have a second hand? Most of us can't say. We look at our watch a dozen times a day, but never actually see it.

The third problem is you're too close to the problem. See if you can solve this problem: Draw a straight line that goes through New York, Dallas, and San Francisco. It's a difficult problem to solve because you're so close to it. In your mind, you automatically see a map of the United States. You see New York in the East, then you see Dallas down South, and San Francisco in the West. You automatically say, "You can't draw a straight line that goes through those three cities." Yet, I can add another condition to that problem, and you probably can solve it immediately. Let me rephrase the question. I want you to draw a straight line that goes through these three cities *in this order*—New York, San Francisco, and Dallas. That makes it easy, doesn't it? You realize all you have to do is draw a line around the globe.

Another example of being too close to the problem is the development of the subway system in the San Francisco Bay area. The planners set out to solve the Bay area's traffic problems.

However, they got so absorbed with building a technologically brilliant system that they lost sight of the objective. Original estimates put the maximum cost at $722 million for 123 miles. It ended up costing $1.6 billion for 71 miles of track. Operating costs are 465 percent of forecasted costs, and only half the people they expected to ride it do so. The result of this inability to see the big picture is a technologically perfect system that nobody wants to ride, or pay for.

The fourth problem when Blueprinting the decision is that you're too obsessed with overcoming barriers and lose sight of the original objective.

John Sculley was head of marketing at Pepsi Cola before he became president of Apple Computers. Pepsi thought for many years that one of its major problems was the distinct shape of Coca-Cola's bottle. Convinced it was a major reason for Coca-Cola's success, Pepsi people tried everything they knew to come up with a bottle design equally distinctive. They couldn't come up with much, and finally settled for a mediocre swirl design.

John Sculley was smart enough to wonder if their obsession with the problem was blinding them to opportunities. He started approaching the problem from a different angle. Throwing away his preconceived notion of bottle advantage, he commissioned a survey to see how the public consumed soft drinks in the home. An interesting fact came to light. By giving away Pepsi to test families, Sculley found out people will drink an almost unlimited amount of Pepsi as long as it is available in the house. He saw that the way to increase sales was to get larger bottles of Pepsi into homes. Coke was at a distinct disadvantage here, because it would be impractical to make its hourglass bottle in larger shapes. By leading the industry into bigger containers, Sculley eliminated the Coke bottle-shape advantage.

And the fifth problem when Blueprinting is misstating the problem. "Should I trust this person enough to go into a new business together?" is different from "Should I start a new business?'' In order to get an accurate blueprint of a problem, we need to carefully pinpoint it.

To review, the five obstacles to accurate Blueprinting are:

- I'm too far from the problem.

- I'm too familiar with the problem.

- I'm too close to the problem.

- I'm too obsessed with the problem.

- I have misstated the problem.

Remember, the key steps to Blueprinting are: (1) Define problems accurately, so you can get a clear picture of the decision you're facing; (2) Beware of Information Drifts that cause you to make decisions using inaccurate information and narrow your field of opportunity; and (3) Be realistic when laying out a problem. The time for optimism is after you've made your decision. Confident Decision Makers understand that it's much better to know some of the right questions than to think you know all of the right answers.

# CHAPTER FOUR

# Intuitive Decision Making

## What It Means to Be Intuitive

Wouldn't it be wonderful to be that one person in a million who appears to have a surefire, never-miss intuition? C. R. Smith, the first president of American Airlines, seemed to have it. Although he'd never worked at an airline before, he had a natural feel for how to run one. On his very first day on the job, he ordered a change in pilots' uniforms that became the standard to this day. After one flight in a DC-2, he called up Donald Douglas, the head of Douglas Aircraft, whose company made the plane. He said, "Don, I want you to expand this plane so it'll carry twenty-one passengers in the daytime and sleep fourteen at night." Douglas told him he was crazy, that his suggestion wouldn't work. Smith wouldn't give in. He kept Douglas on the phone for two hours. He promised to buy twenty of the planes on the spot. Finally, Douglas agreed to have one of his engineers take another look at it. The improvements Smith suggested resulted in the most successful plane in aviation history, the DC-3. In another instance, he virtually ignored a foot-high study the company had done on swapping routes with Pan Am. Instead, he simply walked over to Pan Am president Bill Seawall's office and made the swap. The company once spent $100,000 on a study to cool airplanes. The recommendation? Paint the planes white. Smith wouldn't even read the study.

"Forget it," he said. "If you want to cool them, find some other way."

His persistence led to the air-conditioning that we enjoy today.

Stories about the amazing intuitive abilities of successful businessmen are not hard to find. C. R. Smith wasn't the only one to perform feats of intuition that defy rational explanation.

Going against the advice of his father and all the experts in the oil industry, Nelson Bunker Hunt played a hunch he could find oil in Libya. He drilled into the Sarir field, which turned out to be one of the largest reserves of oil on the planet. Soon he was pumping $100,000 worth of oil a day, and his hunch made him $16 billion.

Gustave Leven, a Paris stockbroker, tried to find a buyer for an almost defunct company that bottled spring water. Although the French show little interest in drinking water of any kind, he bought the company himself, on a hunch. Part of it was fascination with the unusual shape of the bottles, which were fashioned after the Indian clubs the eccentric English founder of the company used when he exercised. Gustave Leven went on to build Perrier into a billion-dollar company.

Conrad Hilton claimed he built his hotel empire on hunches. I've already told you how he bought his first hotel on a hunch, when he'd set out to buy a bank. Another example of his intuitive ability was when he bought the corporate assets of the Stevens Hotel in Chicago. He submitted a bid for $165,000. "Then somehow that didn't seem right to me," Hilton later explained. "Another figure kept coming, one hundred eighty thousand dollars. It satisfied me. It seemed fair. It felt right. I changed my bid to the larger figure on that hunch. When they were opened, the closest bid to mine was one hundred seventy-nine thousand, eight hundred dollars. I got the Stevens Corporation by a narrow margin of two hundred dollars. Eventually, those assets returned me two million.''

Jonas Salk said, ''Intuition is my partner, I wake up every morning to see what gifts it will toss me.'' Johann Sebastian Bach used to say his problem wasn't finding melodies, but avoiding stepping on them when he got out of bed.

Earl Nightingale, founder of the audiotape company Nightingale-Conant, said, ''Ideas are elusive, slippery things. Best to keep a pad of paper and a pencil at your bedside, so you can stab them during the night, before they get away.'' To which I would add, ''Intuition is like a deer nuzzling your sleeping bag on a chilly October morning. Don't be startled by it, or you'll scare it away.''

## Is Intuitive Decision Making a Thing of the Past?

In many ways, it seems that in America we've moved away from intuitive decision making, and we've become obsessed with logic. That we've turned our back on what made us great. One of the reasons we've moved away from intuitive thought is that we feel its usefulness has been supplanted by scientific thought, which is rooted in logic. In the Western world, scientific discovery has been so astonishingly successful for us that we put intuitive thought on the back burner.

The stream of scientific discovery that started in the seventeenth century turned into a river in the eighteenth century, a torrent in the nineteenth century, and became a tumultuous flood of progress as it swept into the twentieth century. In the 1980s, there was one final, enormous swing from intuitive decision making to logical decision making. It was fueled by two key factors—computers, which brought us into the information age; and the move to larger and larger corporations.

When a mainframe can produce a decision tree or a fault tree in seconds, what use do we have for intuitive decision making? A corporate-systems department can now develop payoff tables that can coherently juggle a thousand different factors in minutes. Isn't it an anachronism to have an expensive executive sitting behind a closed door waiting for intuition to inspire him in a blinding flash of light? Probably. Except that scientists are frequently wrong. In fact, there have been two major themes dominating scientific thought during this century, and both are directly related to decision making. Both of them turned out to be wrong.

First, Reductionism. Scientists became obsessed with the thought that if they could understand how the smallest component of the universe worked, then they'd know everything. If we could comprehend the smallest component of the problem, we could understand the whole. There turned out to be a big problem with that line of thinking: There doesn't seem to be a smallest component. Scientists can't comprehend the smallest picture any more than they can grasp the huge picture—what's beyond the universe. They used to think that the atom was the smallest element. Now they don't know.

Second, Universal Predictability, or the belief that everything is predictable. Scientists thought that computers, by their sheer ability to process huge amounts of information, would make human decision making obsolete. Back in the 1960s, scientists began combining the basic laws of physics with the incredible computing power of the mainframe, in order to make remarkably precise predictions. They could send a space probe to the far reaches of our galaxy and predict its course with unbelievable accuracy. Suddenly, they could create robotic factories that would manufacture complex or miniature items with almost no chance of error, because they could predict any problem and compensate for it.

It was then that scientists began to believe in Universal Predictability. They thought that if they could generate enough information and process it through a big enough mainframe fast enough, they could eliminate the need for guesswork. All decisions could be made with computers. They'd never make a mistake again. It turns out they got a bit carried away.

Suddenly, one of them looked up from his computer and said, "If we can do all that, why couldn't we predict the Soviet economy was about to collapse? Why didn't we know the *Exxon Valdez* would run aground in Prudoe Bay? Why didn't we know Saddam Hussein would invade Kuwait?"

Scientists realized that some things are inherently unpredictable. They knew they'd goofed when they tried to make long-term weather predictions. Scientists spent $500 million on satellites and computers in the belief they could solve one of mankind's biggest problems—the unpredictable nature of weather. It turned out to be a complete waste of money. Weather is unpredictable beyond a few days. Scientists determined that any activity that involves nature or human beings is unpredictable on a long-term basis.

The name given to this new theory was Chaos Theory. Any small deviation from normal behavior can become magnified as it moves through the system. This magnifying effect explains why a cormorant diving into the water in Central China could affect the weather in New York. The Chaos Theory is one of the reasons why you can never depend on computers—or any completely logical system of analysis, however sophisticated it may be—to make decisions for you. Confident Decision Makers use logic as a tool, but to be a great decision maker, you must blend in the magic of intuition. If you can do that, you can empower logical decisions with the magic of intuition. No amount of analysis will ever replace a human mind perfectly trained to access and process intuition. Logical decision making reduces the possibility of error. Intuitive decision making develops creative alternatives. By turning our back on old-style intuition, we're missing a great opportunity to develop new and exciting solutions to our problems.

## Intuition Is a Learned Skill, Not a Talent.

So once again, we're beginning to look inward for solutions. Can we rediscover our power of intuition and put it to work for us? Intuition is an awesome power, no question about it. However, I don't think it's a gift given to a chosen few; I think it's a skill we can all learn.

Remember the quiz on logic versus intuition in Chapter One? Were you someone who tended to trust your intuition over logic? You might have been surprised to find out how often you rely on your intuition. In fact, many professionals in occupations such as medicine, police work, and the social sciences use their intuition regularly to handle complex problems that don't have obvious solutions. Because we're not really taught to pay attention to our intuitive ability, they might not realize that that is what they're doing. However, if we saw intuition as a skill to be accessed regularly, think how much easier it would be to handle complex situations.

The realization that intuition is a learned skill came to me as I reread the story of a dirt-poor young schoolboy whose dead-beat father had died before he was born. His mother was raising him in the small town of Woolsthorpe, in northern England. He was doing very poorly in school, and his frustrations led him into a fight with a bigger classmate. He won the fight, but his teacher pointed out that since his schoolmate was doing so much better in school than he, the other boy was obviously still better.

This challenge changed the world. The young boy was Isaac Newton; and that day, he promised himself he'd always get better grades than the other boy. He rose from the bottom of his class to the top, and his uncle arranged to get him into Cambridge University. The year he graduated, another chance incident changed his life. The Great Plague broke out, killing 10 percent of the population. This affected him so much that he gave up the thought of continuing his education and returned home to meditate.

During this time Newton developed a remarkable ability to concentrate on a problem. This ability led to an incredible flow of discovery, including the laws of gravity, motion, and tides. He invented calculus and the reflecting telescope. The poverty-stricken boy who showed no special talent grew up to spell out the mechanics of our universe.

Newton attributed all this, not to any innate wisdom, but to the power of continuous and concentrated thought. He once remarked, "If I have done the public any service, it is due to patient thought."

Someone once asked him, "How did you discover the Law of Gravitation?"

"By thinking about it all the time," he replied. "I did it by keeping the subject constantly before me until the first dawnings opened little by little into the full light."

A neighbor who didn't know who Newton was once complained that she lived next door to a madman. "Every night, when the evening sun shines through his window, he sits in front of a tub of soap suds. Hour after hour he sits there blowing bubbles through a clay pipe, watching them burst." Newton was actually studying the refraction of light on the thin skin of the bubbles. Remember, of course, that Isaac Newton died celibate at the age of eighty-five. You may not want to remain that focused for that long!

In an earlier age, this power of concentration cost Archimedes his life. When the Roman general Marcellus invaded, he ordered his soldiers to spare Archimedes' life. When they reached him, he was concentrating on a problem, drawing circles in the sand. "Don't disturb my circles," he said as he waved the soldier away. It so frustrated the soldier, that he drew his sword and killed Archimedes.

Isaac Newton didn't claim any oneness with God. His discoveries didn't come to him in a dream or in a flash of blinding light. He was an expert in his field, and he made his discoveries by focusing his powers of concentration on the problem.

On his deathbed, he said, "I found myself standing in front of an ocean of truth. All I did was divert myself by picking up an unusually smooth pebble or an exceptionally pretty seashell."

In other words, by using his concentrated thought, or what some people might think of as intuition, he was able to come up with a solution based on the sea of information he had gathered before him. I call this process Rapid Reasoning. I'll tell you how you can learn to access it, too.

# Rapid Reasoning: Creating Order from Chaos

What gives you the power of Rapid Reasoning? First, realize that your ability to reason is limited by three things:

- Your short-term memory

- Your working memory

- Your attention span

Rapid Reasoning is your ability to pull together unrelated facts from your pool of knowledge and focus them on the decision. The reason experts like Sir Isaac Newton have Rapid Reasoning powers is that they chunk information. *Chunking* describes what the mind does when it stores information in parcels rather than individual pieces. Although you're bombarded by millions of bits of information, you can only comfortably juggle about seven pieces of information at one time. If you try to handle any more than seven, your mind overloads.

Let me give you a very simple example of chunking. Remember when you first learned to tie your shoelaces? You learned to pull both ends tight, cross them over into a simple bow, fold one loose end in half, and wrap the other around it. Now, how many times do you think through all these steps when you put on a pair of sneakers? See what I mean? We no longer know what it takes to tie a shoe because we've chunked all those individual pieces of knowledge together.

A really good auto mechanic chunks everything he knows about fixing cars. I once took a car into my mechanic because it sounded as though it were falling apart. I felt sure it would take a major engine overhaul to fix it. As I pulled up, expecting the worst, he said, "You've got a loose engine mount. Give me ten minutes, and I'll fix it for you." If I had asked how he knew it was the engine mount rather than a dozen other problems, he probably couldn't have told me. But long ago, he chunked the information on the make of a car, the model, the type of driving I do, the time of year it was, and many other factors that helped him to conclude my problem was the engine mount. If I'd congratulated him on his powers of Rapid Reasoning, he would have said, "Huh?" Because he's no longer aware of the thinking process he goes through.

A wrinkled old rancher in Kansas may sit on his front porch and say, "We'll likely get some rain tomorrow." He's not aware of Rapid Reasoning either. Ask him how he knows, and he won't be able to tell you. He long ago chunked all he knows about weather.

People who appear to have great intuition really have become very adept at chunking information. It enables them to access huge amounts of information in seconds. The key to intuition, then, is saturating yourself with information about the decision, and then chunking that information to make Rapid Reasoning possible.

## Some Examples of Successful Rapid Reasoners

Many inventions attributed to intuition were really not intuitive at all. They were a result of Rapid Reasoning by experts who could think fast by chunking underlying knowledge. Listen to these examples and decide whether they're really intuition or simply Rapid Reasoning.

Art Fry first thought of Post-it Notes while singing in church. His initial idea was for a bookmark that wouldn't fall out, rather than a note on which to write. It was fortunate he worked for a company like 3M, which encourages its employees to follow up on their hunches. Lewis Lehr, the chairman of the company, says its corporate structure is "designed specifically to encourage young entrepreneurs to take an idea and run with it." He calls it the heart of their design for growth.

Louis Pasteur, the French chemist and microbiologist, was examining some fermented grapes when he realized that grapes ferment only when the skin is broken. He then knew that bacterial infection was caused by germs in the air, not by the spontaneous internal generation he previously thought responsible. His discovery saved the French beer, wine, and silk industries, and led to the process we now know as pasteurization.

When Ray Kroc tried to buy the McDonald brothers' share of his company, they stunned him by asking for $2.7 million—an amount that would leave them a million dollars each after taxes. Kroc recalled, "I'm not a gambler and I didn't have that kind of money, but my funny-bone instinct kept urging me on. So I closed my office door, cussed up and down, and threw things out the window. Then I called my lawyer back and said, 'Take it!' " It was a smart move, however much it hurt. Their share was soon worth $15 million a year to Kroc.

In 1928, Alexander Fleming was about to throw away some bacteria he'd been cultivating. A mold growth was contaminating the culture. But before disposing of the culture, he noticed a bacteria-free circle around the mold growth. A hunch led him to investigate it further. He found a substance in the mold that prevented growth of the bacteria even when he diluted it eight hundred times. He called it penicillin. Years later, Fleming was given a tour of a modern research laboratory with a perfectly sterile environment. His guide commented, "What a pity you didn't have a place like this to work in. Who can tell what you might have discovered?" "Well, certainly not penicillin," Fleming said, laughing.

King Gillette was a salesman who sold cork that went inside bottle caps. It fascinated him. "Isn't that something?" he'd say, "I make my living selling something people throw away and keep on rebuying. I wonder what else would people buy, throw away, and buy again?" That's when he hit upon the idea of the disposable razor blade.

All of these appear to be examples of a magical intuition, when really they are examples of Rapid Reasoning. Every one of these people was an expert in his field. Their expertise had caused them to chunk their knowledge so they could access it easily. Ray Kroc had visited so many restaurants as a malted-milk-machine salesman that he could quickly analyze what the McDonald brothers had going for them.

Louis Pasteur had spent eleven years studying fermentation before he tied it together in his mind with exposure to air. And

King Gillette had spent his entire business life working with people who sold disposable items to the public.

## How to Access Rapid Reasoning

Obviously, it's not realistic to suggest that you should develop Rapid Reasoning by spending a decade or more becoming an expert in the area of the decision. However, you can simulate that condition using the Seven Steps of Confident Decision Making, the first three of which we have already covered. They are:

1. Accurately categorize the situation so you can start looking for the solution in the right direction.

2. Blueprint the problem accurately, so your mind totally focuses on the problem it has to solve.

3. Saturate your mind with facts about the problem. General Schwarzkopf totally saturated his mind with information about Saddam Hussein's battle strategy. Afterward, Barbara Walters asked him what surprised him most about the war. He responded, "It was Saddam's total predictability. He didn't make a single move that we hadn't already anticipated." Sounds like intuition, doesn't it? Not really. It comes from saturating your mind with information, which leads to Rapid Reasoning.

## Do You Have a Golden Gut?

Generating intuition may come naturally to you, or you may have to work at it. To find out how naturally intuitive you are, let's take the golden-gut test. I'm going to ask you fifteen quick questions. See how many of these sound as though they describe you.

---

1. *I think the best way to learn new computer software is to install it and play with it for a while. Later, I read the instructions. Yes or No?*

2. *I should be allowed to set my own work hours. I know when I perform best, and it's not necessarily the same hours each day. Yes or No?*

3. *People think my desk is a mess, but I know where things are. Yes or No?*

4. *I think of myself as an honest and moral person, but sometimes I'm still not sure I'm doing the right thing. But that's okay. Yes or No?*

5. *When the evidence tells me I should decide one way, but I've a strange feeling I shouldn't, I usually follow my feelings. Yes or No?*

6. *When I don't have precise directions to get to a party, it doesn't bother me. I'll go to the general area and ask somebody the way. Yes or No?*

7. *I like problem solving because it gives me a chance to play with possibilities. Yes or No?*

8. *I get bored easily. Yes or No?*

9. *I'll listen to expert advice but don't always follow it. Yes or No?*

10. *I know a lot of people who play their hunches. Yes or No?*

11. *I like novels, as well as nonfiction books. Yes or No?*

12. *Multiple-answer questions are not very effective, so students should have to give essay answers. Yes or No?*

13. *No one ever accused me of being a detail person. Yes or No?*

14. *Making an appointment for a precise day and time ties me down. Yes or No?*

15. *I enjoy taking risks. Yes or No?*

*Total number of Yes answers* _____

Here are the golden-gut test score results:

**TWELVE OR MORE.** You have a twenty-four-karat golden gut. I suggest you follow your hunches whether you think they're right or not. Since you won't be right all the time, have a good attorney on retainer.

**NINE TO ELEVEN.** You have an eighteen-karat golden gut. Trust but verify your hunches.

**SIX TO EIGHT.** You have a brass gut. You sometimes get good hunches, but don't trust them yet. You need this book to help you develop your intuition.

**LESS THAN SIX.** You have a lead gut. You do everything by analysis and almost never take chances. The federal government should have bought you this book!

---

What was the golden-gut test all about? It was a test of your ability to function in, and even relish, a world that's not totally logical. Human beings have an incredible desire to know what's going on. You can put a cow in a field, and it will stay in that field all its life and never wonder what's happening on the other side of the hill. Human beings will spend $1.5 billion to put a Hubbell telescope up in space. We've simply got to know and understand what's happening in our universe.

## How Well Can You Handle Ambiguity?

Your ability to develop intuition is in direct relationship to your ability to accept this truth: Sometimes you can figure out why things happen, and sometimes there just isn't any way you can figure them out.

Remember earlier in this chapter, when I talked about the two scientific theories that have dominated Western thought throughout this century? First, Reductionism, scientists' belief that if they could only understand the smallest component of the universe, they could understand everything. Second, Universal Predictability, scientists' belief that everything is predictable, if only they could build a big enough computer. Both turned out to be completely wrong. Smart scientists now accept Chaos Theory: because we live in a world dominated by nature and human behavior, many things are inherently unpredictable.

The ability to work with ambiguity makes you a better decision maker, and it makes you a better businessperson. Not every decision offers a perfect solution. The willingness to admit you can be wrong is a key to Confident Decision Making. Be willing to make mistakes, and be willing to let your people make mistakes.

Joel Bruckner, professor of management at Columbia Business School, says, "The need to prove we're right overwhelms our ability to think rationally. It blinds us to the early warning signals that a project is failing and creates false hope of a turnaround." Be sure you're letting your people know that it's okay to make mistakes. Perhaps one of the reasons Johnson & Johnson has been so successful is the story CEO James Burke loves to tell about his early days with the company. He had spearheaded a project to market a chest rub for children. It died a horrible death in the marketplace. He was called in front of the company's chairman, General Johnson, who said, "Are you the person who cost us all that money?"

"Yes, sir," he fumbled, feeling sure he was about to get fired.

"I just wanted to congratulate you," the General said. "If you're making mistakes, it means you're making decisions and taking risks. We won't grow unless you take risks."

The best way you can let the people in your organization know that it's okay to make mistakes is to admit quickly when you make a mistake.

## The Biggest Mistake Is Not Knowing When to Cut Your Losses.

Perhaps the biggest mistake you can make is hanging on to something in the hope that a situation will improve. One thing I learned early on is to put in a sell order when initiating a project. Make the decision and budget for a potential loss of $X$ dollars—it may be ten thousand dollars, or $10 million, or $100 million. But when it's gone, seriously consider pulling the plug, just as investors do on Wall Street. Let's say someone buys stock at $100, just before it drops to $75. His broker tells him, "Sell before it gets any worse."

The investor says, "I don't want to sell the stock when it's gone down this far—it has to go back up."

Smart decision makers know to cut their losses. The broker says, "Would you buy the stock today at seventy-five dollars a share?"

He probably would say, "Well, of course not."

"But that's exactly what you've done. By refusing to sell the stock for $75 a share, you've just bought your own stock for that." It's basic logic, but it's seldom obvious.

When I was an active real estate broker, we'd have a seller trying to get $200,000 for his property. We'd present an offer to the seller at $190,000, and he'd refuse it.

I'd teach the salespeople to say, "Let me make another proposal to you. There's an identical house down the street that's for sale. I can get it for one hundred ninety thousand dollars. Would you like to buy it?"

He'd say, "Well, of course not, I'm trying to sell the one I've got."

So we'd tell him, "But when you turned down this offer for one hundred and ninety thousand dollars that's exactly what you did. You just bought your own house back for one hundred and ninety thousand dollars. You just told me that was a poor investment."

Understanding the basic logic in this will make you a better decision maker. Remember, you have to forget what you've lost and reevaluate the situation as it exists today. In my company, Roger Dawson Productions, we once invested a lot of money in a promotional program and lost it. A few months later, I raised the question of starting up the program again with the president of my company.

She said, "I don't think that's a good idea."

"Why don't you think it's such a good idea? Don't you think it would work?"

She said, "Well, yes, but we've lost so much money on it already."

I said, "Forget what we've lost; that money's already gone. Look at the situation as it exists today. Make a decision on whether, from this point on, it's smart to invest the money to get the program going again."

## Developing a Golden Gut Requires a Leap of Faith.

Coors Brewery made a $425 million deal to buy Strohs Brewery. One month later, Bill Coors took back control of Coors and axed the deal—writing off millions in legal costs. Why? Because he reevaluated the situation as it was on the day he took over. Coors was gaining strength, and Strohs was losing it quickly. On the day of making his decision, Coors felt he could cut a better deal if he waited and then moved.

Your ability to develop a golden gut is in direct relationship to your willingness to accept that when you make a decision, you open the door to ambiguity.

Any military leader will tell you that being in a war is like opening a door to a darkened room for the first time. You simply can't know what's going to happen. We discovered that truth in Vietnam, the Soviet Union discovered it in Afghanistan, and Saddam Hussein discovered it when he invaded Kuwait.

The door I want you to walk through is the door from a logical world in which everything can be explained—into the room of intuition. Where things can happen without your understanding why. Where you move confidently ahead with a decision, even though you don't have every assurance that you're doing the right thing. Pure intuition is like a photographic memory. It would be great to have one. It would make life a lot simpler. However, assuming you don't have a vein of pure intuition running through you—I know I don't—work with the Seven Steps of Confident Decision Making.

## The Illusion of Intuition Is Finally Revealed.

So now you've learned that intuition isn't a gift from heaven, it's the learned skill of Rapid Reasoning. You can develop it by learning how to saturate your mind with information, so that your brain begins to chunk information. That enables you to access huge amounts of information quickly and easily. Then develop the intense focus of Isaac Newton. Finally, train yourself to deal with ambiguity, because you can't be intuitive if you insist on perfection before you feel confident about a decision. While these steps will prepare you for Rapid Reasoning, accessing your intuition is another matter. The next technique I'll show you teaches you when to use your logical, rational side and when to access intuitive thought.

# CHAPTER FIVE

# Developing Rapid Reasoning

## Where Does Rapid Reasoning Come From?

While questioning a rape victim, a police detective senses the victim's assailant lives nearby. Later, police arrest a man living two blocks from her home. In another scenario, a doctor decides to push for tests on a patient who she thinks has an obscure disease. The other doctors won't concur with her opinion. Fortunately, her diagnosis is accurate, and the patient is saved from unnecessary medical treatment.

In both these situations, the people involved were able to rely on their Rapid Reasoning ability to lead them to a viable solution. Yet Rapid Reasoning is not an ability that's often stressed or acknowledged in our society. As I mentioned in the last chapter, we depend more and more on our logical ability rather than our intuitive thought.

Where does Rapid Reasoning come from? There are several theories regarding intuition, otherwise known as Rapid Reasoning. One theory suggests that both sides of the brain gather the same information but make decisions differently. The left brain codes the information in verbal form and uses logic to make decisions. The right brain absorbs the information emotionally and makes decisions intuitively. We're still learning and speculating about how all this affects our behavior.

Some researchers wonder if what Sigmund Freud called the subconscious is really just the nondominant side of the brain. In this country, 85 percent of us favor the left brain, the logical side. This means that your left brain dominates your conscious thought. The subconscious, then, may just be the influence of the right brain.

Left-brain dominance also may explain *déjà vu*, that sudden feeling that you've been there before. It may just be one side of the brain transmitting an image a split second ahead of the other side.

## The Unique Functions of the Right and Left Brain

Dr. Benjamin Libet, a psychologist with the University of San Francisco, points out that the brain starts to seek information about four tenths of a second before we're aware of it. This isn't speculation. He proved it in scientific tests. Four tenths of a second is a significant amount of time, which in itself may explain intuition. The right brain starts working on a problem four tenths of a second before the logical left brain becomes aware of it. Sometimes the right brain will come up with the correct answer a split second before the left brain realizes it.

Some other interesting facts to note about the right brain—the right brain gets drunk first; when the right brain is aroused, it impedes the judgment of the left, causing slurred speech and impaired decision making.

The right brain goes to sleep first and wakes up last. That explains why you have those wonderfully creative ideas as you drop off to sleep. When you wake up in the morning, your left brain is screaming, "How could you have ever thought a dumb idea like that would work?"

The right brain shuts down under stress. It has a very delicate "tilt" mechanism. The left-brain engineer can plow through adversity without any problem. It says, "Oh, so the rocket blew up when we launched it? That's interesting, well, we'll keep working at it until we get it right."

The right-brain playwright will be so upset over one bad review that he'll go drive a cab for a year. Noël Coward was once offended by the famous actress Diana Cooper, who cruelly told him she'd seen one of his plays and didn't think it was very funny. "Well, my dear," Coward responded, "I saw you play the Madonna in *The Miracle* and thought you were an absolute scream."

The creative mind shutting down under pressure causes many problems in decision making. Very often stress and decision making go hand in hand. Just when you need your creative right brain the most, it shuts down. The ability to control the left and right sides of your brain when making decisions is a key skill leading to Confident Decision Making.

# The Difference Between Left-Brain Decision Makers and Right-Brain Decision Makers

Whether you're predominantly left-or right-brained makes a big difference in the way you make decisions. Left-brained people like to solve problems with an organized approach. They do research, make lists, and analyze possible solutions. Then they assign possibilities to the different options. They like to research if anyone has faced the problem before, and if so, go with proven solutions.

Right-brained people like to solve problems by getting a feel for what works and finding out how other people feel about it. This is the "Throw it up against the wall, run it up the flagpole" brigade. They may find out that somebody else has faced the same problem before, but they're equally likely to pick a different solution—just to see what happens.

There's a further dimension to this that becomes really important when you consider decision making. That's how assertive you are as a decision maker. Assertive people will make decisions quickly. Nonassertive people will make decisions slowly. When you recognize that both left-and right-brain people can be either assertive or nonassertive in their thinking, you now have a quadrant of personality styles.

## The Four Types of Decision-Making Personalities

Imagine a window with four panes of glass. Put left-brained people on the left-hand side of the window and right-brained people on the right. At the top of the window, place assertive people, and at the bottom of the window put nonassertive.

So, in the top left-hand corner you have the unemotional, left-brained, assertive person, whom I call the Pragmatic. In the top right-hand corner, you have the assertive, emotional right-brained person I call the Extrovert. In the bottom right-hand corner, you have the nonassertive, creative person, whom I call the Amiable. And in the bottom left-hand corner, you have the nonassertive, unemotional, left-brained person, whom I call the Analytical.

Remember, the vertical dimension is assertiveness: high at the top and low on the bottom. The horizontal dimension is emotional disposition: left-brained unemotional on the left; right-brained emotional on the right. To see what I mean, take a look at the quadrant below:

| Left-Brained | Right-Brained |
|---|---|
| PRAGMATIC<br>Assertive<br>Unemotional | EXTROVERT<br>Assertive<br>Emotional |
| ANALYTICAL<br>Unassertive<br>Unemotional | AMIABLE<br>Unassertive<br>Emotional |

## THE QUALITIES OF A NO-NONSENSE PRAGMATIC

Would you like to know which you are? I can help you figure it out very quickly. Imagine you're attending one of my Confident Decision Making seminars. If you're a Pragmatic, you're there for one reason and one reason only, that's because you want to learn. You're very much a bottom-line kind of person. You're saying, "Don't razzle-dazzle me with a lot of wild stories, I don't need motivating, I just want information. You can use a little bit of humor, but only if it's relevant to what you're talking about. I didn't come here to listen to a bunch of jokes." You're a very time-management-conscious person. Perhaps you subscribe to a condensed-book service. That's where they take a five-hundred-page book and condense it down to four pages. Then you get your highlighter and go through that just to get the essence of it. On the way home, you'll be saying, "Well, that was a pretty good seminar on decision making, wasn't it? But did it really have to take three hours? I bet if he'd cut out the stories and jokes, he could have given us the same amount of information in half the time."

Philip Armour, the founder of Armour Meat Packing Company, was clearly a Pragmatic decision maker. In the early days, he had developed an admirable plan for training his second and third echelons in the techniques of management. He set up a junior board of directors and occasionally submitted important company problems to the group. One day, after a lively discussion, one of the young people made a motion that they go ahead with the project. There was a second for the motion. Then Mr. Armour, as chairman, called for a vote. Every person voted yes, feeling proud of his decisiveness. But Armour had no intention of letting it happen, or spending any time explaining his reasoning. He simply said, "The motion is lost," and went on to the next order of business. This is a classic example of a Pragmatic decision maker. Making decisions quickly and unemotionally—and expecting everyone else to be the same way.

While Armour was a Pragmatic, he did manage to maintain a keen sense of humor. He was once so pleased with the performance of a department he decided to buy each of the workers a new set of clothes. He asked everyone to order the suit of his choice and send the bill to him. One particularly greedy young man selected an expensive tuxedo. Armour reluctantly agreed to pay the bill, saying, "I packed a great many hogs in my time, but I never dressed one before."

## THE LIVELY WORLD OF THE EXTROVERT

If you're an Extrovert, in the top right-hand corner of the chart, and you're going to spend three hours in my seminar, it had better be fun. You love the humor and write down all the jokes. You're saying to me as the speaker, "Don't bore me with statistics. I hope you're not going to throw a bunch of charts, graphs, and projections up there, because I really get bogged down in all that kind of detail work. Tell me stories of triumph and disaster. Tell me about people who started out with nothing and really made it big, because when I leave here today, I want to feel good!"

You probably already have pretty good intuition. For example, if somebody in the audience asks me a question, you can often think of the answer faster than I can say it. You don't mind if I skip supporting evidence and go straight to a conclusion.

An example of Extrovert decision making might be the SmithKline Pharmaceutical Company, which became obsessed with finding a treatment for ulcers. The SmithKline people's thinking was, If we throw enough research money at the problem, we're going to come up with something we can market. They committed $2.5 million a year to research, blissfully unaware of the amount of work it would take. In theory, it could have meant testing 30 billion different compounds, which 15 million scientists working for thirty years couldn't have done. Then they committed $10 million to building a plant in Cork, Ireland, before knowing they had anything to sell. Once they had the drug approved, they told the plant boss that money was no issue. He was to make as much of the drug as he could. This is a typical Extrovert type of decision—made emotionally and quickly. Often it bombs, but here it really paid off. The drug SmithKline developed was Tagamet. It blocked the secretion of gastric acid into the stomach the way antihistamines block a runny nose. Tagamet became the first drug ever to exceed $1 billion in annual sales.

## THE AMIABLE PERSONALITY LIKES PEOPLE.

If you're an Amiable, in the bottom right-hand corner of the chart, you probably like being at the seminar simply because you enjoy being around a group of people who have similar interests. The ambience in the room is the most important thing to you. You probably worry about the other people in the room. You may raise your hand and ask me a question, not so much because you're confused, but because you think someone else in the room is confused. You're saying to me, "Talk to me. Please don't yell at me. I hope you're not one of those high-powered motivational people who races around the room, jumps up on the table, and gets us all to stand up and chant things together. Because I can't stand that.''

You also don't like put-down humor. You don't want to hear any attorney jokes or any mother-in-law jokes. Speakers like Amiables, because you often give positive feedback with smiles and nods. But you don't like it if I take a question from the audience and my response, heaven forbid, is insensitive.

Amiables make decisions slowly, because they're emotional and also because they want to involve other people in the decision. A good example of this would be the Canon Camera Company. The company appointed a new president, because it was in serious trouble and rapidly losing ground to its major competitor, Minolta. Instead of storming into his office and starting to make drastic changes in policy, the new president spent the first six weeks on the job visiting camera stores across the United States. He knew the key to Canon's success was its relationship with dealers. He found out the dealers weren't giving Canon much support because they seldom saw a Canon salesperson. He carefully and slowly accumulated information on what kinds of cameras would get the stores excited about Canon again. Eventually, he decided to have Canon deal exclusively through specialty outlets, with products priced just below Nikon, at the high end of the market. Minolta, which did business primarily through discount and drugstores, very quickly lost its number-one position.

## AN ANALYTICAL DECISION MAKER WANTS ALL THE FACTS.

If you're an Analytical, in the bottom left-hand corner of the chart, you relish lots of facts and data. Unlike the Pragmatic, who's likely to get bored in a three-hour seminar, you can sit through a ten-day symposium on the use of decision trees and reaction tables in resolving aerospace problems. After ten days, you come away feeling, "Boy, they just scraped the surface of the topic, didn't they?" You're not at the seminar for entertainment value, you're there for information, and the more you can get and write down, the better off you feel. You probably take the best notes in the audience. You're saying to me as the speaker, "Give me both sides of the story. If you have a bias, I want to know about it. Otherwise, I can't evaluate this." Also you're saying, "Tell me your sources of research, so I can validate this information." You'd hate it if I presented a conclusion without supporting evidence. You love it when I back conclusions with detailed slides, charts, and handouts.

A classic example of an Analytical decision maker was Harold Geneen, the head of ITT. Obsessed by facts, he'd never make a decision until he was absolutely sure he had them all. An embarrassing incident probably caused him to feel this way. Soon after taking over ITT, he became enthusiastic about the potential for manufacturing in Portugal. The labor rate was only nineteen cents an hour, and land was unbelievably cheap. He was aware that ITT had a components operation in Portugal, so he suggested converting it into a factory for telecommunications. With the low-price labor break, the Portuguese operation would be the main supplier for exporting high-technology parts around the world. One of his executives started to grin. Geneen wasn't amused and growled, "What's so funny?"

The man responded, "Mr. Geneen, I've been there. Our Portuguese operation is literally—not figuratively—literally one man and one boy."

He was never to make that embarrassing mistake again. He'd always get angry at his executives if they didn't know the facts. Much later he stormed out of a meeting and wrote a memo entitled

*Facts* that became compulsory reading for all ITT executives. It said, in part:

"There is not a word in the English language that more strongly conveys the intent of incontrovertibility than the word 'fact.' However, no word is more honored by its breach in actual usage. For example, at yesterday's meeting, we got apparent facts, assumed facts, reported facts and hoped for facts. In most cases, they were not 'facts' at all."

The message was clear. To Geneen, it was either a fact or it wasn't, and look out if you confused the two.

## Assessing Your Decision-Making Ability

Could you see yourself in one of those four personality styles? The value of this quadrant is that it clearly illustrates the way you make decisions. If you can easily place yourself in one of these personality quadrants, it doesn't mean you have exceptional decision-making ability. Or that you're doomed to failure as a decision maker. It does mean that you should understand your decision-making style and realize its strengths and weaknesses.

If you're a Pragmatic, you can make decisions quickly and make tough decisions unemotionally. Your weakness is that you may overlook the more creative decisions. And you may make decisions without being mindful of how they'll play out in the organization.

If you're an Extrovert, you can make fast intuitive decisions that everyone will support. But you get into trouble because you don't check out the facts before you move ahead.

As an Amiable, you're always considerate of other people's feelings, and you're very good at getting input from other people. But your emotional, nonassertive character makes you less bold and decisive than you should be.

It's interesting to see a Pragmatic interacting with an Amiable. Because the Pragmatic can always become less assertive, but the Amiable has difficulty being more assertive. Winston Churchill, who was a classic Pragmatic, once presented the Victoria Cross to Sergeant James Ward, who was a very introverted New Zealander. He'd performed an incredible act of bravery, climbing out onto the wing of his Wellington bomber during battle to extinguish a fire in the engine. Ward was struck dumb with awe in front of Churchill and couldn't speak. Churchill said gently, "You must feel very humble and awkward in my presence."

"Yes, sir," Ward managed to get out.

"Then you can imagine how humble and awkward I feel in your presence," said Churchill.

If you're Analytical, you have the most trouble making decisions, because you love to analyze everything. But analysis can lead to paralysis. For example, when the Germans overran Brest at the start of World War II, they captured a new French secret weapon, the fifteen-inch Richelieu gun. They were delighted, knowing that if they could get it quickly into production, it could cinch the war for them. They made the mistake of turning the project over to an extreme Analytical. It took him four years to complete his analysis, during which time he produced hundreds of pages of analysis and used up all the gun's ammunition conducting tests! The Germans lost the war without putting their miracle weapon to work. An Analytical like this is probably not going to make many bad decisions. The question is, will he make any decisions at all?

Take a look at your own decision-making style. Can you relate it to the strengths and weaknesses I've listed?

|  | Strengths | Weaknesses |
|---|---|---|
| **Pragmatic** | Decisive<br>Logical | Overlooks creative solutions<br>Not a people person |
| **Extrovert** | Decisive<br>Intuitively popular | Overlooks facts<br>Jumps to conclusions |
| **Amiable** | Considerate<br>Listens to others | Won't make tough decisions<br>Hesitant |
| **Analytical** | Gathers facts<br>Logical | Delays decisions because of<br>paralysis of analysis. |

# Controlling the Left and Right Sides of the Brain

Now let's look at how you can use this information about left- and right-brained personality styles to generate intuitive decision making. Your ability to be intuitive depends on the degree of access you have to the deepest levels of your mind. You prepare your mind for intuition by forcing your logical left brain to shut down and letting your creative right brain dominate. By shutting down the left brain and letting the creative right brain take over, you prepare your mind for intuition.

Strangely enough, you can do this in two diverse ways— either by stimulating your brain waves or relaxing them. In a high state of arousal, your right brain dominates, and you become more creative. This is what happens at football games, sales rallies, and in trading pits. Jogging and other forms of exercise also keep you in a high state of arousal, because the improved blood circulation pumps glycogen to your brain, and glycogen is rich in energy.

The opposite is also true. In a low state of arousal, the right brain also dominates. A boring assembly-line task shuts down the left brain and causes daydreaming. Hypnotists also use this technique when they put you under. They freeze the left brain with the boredom of a pendulum or metronome, and monotone talk, and then implant suggestions in the right brain. Attorneys use the same procedure in court by making a witness answer question after question for hour after hour. The left brain effectually goes into a coma, which causes the right brain to take over, and they emotionally blurt out something they had no intention of revealing.

I once attended a four-day seminar that exploited this phenomenon of shutting down the left brain. We sat in a hotel ballroom listening to a trainer drone on. We'd submitted ourselves to a very controlled environment, unable to do anything outside the very rigid rules that were set up. We soon learned that it was a waste of time to challenge the viewpoint of the trainer. The seminar was designed to numb our ability to be creative. However, we stayed in the room because of the trainers' constant assurance that on the fourth day we'd "get it." What we eventually got was a heavy dose of behavioral psychology for the masses. The speakers told us not to worry about life, and that we were so strongly conditioned by our experiences, we'd always react the way we'd been programmed to react, regardless of what we tried to do. So we should relax and let life happen to us. The audience greeted this astounding assertion with cheers of delight and left the room thrilled with their four-hundred-dollar investment. All I got out of it was a sore butt.

# Recognizing the Left-Brain-to-Right-Brain Shift

You can experience a shift from left-brain to right-brain thinking in many little instances in your life, once you're aware of the phenomenon. For example, analyze how you decide what to do the next time a homeless person asks you for a handout. If I have to walk through a poor area of a city, I very often put some dollar bills into a separate pocket. Then, if I'm approached by a needy person, I can be generous without having to bring out my money clip. I call it benefaction without buffoonery. Once, I was in downtown Chicago and saw a shabbily dressed man approaching me for a handout. My right brain was reaching into my pocket for a dollar bill, when he asked me if I could spare a quarter. My logical left brain immediately took over. I thought, What on earth can you do with a quarter? Since, as any salesperson will tell you, a confused mind says no, I moved on without giving him the dollar.

Flamboyant actress Tallulah Bankhead once dropped a fifty-dollar bill into a Salvation Army tambourine. "Don't mention it," she said, "I know what a perfectly ghastly season it's been for you Spanish dancers."

Reacting to a request for a handout is only one of many instances where you can experience your mind shifting from one side of the brain to the other. Once you become aware of this syndrome, you'll find yourself experiencing it all the time.

## When to Shut Down the Right Brain

If both stimulation and boredom can arrest the left brain and let the right brain dominate, then what about the right brain? What arrests the right brain, and why would you want to do that? If you're in a fearful situation, it's very good to know how to shut down the right brain, which loves to exaggerate danger. Let the left brain take over for a while.

My son Dwight recently talked me into doing a bungee jump, the craze in California that involves going to a high place, tying elastic cords to your ankles, and diving off. The bungee rope is a hundred feet long, but it has a huge amount of stretch in it. It's the kind of rope the military uses when they parachute jeeps into a battle zone. When you jump, you free-fall a hundred feet, then the stretch in the rope lets you fall another hundred feet—almost to the ground. If all goes well, just before you hit the ground, the rope catches, and you bounce back up in the air. So there I was, standing on the platform, which was so far up in the air that the people down below looked like ants. The wind was whistling past me, and fear clutched me with a viselike grip.

If I'd been asked to stand on the platform and told, "Just go ahead and jump whenever you feel like it," I'd still be standing there. I could feel my right-brain imagination taking over. I imagined the rope breaking or being too long, and saw myself smashing into the ground below. Luckily, to shut off that creative right brain, all the other jumpers gathered on the ground below. They peered up at me and yelled, "Five! Four! Three! Two! One!" My left-brain concentration on counting momentarily shut down my right brain. Instead of imagining all the things that might happen, I was concentrating on what I had to do.

On the count of "One," I reached my hands above my head, bent my knees, and launched myself off into space. Suddenly, I was free-falling, and the ground hurtled toward me at sixty miles per hour. Just when I was convinced that something had gone horribly wrong, and I was going to smash into the ground, my fall was magically arrested. For a brief second, I hung there, neither going down nor up. Then the stretch in the rope won the tug-of-war with gravity, and I hurtled back into the sky again. During the ascent, I experienced what only a handful of astronauts have experienced in the past—complete weightlessness. I was aware that I was going up, but the tug of the rope and the tug of gravity were so evenly balanced, I felt as though I were floating. But at the top of the float upward, panic again overcame me as I started back down. Three or four times I bounced up and down, until the stretch in the rope was exhausted.

It was the countdown from the other jumpers that helped me overcome my fear. It had a magical effect by shutting down the right side of the brain and letting the left side take charge. The logical left side of the brain isn't creative enough to conjure up all the horrible things that might happen to you, so it enables you to jump. Believe me, it's the only thing that pried me off that platform!

## A Business Application for Left- and Right-Brain Thinking

Typically, salespeople are in the business of stimulating right-brain thinking, because emotion is what sells. But sometimes it's necessary to do the reverse. For example, in real estate I found that sellers often have a tremendous amount of emotional involvement with their homes, because they've lived there for years. Unfortunately for the salesperson, the buyer isn't going to have that emotional attachment to the house. The real estate agent must arrest the owners' right-brain thinking and bring them back to the logical world. They start by calling it a house, not a home. In real estate terminology, people buy a home but sell a house.

This is just one of the many ways understanding left- and right-brain thinking can be useful in the business world. With a little practice, you'll find that you're quickly able to control which side of the brain dominates your thinking. When you can do that at will, you're closer to being able to access what others will call intuitive flashes of inspiration, what we know is really Rapid Reasoning.

# The Value of Distancing Yourself from the Problem

So far I've covered four of the Seven Steps to Confident Decision Making:

*Step One:* Categorize the type of decision.

*Step Two:* Blueprint the problem accurately.

*Step Three:* Saturate your mind with facts about the problem.

*Step Four:* Position your mind for intuitive thought by shutting down your left brain and stimulating the right.

The fifth step is to move away from the problem, either physically or mentally. By doing this, you more clearly focus your concentration on the problem. Some impressive thinkers have seen the value of mentally moving away from the problem. Thomas Edison was famous for the catnaps that he took during the day, saying they gave power to his thinking. In December 1914, he faced the biggest challenge of his life when a fire destroyed his movie-and record-producing plant. It was the only money-making venture he had at the time, and the profits from it were needed to support his laboratory. According to his son Charles, as soon as the fire was under control, he took off his coat, rolled it up to make a pillow, and fell asleep at the table. When he awoke, he announced that he was rebuilding. Almost as an afterthought, he added, "Oh, by the way. Anybody know where we can get some money?"

Hulki Aldikacti, the chief engineer on Pontiac's Fiero, first had a mock-up of the driver's cockpit built. During his lunch break, he'd go sit in the cockpit, close his eyes, and daydream about the look and feel of the rest of the car. By thinking about the car in this manner, he was able to design one of Pontiac's best-looking cars.

Much Rapid Reasoning has also been attributed to physically moving away from the problem. John Moran, the founder of Hycel Corporation, worked for months on a design for an automatic blood analyzer. He finally gave up and left on vacation. When he woke up the next day at a resort hotel, he could see the right design in his mind. He hastily sketched it out, flew home, and built the prototype. He sold his company to a German conglomerate fourteen years later for $40 million.

Debbi Fields, the founder of Mrs. Fields Cookies, headquarters her $30 million business in Park City, Utah, partly so that she can slip out onto the ski slopes when she needs to mull over a tough decision.

Getting away, particularly to a foreign country, removes any preconceived parameters you've put on the decision. When you're in your working environment, you're surrounded by invisible chains of what's done or not done in your industry. Just as people will do things in the tropics they'd never dream of doing at home, so, too, will the mind loosen its inhibitions in a foreign land. One of the smartest business decisions I ever made came to me when I was sitting on a beach in Tahiti, looking out over the peaceful waters at the magical island of Bora Bora. Often an idea has popped into my mind as I've absentmindedly browsed through a street market in Peru or Ecuador. Physically removing yourself from the decision-making arena reduces your anxiety level and helps you stay calm and self-assured. Also, of course, it reenergizes a mind that may be drooping from mental fatigue.

But you don't have to fly to Tahiti to get away from the problem. You can mentally get away from the problem by just closing your office door and having your calls held. And the length of time away from a problem may need to be only microscopic. I'm sure you've had the experience of trying desperately to recall a name. It wasn't until you stopped thinking about it that it came to mind.

Okay, so you're in the middle of making a big decision. How do you know if you should keep on pressing for a solution? Perhaps you need to move away from the problem and say what Beethoven would say when inspiration wouldn't come to him. "Nothing comes to me today; we shall try another time."

It's time to move away from the problem when the same solution keeps recurring but doesn't seem to be the perfect answer. Or when you're having trouble concentrating, feeling frustrated, and you can't focus clearly on the problem. When irritability sets in, when you see physical signs of stress or fatigue, and when you're having trouble articulating what you're thinking are all signs that tell you to take a break.

Once you've moved yourself away from the problem, whether it's to a beach in Tahiti or simply into your office with the door closed, you need to induce intuitive thought. It's time to develop inner calm, because at the very center of inner calm is mental clarity.

## An Exercise to Induce Intuitive Thought

The following is a form of meditation that will help you to access your right-brain thinking.

Close your eyes and roll your eyeballs up slightly, until you feel the slight pressure of them touching the optic nerve. Stay perfectly still and start thinking of the muscles in the toes of your right foot. Let your muscles go limp, like a handful of rubber bands. Do the same thing with your left foot. Gradually work your way up through your legs, mentally relaxing each muscle. Let this wave of calm relaxation work its way up through your body, until your shoulder and neck muscles start to go limp. Then move it up into your brain, until your thoughts stop dancing around, and you're at perfect peace.

The objective of this minimeditation is to reduce mental noise and create a lowered state of arousal. A lowered state of arousal shuts down the left brain and stimulates the right. "Mental noise" is a term psychologists use to describe thoughts and images that come to you solely from your memory. It interferes with intuition because any thought that comes from memory carries with it preconceived views.

It's a fascinating contradiction—Rapid Reasoning is hard work. Yet the harder you work, the less you generate Rapid Reasoning. It happens when you work hard at moving your mind away from work. "I've never heard of a completely out-of-the-blue insight," says Dr. Perkins of Harvard University, author of *The Mind's Best Work.*

## Confident Decision Making Blends Logic with Rapid Reasoning.

Rapid Reasoning reflects your ability to make connections between completely separate pieces of information stored in the brain. Experts do it by chunking information together, so their minds can better juggle the complexities of the problem. You can do it by learning how to subdue the left brain and letting the right brain go to work for you. Lowering mental noise induces Rapid Reasoning and helps you make those connections better and faster. Confident Decision Making requires you to perfect your left-brain ability to sift details, and to blend it with right-brain creativity. Finally, you return to left-brain logic to verify your hunches.

In our next chapter, I'll teach you Creative Synthesis—for a very specific reason. You must put the largest-possible number of options on the table before selecting the best one. The more options you have, the better your decisions will be. That's called *divergent thinking*, or increasing opportunities. Once you learn Creative Synthesis, then I'll move back over to the logical side of decision making, with some very precise ways of selecting the best option available to you. That's called *convergent thinking*, which means zeroing in on the decision. Remember, the more opportunities you have for understanding how to approach a decision, the greater the chance for selecting the best possible solution.

# CHAPTER SIX

# Expanding Your Options

## The Magic of Creative Synthesis

We've all experienced it—those moments when we find ourselves at our desks with our heads in our hands agonizing over a decision. We wonder if there might be more options of which we're not aware. We know that somewhere out there is the answer we're looking for, but we haven't found it yet.

President Warren G. Harding once found himself in the same situation. "I can't make a damn thing out of this tax problem," he said at one point. "I listen to one side, and they seem right. I talk to the other side, and they seem just as right. And there I am where I started. I know somewhere there is a book to read that would give me the truth, but . . . I couldn't read the book. I know somewhere there is an economist who knows the truth, but I don't know where to find him. God, what a job!"

Finding that missing answer is where Creative Synthesis comes into play. To synthesize a decision is to bring together many possible partial solutions into a perfect decision. In this chapter, I want to take you through a series of steps that will help synthesize additional options for you to consider. Even if you've already come up with a good answer to your problem—a perfect answer to your problem—try performing these steps. Once the pressure is off to find an acceptable solution, you can practice Creative Synthesis and often come up with an even better idea. That's because there's magic in the second solution.

Experts in Creative Synthesis talk about vertical and lateral thinking. *Vertical thinking* is the traditional thinking, building on one thought at a time as you move to a conclusion. *Lateral thinking* doesn't require that kind of foundation of thought. It attempts to trigger great leaps in thought. With this new way of thinking, you can jump to a conclusion without taking all the steps in between. I'll show you how to do this by taking you through a ten-step checklist of right-brain Creative Synthesis ideas.

## The Sixth Step Toward Confident Decision Making: Ten Ways to Expand Your Options

We might think of the ten steps of Creative Synthesis as disciplined daydreaming. Like me, you've probably been conditioned against daydreaming by criticism from teachers and parents. It's cruel and unusual punishment in this country, but when I went to school in England teachers were permitted to throw chalk at the students. From clear across the room they could hit a daydreamer on the head with the accuracy of a Patriot missile. To this day, it's hard for me to feel comfortable when I see one of my employees sitting at his desk, just thinking. No doubt it's the most valuable thing he could be doing, but it doesn't seem right to me.

An efficiency expert once told Henry Ford he should fire one of his executives. He told Ford, "Every time I go by his office, he's just sitting there with his feet on his desk. He's wasting your money."

Ford replied, "That man once had an idea that saved us millions of dollars. At the time, I believe his feet were planted right where they are now."

Unfortunately, we live in an age where we glorify machines that think but condemn people who try to. For effective Creative Synthesis, we need to learn the art of disciplined daydreaming. The way to prepare your mind is to shut down the left brain and let the right brain dominate, the way I showed you in the previous chapter. Then, by following the ten right-brain ways to expand your options, you can begin Creative Synthesis.

## STEP ONE: VISUALIZE THE OPPOSITE OF THE SITUATION.

The first technique to expand your options is to visualize the opposite of the situation. There are many ways to do that; one way is to reverse the objective. A distributing warehouse company in New England did this with great success. I learned about it when I trained their buyers to negotiate better. The company was in a situation where the warehouse workers weren't filling the orders fast enough. The obvious solution was to put in more supervision, so a better job would be done by the workers. Instead, management reversed the objective and considered no supervision at all. Then what would it take to make it happen? Well, it would take incentives for the workers. It would take a system of teams, where each team member policed the action of other team members, because they were competing for the choice of work schedules and other benefits. The company decided to take a chance on it. It was the best move it ever made. The money previously paid for supervisors could now be allocated to worker incentives. Both production and morale went up.

Let's look at another situation where reversing the objective may be effective. Los Angeles, where I live, has a horrendous traffic problem. The average daily commute increased from forty-five minutes to one hour and fifteen minutes in the last two years. CalTrans, which is the state agency that handles highways, sees carpooling as the answer to the problem. The CalTrans people think all we have to do is cram a million people in a car, and all our problems will go away. What if we reversed the objective to see how *few* people we could get into a car? Well, we could have smaller cars. What's smaller than a car? A motorcycle. If everybody rode a motorcycle to work, we could make traffic lanes half the size. Overnight we could double the capacity of our freeways, to say nothing of solving our fuel crisis and pollution problem. Well, that's too extreme, but we could add motorcycle lanes to the shoulder of the freeway right now. But motorcycles are unsafe. Why can't we develop a safe motorcycle? One with a protective bubble around it for weather and safety? See how reversing the objective stimulates creative solutions?

The decision you're working on right now probably has the objective of increasing profits as quickly as possible. What if you reversed that objective and thought of it as being to lose money as quickly as possible? How would you go about that? By uncovering the ways you lose money, perhaps you'll discover where your profit is slipping through the cracks.

Fred Smith wanted to start a business that would move envelopes and packages from one place to another overnight. Everybody knows the fastest way between two points is a straight line. Try reversing that objective. Visualize the opposite of a straight line. To him, it was the notion of shipping everything first to his hometown of Memphis and then shipping it back out. From this came Federal Express.

Scientists have for years been baffled by what to do about noise. Ever-increasing levels of noise have become a plague on our modern society. All their attempts to do something about it centered on baffling the noise, to reduce the sound waves that reach us. Then somebody tried visualizing the opposite of that. What if, instead of reducing the noise, sound waves, we increased them? It didn't seem to make any sense, but they tried it anyway. What they discovered was very intriguing. If you exactly duplicate a noise, the two sets of sound waves cancel each other out, and the human ear can't hear either one. They created a device that would listen to the noise, digitalize the sound, and recreate it. Remarkably, it works well—the two sounds cancel each other out, and what you hear is silence. Now they are developing devices that will fit on car mufflers, and other sources of noise, to make them silent. Isn't that something?

Another form of reversing the objective is *contrary thinking*. When everybody in your industry is thinking one way, start looking in the opposite direction. The Gillette Razor Company knew that 60 percent of razors sold were the ten-for-a-dollar disposable kind. Instead of introducing even cheaper razors, Gillette introduced the Sensor Razor. It sells for 25 percent more than the existing best-selling razor, and it's a huge success.

So always question conventional wisdom. Why is everybody thinking this way? What would happen if they were all wrong?


## STEP TWO: EXAMINE THE ENVIRONMENT.

The second step of Creative Synthesis is to examine the environment in which the problem exists, not the problem itself. When President Reagan got to the White House, he found he'd inherited a world gone mad. Ironically, mad is also the acronym for the insanity I'm talking about—MAD as in Mutually Assured Destruction. Since the Soviet Union first developed ICBMs, we'd relied on this policy to save the world from destruction. The policy said: If you attack us, we'll have a big enough second-strike capability to destroy you in return. Over the years, each side kept increasing its arsenal of nuclear warheads to maintain the balance. By 1981, the superpowers were looking like two people standing at opposite ends of a swimming pool filled with gasoline. Each of them with a stockpile of cigarette lighters, threatening to ignite the gasoline and destroy the other, and himself. This must have confused Ronald Reagan, too, because when asked about it, he said, and I quote word for word, "If they realized that we—again if—if we led them back to that stalemate only because that our retaliatory power, our seconds, or strike at them after our first strike, would be so destructive that they couldn't afford it, that would hold them off." End quote. And if you think that's scary, Idi Amin, the president of Uganda, once seriously proposed that the United Nations ban all conventional weapons in favor of low-priced hydrogen bombs distributed equally around the world!

Instead of looking at the problem, President Reagan looked at the environment in which the problem existed. He realized it existed only because the Soviet Union could afford to continue the buildup. What would cause them to say, "We can't do this anymore?" The brilliant strategy he came up with was Star Wars. We'll probably never know whether Star Wars was the biggest bluff of all time, but it worked. The Soviets said, "We can't afford to stay in this game," and folded their hand. Most scientists doubt that Star Wars was ever feasible, but the research did produce the Patriot missile that was so effective in the Iraqi war. Remember the Patriot? According to Saddam Hussein, that was the missile the Israelis were launching toward Baghdad, which the glorious Iraqi Air Force could hit every time with their Scud "defense system!"

This idea of looking at the environment, rather than the problem, is invaluable in raising children. If you have three or more children, chances are you have one who's giving you fits. And you know there's nothing wrong with children that reasoning with them won't aggravate. Instead of worrying yourself sick about them, start examining the environment in which they exist.

I learned this the hard way, with one of my sons. He was doing so poorly in school that I was being called in every week for counseling sessions. So I put him through an extensive evaluation program to see if he had any learning disabilities, then had him evaluated by the school-district psychologist. He said nothing was wrong with him. Finally, instead of concentrating on him and his problem, I started to look at his environment. The problem was the friends with whom he was hanging around. Their attitude toward school was so bad that they were dragging him down. By the time I realized what was causing the problem, it had gone too far. Only by moving the family to another city could I break their hold on his thinking.

So, if you have a problem with one of your children, examine their environment. With whom do they hang around? What books are they reading? What movies are they watching? That's where you'll find the answer to your problem.

## STEP THREE: VISUALIZE YOURSELF FINDING THE PERFECT ANSWER.

The next step in Creative Synthesis is to visualize yourself finding the perfect answer. Visualization may seem old hat to you, but there's no denying its power. "You become what you think about," Earl Nightingale said. This wise saying was to have a profound effect on my life. More than twenty years ago, I was living in Yakima, Washington, where the local mortuary sponsored Earl's daily radio program *Our Changing World*, one of the most widely syndicated radio shows at that time, and was offering free copies of his scripts. When I went down to get them, I was taken into the conference room and brought a box of scripts that covered the previous year's programs. "Help yourself," I was told, so I went through them all, hungrily pulling out one script from each bundle. I can still remember sitting in that mortuary with the awful smell of the embalming fluid all around me. I took the scripts home and started to read them. Then I started to wonder what I'd sound like if I recorded them. Would I sound anything like Earl Nightingale? So on a very cheap little tape recorder, I read some of his scripts, just to see what it would be like. This was fifteen years before I ever thought of becoming a speaker; before I ever thought of recording a cassette program myself; before I'd even heard of the Nightingale-Conant Corporation. But Earl was right: You do become what you think about. Twenty-five years later, I was recording programs for his company.

Jack Nicklaus said, "I never hit a shot without having a very sharp, in-focus, picture of it in my head. It's like a color movie. First I see the ball where I want it to finish, nice and white and sitting up high on the bright green grass. Then the scene changes quickly, and I see the ball going there. Its path, trajectory and shape—even its behavior on landing."

Visualization really does work. However, in a stressful decision-making situation, we tend to picture negative results. Instead of visualizing the favorable results of a good decision, we become obsessed with the penalties of a bad decision. I think it's very revealing that there are at least fifteen words in the English language that describe a mistake: error, blooper, blunder, boner, bungle, fluff, lapse, miscue, misstep, fault, slip, slipup, trip and oversight. But there isn't a single word that describes the opposite of a mistake, *the act of doing something right*. With such a focus on negativity, it's no wonder we have trouble making the right decision!

Visualization is especially helpful in dealing with people. When I'm about to go into a meeting where I think people will raise objections to my proposal, instead of worrying myself sick about the conflict, I shut my office door, close my eyes, and visualize their warm response to me. It has a magical effect on people. I don't know why it works, but then I don't need to understand how a plane works to get to New York, either. I just know that when you push thoughts of love and encouragement out into the world, they don't dissipate, they circulate. The power of visualizing a warm response to your proposal is an awesome force.

## STEP FOUR: IMAGINE ALL THE ASSUMPTIONS YOU'VE MADE ARE WRONG.

The fourth Creative Synthesis step is to imagine that all the assumptions you've made about the decision are wrong. What if all the expected opposition to your plan fell away? For example, let's say you were nervous about introducing a price increase. What if your customers said, "That's great, we were wondering why you didn't do it a long time ago." It's possible they might even respect you more when you place more value on your services.

My friends Dotty and Henry Hoche turned their Victorian-style mansion, the Innisfree in Glenville, North Carolina, into a beautiful bed-and-breakfast inn. They assumed I'd still want to come and stay with them without charge. Not so—I'd rather pay and know I'd be welcome again.

What about a company that increases its staff but then doesn't have enough parking spaces? It assumes it has a problem because everyone wants to park close to work. Let's imagine for a moment that that assumption is wrong. Instead of people wanting to park close by, they really want to park as far from work as possible. From this thought, the idea of van pooling was born. If companies could arrange stops to pick up employees in a company van and drive them to work, everyone would save on gas, and it would cut down on traffic congestion.

This exercise of imagining your assumptions are wrong moves you away from the obvious solutions to your problems and generates more options.


## STEP FIVE: WHAT IF YOU KNEW YOU COULDN'T FAIL?

The fifth Creative Synthesis step is to imagine what you'd do if you knew you couldn't fail. If you could work miracles, what would you do to solve the problem? When I was young and knew everything, I thought it was self-defeating to set unrealistic goals. If you weighed three hundred pounds, you shouldn't dream of becoming a racehorse jockey. Now I'm not so sure. That kind of thinking didn't get fifty-two-year-old Dick Bass to the top of Mount Everest.

The "what if" line of thinking is absolutely fascinating. What if we didn't have to ship things, but we could transport them by beaming them up as Scotty does in *Star Trek*? Perhaps it was just such a thought that developed the fax machine. What if children didn't have to learn everything their parents knew? What if we could genetically implant a brain cell that would transmit all current knowledge to them?

It was this kind of "what if" thinking that caused Albert Einstein to discover the Theory of Relativity. He probably said, "What if I could travel from point A to point B faster than the speed of light? Well, the people at point B could clearly see I was with them. On the other hand, they could look back to point A and see I was still there. Since my image was traveling at the speed of light, it would appear I'd be at point B before I'd left point A."

Einstein's son was visiting London when Einstein called him from Munich. He said, "Son, do you realize that you hear what I'm saying before your mother can? My voice is traveling to you at the speed of electricity, but it's traveling across the room at the speed of sound. So you hear me before she does. Did you know that?" His son said, "Of course I know that, Papa . . . it's six in Munich and it's only five in London."

From Einstein's "*what if*" thought about the speed of light, came the Theory of Relativity and also his theory that time isn't a sequential thing and that all time is happening at one instant. We've just translated it into a sequential thing so we can better comprehend it.

You don't have to be an Einstein to have the "what if"

theory make a big difference in your life. I always used to feel that, in life, I was limited by what I could afford to do. For example, I'd drive into a town and make a decision on a hotel based on what I could afford to pay. Then one day I was driving into Geneva from Paris. Geneva's one of the most expensive cities in the world, so I knew the price of a hotel room would be outrageous. I started thinking, Where would I want to stay if money was no object? Ah, yes, this beautiful luxury hotel next to the lake, in a corner suite with two balconies. So what if I knew I couldn't fail to negotiate the price with the desk clerk? First you select the hotel, and then you figure out how you can afford to pay for it. As luck would have it, the desk clerk was from England. We struck up a conversation, and he gave me just the room I wanted at a bargain price.

From then on, I quit limiting my vacations to what I felt I could afford to pay. Instead, I started thinking, Where in the world would I like to go, and what would I like to do when I got there? Having decided that, I'd then rather figure out how I was going to pay for it. That may seem like strange thinking to you, but it will make an amazing change in your lifestyle. In decision making, we all too often limit our thinking to preconceived parameters. Don't exclude any possibilities until you've decided what you'd like to accomplish if you could work miracles.

## STEP SIX: RUN THE DECISION BY A SERIES OF ROLE MODELS.

The sixth Creative Synthesis step is to run the decision by a series of role models. The role models don't have to know they're role models. In the speaking industry, there are several people I admire greatly, and whenever I'm faced with a decision, I run it by them. I don't call them, and they never know. I just bounce it off them in my mind. It's amazing how often I've stopped myself from making a stupid mistake because I knew my role model would tell me to forget it. It's also amazing how often creative solutions have opened up to me because of running my decisions by a role model.

For example, a couple of times I've faced what appeared to be an impossible travel schedule. I'm booked to speak at a large convention in Maui, and I have an opportunity to earn a large speaking fee talking to another group in Orlando the next day. But I call the travel agent, and she tells me it's impossible, it can't be done. The last flight that would connect to Orlando leaves Maui at 2:00 P.M., so there's no way I could make the engagement.

In my mind, I run it by one of my role models. My line of thought is, "Well, my role model wouldn't have a problem with this, because he could afford to rent a private jet to fly him there. I can't afford to do that, but have I checked the possibility that there may be a corporate jet with an empty seat? Could I get as far as Los Angeles on a commercial flight and then rent a corporate jet and still have it pay off for me? Perhaps the company in Orlando has a jet that's flying in from the West Coast that could take me."

Another thought that might come into my mind is that my role model wouldn't have a problem with this, because he'd have enough clout to move the date of one of the speaking engagements. I haven't approached the companies on this possibility, but maybe I should talk to them about it.

In your business, you might be faced with a major financial problem, and you say to yourself, "Okay, my role model is Alan Greenspan, chairman of the Federal Reserve Board. What would Alan Greenspan do?" You think, Well, that's ridiculous. Alan Greenspan wouldn't have a problem with this. He could pick up the phone and talk to a dozen people who could restructure debt for him and resolve the problem. And that triggers the thought, Well, why couldn't I do that or Who could I contact who could do it for me?

Perhaps you have a security problem at your plant in Nebraska. Your role model for this kind of problem is the director of the FBI in Washington. The moment you run it by your role model in your mind you think, Well, sure, he wouldn't have a problem with that. He'd simply pick up the phone and call the attorney general of the state of Nebraska, and things would start to move. Then you think, Well, wait a minute, why can't I pick up the phone and call the Attorney General's Office? I may not get to talk to him or her, but I'd get to talk to somebody there.

Tom Monaghan, who turned a five-hundred-dollar investment into a $480 million fortune with Domino's Pizza, had Ray Kroc, the founder of McDonald's, as his silent role model. He didn't get to meet Kroc until he was already a huge success, selling over $200 million a year. Ray Kroc said, "I'm gonna give you some advice. You've got it made now. You can do anything you want, make all the money you can possibly spend. Slow down, take it easy. Open a few stores every year, but be very careful. Don't make any new deals that could get you into trouble. Play it safe."

Finally, Monaghan blurted out, "But, Mr. Kroc, that wouldn't be any fun!"

Kroc jumped up from behind his desk and pumped his hand. With a big grin, he said, "That's just what I hoped you'd say!"


STEP SEVEN: THINK BACKWARD FROM THE SOLUTION
OF THE PROBLEM.

Thinking backward is the next step of Creative Synthesis. With this one, you imagine the desired solution, and you start working back and visualizing how it all came together. It's a great way of forcing the subconscious mind into play. It's also a terrific technique to identify the missing link in a problem. What's the one thing that's creating the problem? What's the one thing that would solve the problem?

Many years ago, when I was a retail-store executive, we had a shoplifting problem. Experienced shoplifters knew how to approach a rack of clothes near the door and swoop up a great armful. They'd jump into a waiting van and drive off before we even had a chance to get a description of them. We knew, since we wanted to run a store that was customer friendly, that we must have goods exposed to shoplifters, and they'd continue to steal from us. But we identified the missing link as the short amount of response time we had for this occurrence. We started to think, How could we slow them down? The solution came to us that we'd simply alternate the direction of the hangers on the rack. So when the shoplifters tried to swoop up an armful of clothes, they wouldn't come off easily.

When Ulysses S. Grant was a little boy, he won a prize at a carnival for riding a wild mule. He stood there watching as the bad-tempered animal tossed off man after man. Then he got on it, wrapped his legs around its stomach, and hung onto its tail for dear life. He had simply identified the missing link—something to hold on to. Once he identified that, he knew the simple solution was just to sit on the mule backward.


## STEP EIGHT: LOOK AT THE PROBLEM FROM ANOTHER PLANET.

You might be surprised that my next suggestion is to look at the problem from another planet. But sometimes we're so close to a problem, we can't see it in proper focus. We don't know who discovered water, but we know it wasn't a fish. We don't know who discovered stress, but we know it wasn't a corporate executive, because they're swimming in it all the time.

On the wall in my office, I have a large poster with a graphic depiction of the planets. On one side, the sun is a huge ball, and stretching off into the distance are Mercury, Venus, then Earth, Mars, Jupiter, Saturn, Uranus, Neptune, and Pluto. Pointing down at the little blue-and-white planet Earth is one of those directional markers that says, "You Are Here." That puts things in perspective for me!

When I'm faced with a problem, I like to take myself away in my mind to one of my favorite places. In my mind, I ride the train up to the top of Victoria Peak overlooking Hong Kong Harbor—not the modern new railway but the rickety old one that existed when I first went there in 1960. I go to the Peak Cafe at the top and have a cup of tea and look out over the view. It's a great mental hideaway, and I've solved many a thorny business problem there because I'm reminded that nothing lasts forever—in just a few years Hong Kong will no longer be a British colony—and that any problem can be resolved with care and patience. So my trip takes me across an ocean, and more important, back through a few decades. It helps me to put everything into perspective, even though it's a trip I'm taking only in my mind.

It's the same sort of perspective that an executive from the main office of a company has when he visits a factory and sees a problem of which its manager might be unaware. The executive who works somewhere else has a different perspective on the problem than a local manager might; he has more distance. In fact, another technique that will help you to take yourself away from a problem is to envision yourself playing another role at your company. If you work at a factory in Alabama, pretend you're the chairman of the board and work at company headquarters on Wall Street. Ask yourself, "How would I feel about the problem then?" By transporting yourself to another place, another time, or even to another person, you can let go of some of your old notions and find new ones.

## STEP NINE: DEFOCUS THE PROBLEM.

It's just as important to defocus the decision as it is to focus on it. One illustration of this is Mary Kay Ash, founder of the cosmetics giant Mary Kay Cosmetics. She was working in catalog sales and wanted to write a book to help women like herself, who were being underutilized in business. Her idea was to help other women overcome the obstacles she had encountered. Yet she didn't know how to write a book, so she began listing the things in business that held women back. Then she listed the positive things that help women succeed. Without realizing it, she had written the marketing plan for her company. The business that intuitively popped into her mind avoided all the traps and offered all the opportunities. From this, she built an $800-million-a-year industry. Had she stayed focused on writing the book, it never would have happened. Eventually, she did write the book, and it became a best-seller: *Mary Kay on People Management.*

Fred Smith really started Federal Express as a courier for federal bank documents, which is where it got its name. When that didn't work out, he was flexible enough to use the same business plan to start a very successful package-moving business.

## STEP TEN: LOOK AT THE PROBLEM
## WITH CHILDLIKE INNOCENCE.

The last step in Creative Synthesis is to look at the problem with the innocence of a child. Remember the movie *Big*, in which Tom Hanks was mystically given a grown-up body and then got a job as an executive at a toy company? Although he knew nothing about toy manufacturing, he was very effective as a creative executive. Why? Because he could cut through the corporate clutter to get to the essence of the problem. That movie may have been based on an actual incident, where a consultant convinced Mattel Toy Corporation to put children on its board of directors.

Look at your problem as if it were being explained to you for the first time. Think about how you'd react. For example, you may be faced with an inventory-shrinkage problem at one of your factories. Your natural tendency might be to bite the bullet and hire detectives or increase the number of security guards at the plant to watch over employees. A child might ask, "How much do all those security guards cost you? How much are the employees stealing?" It could well be that security is costing you more than the stolen goods. Then a child might say, "Why don't you do away with all those security guards and just trust the employees?"

This may be a laughable example to you, an experienced executive, but your innocent side may say, "Perhaps that would work. Perhaps if we trusted the employees more, they'd steal less." In fact, I know of a company that did exactly that. Faced with a problem of employee theft, it eliminated the cost of its security guards, which was more than the amount of the stolen goods. Then the employees were told the company trusted them. And in the future it expected the employees to police each other, so nobody let the team down. To management's surprise and delight, employee theft dropped off to almost nothing, and the reduced cost of security jump-started the company's bottom line.


## NOURISH YOUR DREAMS DAILY, AND WATCH THE POSSIBILITIES GROW.

Creative Synthesis offers ways to expand our choices in making a decision, a technique I call *divergent thinking*, or *expanding the possibilities*. Take a minute to review the steps I've listed below. Perhaps there's a problem right now you might be able to resolve using these techniques. In most of these methods, your imagination is the most important criterion you need. Remember the executive with his feet on the desk? It might not be a bad idea to give yourself a few minutes to daydream every day.

1. Visualize the opposite of the situation.

2. Examine the environment in which the problem exists, not the problem itself.

3. Visualize yourself finding the perfect answer.

4. Imagine all the assumptions you've made about the decision are wrong.

5. Imagine what you'd do if you knew you couldn't fail.

6. Run the decision by a series of role models.

7. Think backward from the solution of the problem.

8. Look at the problem from another planet.

9. Don't be too focused on what you want to come out of the decision.

10. Look at the problem with the innocence of a child.

## The Four Magic Words of Success

I want to let a real expert have the last word on creative thinking. Walt Disney was probably the most creative thinker of the century. He once said to a young visitor to Disneyland, "If you'll remember four words, you'll grow up to be a very wise man. The first word is: **Think.** Think about the values and the principles that guide you. The second word is: **Believe.** Believe in yourself based on the values and principles that guide you. The third word is: **Dream.** Dream about something that you want to do, and then do it based on your belief in yourself about the thinking that you have done, about your values and principles. The last word is: **Dare.** Dare to make your dream become a reality because of your belief in yourself, because of the thinking you've done about the values and the principles that you are going to live by.''

I think that with those four words, Walt Disney gave us the framework with which to make any decision:

- **Think** through the problem, so you thoroughly understand it;

- **Believe** that you can find the perfect answer;

- **Dream** of a creative solution; and

- **Dare** to follow through and make it happen.

## Entrepreneurial Decision Makers Are Masters of Intuition.

Before I explain logical decision making, it's important to examine the entrepreneurial style of decision making. Very often, entrepreneurs get into trouble because they're not able to make the transition from intuitive decision making to the logical decision making that is prevalent in large corporations. It's one thing for an entrepreneur working in his garage to play his hunches, whether they be true intuition or simply Rapid Reasoning. It's another thing in today's large business climate, where competition and stockholders are watching every move. David Mahoney was head of the Norton Simon conglomerate before he left to form his own company. He said, "Today the CEO isn't supposed to say 'I feel,' he's supposed to say, 'I know.' "

It's very easy for the Ray Krocs, the Donald Trumps, and the owners of their own businesses to brag about their flashes of insight. How intuitive would they be if they had to justify their decisions at a stockholders' meeting, or to a left-brain logical thinker like Harold Geneen?

Did you ever wonder why the business successes of entrepreneurs seem so cyclical? One minute they're on top, and the next minute they're struggling to survive. Donald Trump, Allen Bond, Frank Lorenzo, John Elliot, have all gone through the same cycle. The cycle occurs because intuitive decision making is stifled when one or more of these things happen:

1. They lose their self-confidence because they're worried that their luck has run out.

2. They have to start justifying their actions to investors, or to bankers.

3. They're required to work within strict limits set by bail-out bankers.

4. They have to work in an environment of high anxiety.

Entrepreneurs who succeeded because they invented something, or who had great technical expertise, often rise above their managerial expertise. This is called the TM—technical management—balance: the balance of skills between technical expertise and management skills. It's very evident in the computer industry. After the founder's technical expertise causes the company to grow beyond his or her management skills, four things can happen.

First, the entrepreneur clings to power and sinks the company. Adam Osborne was a fascinating character whose father was a countermissionary in Burma, converting the "savages" in the jungle from Christianity back to Buddhism. A chemist, Adam Osborne wrote one of the first books on computing, and then founded a publishing company that he sold for $4 million. He then started Osborne Computers, which marketed the first low-priced personal computer. The first year he was in business, he sold seventy-five thousand of them at almost two thousand dollars each. That's $150 million! Had he realized that he had outrun his managerial skills, he could have survived by bringing in a top manager, but instead he clung to power and sank his company.

The second thing that could happen is what everybody hopes will happen. The entrepreneur learns the management skills he or she needs to run a corporation. Bill Gates at Microsoft is a good example of that.

The third possibility is that he or she gets ousted by the stockholders. Steve Jobs, the founder of Apple Computers, was actually smart enough to realize his management shortcomings. He hired John Sculley away from PepsiCo to take over his little company that had become a giant. But he wasn't smart enough to leave well enough alone. When he tried to get Sculley out and regain control of the company, Sculley's superior corporate smarts ousted Jobs instead.

The fourth thing that can happen is that the entrepreneur gets smart enough to realize his limitations and hires a professional manager to run the company.

Why do entrepreneurs appear to have such high intuition? One reason is because being an entrepreneur requires a high degree of self-confidence. Accustomed to being point men or women, they never have to worry about people second-guessing them. That also means it takes an independent mind-set. Entrepreneurs don't have to worry about convincing other people they're right. And finally, entrepreneurs are usually people who believe that mental rigidity stifles intuition. They're not bound by corporate policies and procedures.

## How to Give Your Ideas a Reality Check

Entrepreneurs are a wonderful example of the power of imagination at work. While their right-brain thinking ability can produce corporate conglomerates from microchips or create new uses for an ancient invention like paper by combining it with adhesives, there are still some situations that call for different tactics, or what I describe as *convergent thinking*. Techniques such as Creative Synthesis will allow you to place more trust in your instincts and broaden your outlook, but consistently relying just on your intuition can also lead you down a narrow path. In the next chapter, I'll show you how logical-thinking skills can back up some of the answers you've found through Creative Synthesis.

# CHAPTER SEVEN

# Logical Decision Making

## Intuitive Decision Making Versus Logical Decision Making

In this section I'll cover the last of the Seven Steps to Confident Decision Making. Remember that the first six were:

1. Accurately categorize the situation so you can start looking for the solution in the right direction.

2. Blueprint the problem accurately, so your mind totally focuses on the problem it has to solve.

3. Saturate your mind with facts about the problem.

4. Position your mind for Rapid Reasoning by shutting down the left brain and stimulating the right.

5. Move away from the problem, either physically or mentally, so your mind can view it objectively.

6. Increase your options through a checklist of ten creative possibilities.

The last step we'll examine is:

7. Using logical decision making techniques to verify your intuition.

Intuitive decision making does seem like a wonderful answer to all our problems—if we can make it work. If it always worked, all we'd have to do is sit back, do a few exercises to shut down the left side of our brain, and put 10 billion brain cells to work on the problem. But intuitive thinking won't work on some decisions. Let me prove that to you by having you consider this mental exercise:

I live in La Habra Heights, which is just outside Los Angeles. Let's say that one morning I decide to drive up the scenic coast road to San Francisco. I'm going to visit my youngest son, John, a student at Menlo College. It's a four-hundred-mile drive and will take me all day. It's a fun drive, through San Luis Obispo, past Hearst Castle, through Big Sur and Monterey. I start at 8:00 A.M. and because I'm driving slowly, admiring the scenery, it takes me eleven hours. Two days later, I start driving back, again leaving at eight in the morning, following the same route. However, this time I'm in a hurry and drive much faster, reaching home in eight hours.

Here's the question:

Will I be at any point on that road at exactly the same time of day that I was there two days before?

Put the book down, and think about it for a while.

Okay, what was your conclusion? Probably you said no, it isn't possible to be at the same point at exactly the same time of day. I did the northern part of the journey in the morning when I was going north. I did the southern part of the journey in the afternoon when I was coming south. If I was driving at exactly the same speed, there would be a point in the middle that I'd pass at exactly the same time. But I wasn't driving at the same speed. So the answer has to be no.

But that's wrong. The answer is yes, there is a place where I would be at the same point at the same time of day, on both trips. This is an example of how intuitive decision making can give us the wrong answer. This question demands a logical decision. Instead of one driver making a round trip, think of two drivers making the trip on the same day. I leave Los Angeles at 8:00 A.M., and my son John leaves his college in San Francisco at the same time on the same day. He drives much faster than I do. Isn't it obvious there will be a point in the journey when we'll pass each other? And when we do, aren't we in the same place at the same time?

## ANOTHER INTUITIVE MIND-BENDING BRAIN TEASER

Here's another example. Cognitive scientist Peter Watson came up with a very interesting experiment. He displayed these four cards:

A Vowel        A Consonant        An Even Number        An Odd Number

Note that there was one vowel, one consonant, one even number, and one odd number. Then he said, "You have been told that any card with a vowel on one side has an even number on the other side. Your challenge is to prove that statement by turning over any two of the four cards. Which two should you turn over?"

Put down the book and see if you can figure it out.

Only 4 percent of the people he tested got it right. Obviously, you turn the A over to be sure it has an even number on the other side. But most people select the 4 as the other card, to be sure it has a vowel on the other side. And that's the wrong answer! The right answer is the 7, to be sure it *doesn't* have a vowel on the other side.

The interesting thing about that is, not only did 96 percent of the people get it wrong, but it's almost impossible to understand why you should turn over the 7, and not the 4. Let's say that the second card you turn over is the 4, and it does have a vowel on the other side. So far so good; but you're still left with the possibility that the 7 has a vowel on the other side. That would dispute the supposition that any card with a vowel on one side has an even number on the other. So you can't prove the supposition that way because you've already turned over two cards, the A and the 4.

So you should turn over the A and the 7. If the A has an even number on the other side and the 7 doesn't have a vowel, you've proven the supposition. But how do you know that the 4 has a vowel on the other side? It doesn't matter whether it has a vowel or a consonant. Your challenge was to prove that if a card has a vowel on one side, it has an even number on the other. If the 4 has a vowel on the other side, fine. If it has a consonant on the other side, it's not relevant to the supposition. However, it's confusing, isn't it?

Just as in the Los Angeles to San Francisco problem, our intuitive mind lets us down.

The point is that some decisions can't be made with intuition, however good at it you become. You simply need logic, and in this section we're going to talk about the three different kinds of single-step decisions you can make—"go or no go" decisions; dichotomy decisions involving two choices; and decisions with three or more possibilities.

## A Guide to Making "Go or No Go" Decisions

There are many ways of statistically evaluating the choices you have. You won't want to use them all, of course. The more important the decision, the more involved the procedure you'll want to select.

In Chapter Three, I taught you how to blueprint the decision, using these categories:

- Does it require analysis, synthesis, or judgment? Or a combination of all three?

- Are you trying to solve a problem or seize an opportunity?

- Does the situation involve a people problem or a money problem?

- Is the choice between "go and no go," or is it a matter of choosing between two or more solutions?

When you determine that the last category applies, the process becomes more involved. Now you must match the problem to a decision-making method. In the business world, this type of decision arises when you have choices such as: Should you accept that job offer, or shouldn't you, or should you buy out your competitor or not? When faced with a ''go or no go'' decision, there are three methods to choose from: the coin toss, check-listing, and quantified evaluation.

## THE COIN TOSS HELPS TO ELIMINATE CHOICES.

Let's start with the simplest method for dealing with this, the coin toss. Hey, don't laugh, this is serious stuff. There's a lot more you can do with a coin than start a football match. My son Dwight taught me this while we were on a tour of Central America. For the last ten years or more, I've had the ambition of driving down to Buenos Aires, but I could never find the six months or so it would take to do it. So I decided to do a test run to Central America and see what it would be like. I think it's important to take trips like this with my kids. It's part of teaching them about the world. In fact, I've taken my three children all over the world, but somehow they always find their way home!

So we drove all the way through Mexico and Guatemala into Honduras. One night we were in Tegucigalpa, the capital of Honduras, and couldn't decide whether to go on down to Managua, Nicaragua, or swing back through San Salvador and head across Guatemala to Belize. We talked about it for a couple of hours over dinner and still couldn't decide. Neither of us felt strongly enough about it to push for one side of the decision or the other. My son said to me, ''Let's toss a coin.''

I told him, ''Come on, Dwight! I don't want to decide something as important as this based on a coin toss. There's a civil war going on in El Salvador. What if we go there and get shot? How's that going to look in my obituary, when people read that I decided to go there based on a coin toss?''

He told me, ''There's more to it than that, Dad. We toss the coin, and then decide.''

"Give me that again," I said. "Have I spent twenty-six years raising a complete fool?"

"Trust me, Dad, you'll love it. You'll be talking about it in your seminars one day."

So we tossed the coin. Heads we go to Nicaragua, tails we go to El Salvador. It came up heads—Nicaragua. Dwight said, "Now how do you feel about it?"

It was amazing. A moment ago, I simply couldn't decide. Now I was clearly disappointed it hadn't come up tails. I really wanted to go to El Salvador and Belize. It sounds stupid, but it's an amazingly effective way of making up your mind. We went into El Salvador, didn't get shot, and then had several adventures in the remote eastern side of Guatemala—putting the four-wheel drive to the test on the worst roads I've seen anywhere in the world; staying on a remote ranch where there had been several random executions; and exploring ancient Mayan ruins with a new Israeli friend.

The coin toss is a great technique to use when you're having trouble making up your mind.

What about in a business situation? Let's say you own a car dealership. There's a Chrysler dealership down the street that's having tough times, and it's up for sale. You've done all the analysis, and you still can't decide. The deal isn't so great that you'd be crazy to turn it down, but on the other hand it looks as though it's a pretty good opportunity. Toss a coin. Now how do you feel about it? Is your mind fighting the decision? Are you thinking, I really didn't want to take on that much extra work? Or are you thinking, Now I know it's the right thing to do?

If you use this method frequently, you may find you don't even have to get as far as tossing the coin. Most people tend to think of heads as positive and tails as negative. Very often you pick heads for the one you subconsciously want to do. You say to yourself, "Heads I'll buy it, tails I won't." So see if a pattern develops. If you're pleased when it comes up tails and disappointed when it comes up heads, you don't even have to toss the coin to know which way to decide.

## A LIST OF POSSIBILITIES TELLS WHEN
## ALL SYSTEMS ARE "GO"

Another effective way of making a "go or no go" decision is checklisting. This is similar to a mission-control countdown, or a pilot's checklist. Your list is made up of items that must be on a "go" status in order for you to proceed.

For example, the decision may be to hire or not hire a particular person for a position in data processing at the bank you run. You list minimum requirements for that position, which might include:

1. Must have five years experience in data processing, of which at least one year must be in banking;

2. Must be willing to relocate downtown later, if that becomes necessary;

3. Shouldn't be taking a cut in pay to come work for us (people who take a cut in pay are frequently dissatisfied, and move on quickly); and,

4. Must be able to pass a physical exam.

You might give this checklist to your human-resources director to establish parameters for the position. Or you may use it yourself to evaluate the choices they bring to you.

With checklisting, you go down the list to be sure the applicant qualifies in each of the areas, or put the person on a "no go" status until the requirement is waived or deleted.

## HOW DOES THE DECISION RATE?

A more complicated way of making a "go or no go" decision is what I call *quantified evaluation*. Using two separate lists, one with those factors that favor making a decision and the other with those factors against making the decision, rate each factor on a scale from 1 to 10.

I used quantified evaluation to decide where I should write this book. I have a second home in the mountains at Lake Arrowhead, about an hour and a half by car from my home. Part of me was saying I'd be better off writing up there, and part of me was saying I'd be better off at home.

First I listed the reasons for going to the lake. I thought of three—there would be fewer interruptions; the lake is a more creative environment; and it's a more relaxing atmosphere.

Then I thought of four reasons for writing at home—I'd have all the reference books from my home library; the public library near home is much larger, so research would be easier; I'd be less lonely at home; and I wouldn't waste time making several trips up and down the hill, taking care of regular business.

The next step is to rate each of these factors on a scale from 1 to 10. Remember that in this system, all the ratings are positive. Five and below isn't a negative, it's just less of a positive.

In favor of going up to Lake Arrowhead, I rated the factors this way:

|  |  |
|---|---|
| Fewer interruptions: | 8 |
| Creative environment: | 6 |
| Relaxing atmosphere: | 5 |
| Total | 19 |

Next I divided the total by the three factors and came up with a score of 6.3 in favor of going to the lake.

In favor of staying home, I rated the factors this way:

| | |
|---|---|
| Access to my home library: | 8 |
| Having a good public library: | 6 |
| Being less lonely: | 4 |
| The time saved by not having to go back and forth: | 9 |
| Total | 27 |

This total score divided by the four factors gave me a final score of 6.8.

Since the score in favor of staying home was 6.8 and the score for going to the lake was 6.3, I stayed home. I hope you agree I made the right decision! Remember that with quantified evaluation, there are no negatives. You rate only the positive factors and then average them.

Now you have three ways to make a decision when the choice is between doing something and not doing something:

• The coin toss

• Checklisting

• Quantified evaluation

## Choosing Between Two Alternatives

But what do you do when you have to choose between dichotomous possibilities? Remember that a true dichotomy is rare. If you use the Creative Synthesis checklist I gave you in Chapter Six, you can usually come up with more than two choices. However, if you have narrowed it down to only two choices, there are three ways of making the decision.

## THE 1-TO-10 RATING SYSTEM

Rating everything on a scale from 1 to 10 makes decision making easy. Once you've assigned ratings, the choice is obvious. The advantage is that it forces you to evaluate the choices systematically. You can't decide whether to open your next frozen-yogurt store in Tulsa or Oklahoma City. Your file on each location is three inches thick. It seems as though the more information you get, the harder the choice becomes. Try the 1-to-10 test. How do you feel about Tulsa? About an 8. How do you feel about Oklahoma City? About an 8.5. Why do you feel that way? You don't know, but those 10 billion brain cells have been working on it, and that's what they're telling you.

Don't use this to override good, solid information. But if you simply can't decide, it's a good way to break a mental deadlock.

The 1-to-10 rating system is also a terrific way to extract information from other people. You're a salesperson and you can't get a fix on whether your customers are ready to place the order or not. So ask them, "Where are you on a scale from one to ten? Ten meaning you're ready to order right now, and one meaning you wouldn't take it if we gave it to you." I've never had anyone refuse to give me a number.

Your customer might say, "Well, I guess I'm at a six."

And you say, "Help me out, what would it take to get you to a ten?"

She might respond, "I'll tell you what's bothering me. I see your figures about the projected savings, but I need something stronger than that. For me to go with this, I'd have to be guaranteed that kind of savings.''

Bingo! In a few short seconds, you've isolated the objection and almost got the buyer's commitment to buy if you can satisfy her one concern.

Or you might be trying to hire a key executive for your company. You need to find out if the money you're offering is going to be enough to get him or her on board. So you ask, ''How do you feel about coming with us—on a scale from one to ten, ten meaning you're ready to accept right now, and one meaning you've already ruled it out?'' You'll get an instant fix on how this person feels, without having to come right out and ask if you're offering enough money.

It's one of the most powerful tools I've ever learned for finding out what's going on in a person's mind, and it seems to work every time.

I've been using the 1-to-10 rating system for fifteen years, but it wasn't until recently I became aware of a significant fact. Not everybody's scale goes from 1 to 10. I have three children: Julia, Dwight, and John. One winter we rented a condominium in Park City, Utah, for a ski vacation together. After skiing for a couple of days in Park City we discussed whether, for a change, we should drive around the mountain and ski Snowbird. We couldn't seem to decide. So I said to John, my youngest child, ''On a scale from one to ten, how do you feel about going to Snowbird?''

He said, ''I'm at a seven,'' which wasn't particularly helpful to me. Then he said something very insightful. He said, ''But remember, on my scale I don't have an eight, nine, or ten.''

That's true—John is very low-key. He never gets particularly excited about anything, but on the other hand, he never gets depressed, either. One summer, I took him climbing in Europe, and he reached the top of the Matterhorn. An incredible accomplishment, considering he'd only climbed two mountains before and this was his first rock climb. I met him at the fourteen-thousand-foot level and threw my arms around him. I said, "I can't believe you made it!"

In his low-key manner, he said, "Wasn't that what I was supposed to do?" In effect, he doesn't have an 8, 9, or 10 on his scale, nor does he have a 1, 2, or 3. His range goes from 4 to 7. On the other hand, Dwight, my older son, has a scale that includes *only* 1, 2, 3, 8, 9, and 10. He either loves something or hates it.

So be aware of this. You may not have an 8, 9, or 10. For you, a 7 may mean "Run with it!"

## THE BEN FRANKLIN BALANCE SHEET

Benjamin Franklin designed a popular decision-making technique that you probably already use. In a letter to British chemist Joseph Priestley, Franklin explained his system this way:

"My way is to divide a sheet of paper into two columns; writing over the one Pro, and over the other Con. Then, during the three or four days' consideration, I put down under the different heads short hints of the different motives, that at different times occur to me, for or against the measure. When I have thus got them all together in one view, I endeavor to estimate their respective weights; and where I find two, on each side, that seem equal, I strike them both out. If I find a reason 'pro' equal to some two reasons 'con,' I strike out all three. If I judge some two reasons 'con,' equal to some three reasons 'pro,' I strike out the five; and thus proceeding I find at length where the balance lies; and if, after a day or two of further considerations, nothing new that is of importance occurs on either side, I come to a determination accordingly."

He called it moral, or prudential, algebra. To follow his approach you need to make a chart like this:

| Pros | Cons |
|------|------|
| 1. | 1. |
| 2. | 2. |
| 3. | 3. |
| 4. | 4. |
| 5. | 5. |
| 6. | 6. |
| 7. | 7. |
| 8. | 8. |
| 9. | 9. |
| 10. | 10. |

After you've listed your pros and cons, match them up in importance. When you see a ''pro'' that equals a ''con'' in importance,
strike out both of them. If you find two on one side that equal
three on the other, strike out all five, and so on. The side that
strikes out first loses! This method works well when the choice
is between doing something or not doing it. It's not very effective
for multiple choices.

   Salespeople find the Ben Franklin approach very helpful in
convincing buyers. On one side of the sheet, they list all the
reasons for going ahead with the decision. On the other, they list
the reasons for not going ahead. Of course, they're very helpful
in coming up with reasons for going ahead, and a lot less helpful
in thinking of the negatives.

## THE REPORT-CARD METHOD

The third method of deciding between two options is the report-card method. Al Neuharth, the newspaper genius who later started *USA Today*, used this method when he was trying to decide whether to move from Knight Newspapers in Detroit to Gannett. He was doing well with Knight Newspapers, and the decision didn't seem as obvious as it appears in hindsight. He listed the ten things that were most important to him, personally and professionally, and rated them on a scale of 1 to 10. A major point was that Gannett was a publicly traded company, which he could eventually control. Knight was family owned, so he could never have complete autonomy. He gave Knight Newspapers a ten-point "loyalty" bonus. Even so, Gannett won, 94 to 92. Close, but enough to change the face of newspaper publishing in this country. At Gannett he expanded the company until it owned small newspapers all over the country. It became the only company with enough printing plants to enable *USA Today* to be composed centrally and printed locally.

Let me explain the report-card method by telling you how I used it to decide which vehicle to buy for our trip to Central America.

My son Dwight, who was taking the trip with me, wanted a Nissan Pathfinder. This is the rugged four-wheel drive that looks like a four-wheel drive should, a real man's vehicle. He had the dealer bring one to the house for me to test-drive, and it impressed me. The other option we'd narrowed it down to was a four-wheel drive Ford Aerostar, which is a minivan.

We listed the factors that were important to us and then rated them. We had considered whether our preference for American-made vehicles should be a factor, but decided this was a prejudice and shouldn't be a part of the decision-making process. Instead, we examined the following points. First, gas mileage, which was important because we'd be driving thousands of miles. We gave the Ford an 8, and the Nissan a 5. Remember that on a scale from 1 to 10, 5.5 is neutral. So 5 or less is a negative, and 6 or more is a positive. If you think of 5 as neutral, you skew the scale with an optimism factor.

Availability of parts in Central America was significant, and had caused us to rule out many other possibilities. We gave Ford an 8 and Nissan a 6. Although we never spent a night in the vehicle, we thought we might have to, so we rated sleeping comfort. We gave Ford an 8 and the much smaller Nissan a 2. For driving comfort, we gave the Ford an 8 and the Nissan a 6. Then we considered how useful the vehicle would be to me after the trip. Here the minivan was a big advantage over the smaller Nissan, 9 to 5. It also got a big plus for carrying space, 8 to 4. The van was eight thousand dollars cheaper than the Nissan, so it got an 8 compared to a 6. For off-road capability, the Nissan was clearly the winner, 9 to 7. For dependability, we considered the fact the Ford was using a new electronic four-wheel drive, so we gave the Ford a 6 and the Nissan an 8. Finally, we rated each on a lust factor. How badly did I want to own them? Here the Nissan won overwhelmingly! It got a 9. The poor old minivan only got a 5.

Then we added up the scores. The Ford Aerostar got a 75 rating, compared to the Nissan's 60, so we went with the Ford and didn't regret it. It behaved beautifully, even in eastern Guatemala, on the worst roads I've seen anywhere in the world.

|                      | Pathfinder | Aerostar |
| -------------------- | ---------- | -------- |
| Gas Mileage          | 5          | 8        |
| Availability of Parts | 6         | 8        |
| Sleeping in Vehicle  | 2          | 8        |
| Comfort              | 6          | 8        |
| Useful After Trip    | 5          | 9        |

| Carrying Space | 4 | 8 |
| Price | 6 | 8 |
| Off-Road Handling | 9 | 7 |
| Dependability | 8 | 6 |
| Desire | 9 | 5 |
| Total | 60 | 75 |

The report-card method obviously has flaws, the biggest one being it doesn't give weight to the various factors. But it worked for Al Neuharth, and it served us well also.

So to recap the three ways to decide when you are faced with a dichotomy:

• The 1-to-10 Rating System

• The Ben Franklin Balance Sheet

• The Report-Card Method

# Handicap When You Have Three or More Choices

Now let's move from dichotomies to more complicated problems. If you have more than two choices, decision making becomes more involved. We need to use not only judgment, but also analysis, and synthesis—bringing many elements together to develop new options. In order to decide between three or more possibilities, when the outcome of each choice is predictable, I use a system I call handicapping.

The first step in handicapping is to blueprint the objective in positive terms. What are you trying to accomplish? Don't focus on what you dislike; consider only the positive aspects of each option. Let's say you're thinking of making a career change. Negative concerns might be:

1. I hate my boss.

2. I'm starving to death on what they pay me.

3. I feel trapped.

4. I hate the weather in Buffalo, and so on.

Dwelling on the negatives like that doesn't induce creative thought, it stifles it. Instead, consider only positive objectives, which might be:

1. I want to move to a larger company that could offer greater opportunity.

2. I want to earn more money.

3. I'd like to live in a warmer climate.

4. I want a better benefit program.

5. I want a greater challenge.

6. A different boss might see me in a more favorable light.

7. If I move, I could improve my position within the company.

8. I could get a better title.

You've now developed a blueprint that encompasses all the objectives that are important to you. Next, on a scale from 1 to 10, consider how you feel about each of these factors. For example, you might give a low rating to money and title. Your major concern might be opportunity and the chance to end up running the company. The importance you give to each of these is a personal thing, but let's say that you rate them on a scale from 1 to 10, like this:

## Importance

1. Greater opportunity:     10
2. More money:               8
3. Better location:          6
4. Improved benefits:        6
5. Greater challenge:        9
6. Better boss:              8
7. Improved position:        7
8. Better title:             4

Next, put your creative mind to work and list all the available alternatives. This might be a list of the companies in your industry meeting your criteria. Evaluate each company against your list of criteria weights. Give them a rating on a scale from 1 to 10 as you feel about them in each of those elements.

Now multiply the weight factor by the rating number. For example, opportunity was a weight factor of 10 for you, and you give this company a 7 for that. Ten times 7 is 70, so that's the score this company gets in that element. Benefits got a weight factor of 6, and you give this company a 7 for its benefit package. So it gets 6 times 7, or 42 points for this. Here's how your chart might look then:

|  | **Importance** | **× Likelihood** | **= Score** |
|---|---|---|---|
| 1. Greater opportunity: | 10 | 7 | 70 |
| 2. More money: | 8 | 8 | 64 |
| 3. Better location: | 6 | 8 | 48 |
| 4. Improved benefits: | 6 | 7 | 42 |
| 5. Greater challenge: | 9 | 6 | 54 |
| 6. Better boss: | 8 | 7 | 56 |
| 7. Improved position: | 7 | 8 | 56 |
| 8. Better title: | 4 | 8 | 32 |
|  | Total Score for This Company: | | 422 |

In that way, you rank each company. This might give you a list of twenty different companies that might have what you're looking for, rated by how closely they meet your objectives. Make a tentative decision on the best alternative, based on the total scores of each company. Then examine that alternative for any possible adverse consequences. Perhaps there's something you overlooked. Perhaps you didn't think of football when you made your list, but when you contemplate a move to Amarillo, you suddenly realize how much you're going to miss pro football. List alternative actions that you'd take in the event the decision doesn't go as you expect. What if none of the twenty companies on your list wants to hire you? What if you move to Houston and can't stand the weather—what are you going to do then?

Make your own chart based on the sample on the following page.

HANDICAPPING CHART

For _____

| | COL. A<br>OBJECTIVES | COL. B<br>SCALE OF<br>IMPORTANCE TO YOU<br>(1–10 WITH 10 THE<br>HIGHEST) | COL. C<br>LIKELIHOOD OF<br>ATTAINING THIS<br>OBJECTIVE<br>_____ | COL. D<br>POINT VALUE FOR<br>_____<br>(MULTIPLY COL.B<br>FIGURE x COL.C FIGURE) | COL. E<br>LIKELIHOOD OF<br>ATTAINING THIS<br>OBJECTIVE<br>_____ | COL. F<br>POINT VALUE FOR<br>_____<br>(MULTIPLY COL.B FIG-<br>URE x COL.E FIGURE) |
|---|---|---|---|---|---|---|
| 1 | | | | | | |
| 2 | | | | | | |
| 3 | | | | | | |
| 4 | | | | | | |
| 5 | | | | | | |
| 6 | | | | | | |
| 7 | | | | | | |
| 8 | | | | | | |
| TOTAL | | | | | | |

Note: When using this blank Handicapping Chart, remember that you need not use all the columns across. For instance, you may only have three objectives rather than the eight shown. Or you may have to add columns if there aren't enough either vertically or horizontally.

You may feel that this is getting to be too complicated to be worthwhile. Remember, however, that you won't be using a handicapping chart to decide where to go to lunch. You'll only be using it for life-changing decisions like a career move or buying a home. Then you'll discover that when critical decisions are considered, it's well worth taking the time.

# Check Both Sides of the Brain Before Answering.

In this chapter, I've shown you how to make single-step decisions when there isn't much uncertainty involved. That means you decide, take action based on that decision, and then finally you find out if you made the right decision. For the three different kinds of single-step decisions:

- I've taught you methods for handling "go or no go" decisions—the coin toss, checklisting, and quantified evaluation.

- You've learned how to handle dichotomies with the 1–10 rating system, the Ben Franklin balance sheet, and the report-card method.

- Finally, I taught you how to choose between three or more possibilities with handicapping.

If the outcome of each choice you make is uncertain, you need a more involved decision-making system—one that will accommodate uncertainty, such as a reaction table or decision tree. That's what I'll teach you next. However, before we go on, let's update the "Categorizing the Decision" chart with the methods I've taught you in this chapter.

# Categorizing the Decision 2

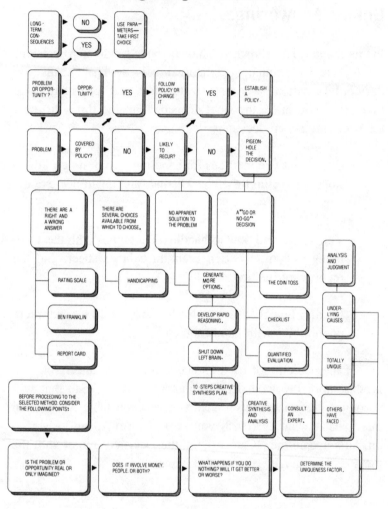

# CHAPTER EIGHT

# Reaction Tables and Decision Trees

## When a Decision Deals with the Unknown, Consider a Reaction Table.

I have already shown you how to decide when the decision is a multiple choice with the outcome of each choice being predictable. But what do you do when you're faced with multiple-choice decisions where the outcome of each choice is uncertain? The solution is to make the best choice using all the information you have available now, and then consider how others will react to the choice you made.

Imagine you own a company called DPC—Data Processing Consultants, a computer consulting firm. You're bidding on a consulting project with a large bank that wants to coordinate all its corporate payroll-processing programs. Here are the variables involved:

1. You know other consultants are bidding on the project, but you don't know how many.

2. You know that price will be a factor to the bank, but you don't know how big a factor.

3. You know the number of experienced programmers you're willing to assign to the project is a consideration, but you don't know how big a consideration.

This type of situation calls for a reaction table. While more complicated than handicapping, a reaction table does a better job of handling the uncertain consequences of the decisions you might make. A reaction table incorporates the three major components of any decision situation:

A. *Alternatives*: the choices that are available to you;

B. *Variables*: the responses that might come from choosing each of these alternatives; and

C. *Reactions*: a projection of how the other side might respond to a combination of each of these alternatives and variables.

You can start by setting up a reaction table with three columns. The left-hand column of the table lists the alternatives, followed by the variables, and finally the reactions. Note that there are more spaces in each column as you move to the right, because each alternative will generate more variables, and each variable will generate even more reactions. Your table should look like this:

## TABLE I.   THE REACTION TABLE

| ALTERNATIVE | % | VARIABLE | % | RESULT |
|---|---|---|---|---|
| | | | | |
| | | | | |
| | | | | |
| | | | | |
| | | | | |
| | | | | |
| | | | | |
| | | | | |
| | | | | |
| | | | | |
| | | | | |
| | | | | |
| | | | | |
| | | | | |
| | | | | |

Instruction: In the lefthand column, list alternatives available to you. In the center column, list the variables; in the event you select one of those alternatives, what might happen? In the percentage column, list the chance of each variable occurring. Eliminate any variable that would have an insignificant effect on the result. Remember that the total percentages for each variable must add up to 100. In the right column, list the likelihood of each possible result.

## LEARN TO JUGGLE THE VARIABLES.

Let's say the alternatives here are:

- *The number of companies bidding on the job.* You might decide that three other companies are in the running for the job.

- *The amount of your bid.* You may decide to consider submitting either a high bid of $400,000, a medium bid of $350,000, or a low bid of $300,000.

- *The number of senior programmers you'll assign to the work.* You've computed it'll take four thousand hours, or roughly eight people working for three months to complete the project. You'll either assign four, three, or two senior programmers to the work, depending on how important this is to the client. With four senior programmers, the cost to you will average $40 per hour, or $160,000. With three seniors, the cost will drop to $35 per hour, or $140,000. With two seniors, the cost will average $30 per hour, or $120,000.

The three alternatives in the first column produce ten variables in the second column. These include:

- The four companies bidding;

- The three levels of your bid; and

- The three possible numbers of senior programmers you'd assign.

## WHEN YOU'RE ESTIMATING REACTIONS, IT ALL ADDS UP.

The next step is to estimate the possibility of the bank's reaction to each of these variables. You examine all the competitors and estimate that you've got a 50 percent chance of getting the job, if you're playing on a level field. That means you all bid at the same price and all commit the same number of senior programmers.

Next you estimate that your chances of getting the job drop to 30 percent if you go with your high bid, remain at 50 percent if you go with the middle bid, and increase to 65 percent if you drop your price to the low bid.

Finally, you consider the number of senior programmers assigned and decide that it's of less importance. You increase your chances of getting the job by 20 percent if you assign four, and you decrease your chances by 25 percent if you're only willing to assign two. The next column on the table, the reactions column, multiplies out the profit for each of these scenarios. You may decide that profit will range from $140,000, if you assign four senior programmers and submit the low bid, all the way to $280,000, if the bank accepts your high bid with only two senior programmers.

When you consider the competition, your experience is that company A always bids high, counting on its national reputation to get them the job. So you project that they'll bid $450,000. Company B is likely to bid $400,000, the same as your high bid. Company C is always the low bidder and probably will match your low bid of $300,000.

Laying all the facts out in a table like this makes your choice much easier. You feel you're almost certain to get the bid at $350,000. That's $100,000 lower than the best-known company, and still $50,000 below your legitimate competitor. It's $50,000 higher than the lowest-price bid, but you feel that by making the point you're willing to assign senior programmers with prior banking experience, you can win the bid.

You're left to choose whether to offer two senior program-

mers and take a $230,000 profit before head-office overhead, or
three seniors and $210,000 profit. You exclude assigning four
seniors as unnecessary in order for you to get the bid on a project
like this. The final decision is that with a $50,000 difference
between the lowest bidder and you, it's necessary to offer three
senior programmers. However, to hedge your bet a little, you also
offer the bank the option of having only two senior programmers
assigned, and saving $20,000.

So you submit a multiple-choice bid at $350,000 with three
senior programmers assigned to the job, or $330,000 with only
two assigned. Take a look at the finished chart below. Notice
how easy it is to see the possibilities involved in this decision
using the reaction-table format.

## TABLE II.    THE REACTION TABLE

Example: Companies Bidding For Project

| Alternative | Variable | Reaction | |
|---|---|---|---|
| companies bidding | Company A<br>Company B<br>Company C<br>Our Company | Bid high:<br>Bids your high:<br>Bid low:<br>Bid : | $450,000<br>$400,000<br>$300,000<br>$350,000<br>with 3 seniors or<br>$330,000<br>with 2 seniors |
| If this is the price you'll bid | $400,000<br>$350,000<br>$300,000 | This is your<br>estimated<br>chance of<br>winning job | 30%<br>50%<br>65% |
| # of programmers | 4 at cost of $160,000<br>3 at cost of $140,000<br>2 at cost of $120,000 | profits against 3 bid levels<br>$240,000; 190,000; 140,000<br>$260,000; 210,000; 160,000<br>$280,000; 230,000; 180,000 | |

## SETTING UP REACTION TABLES

Let's review the process for a reaction table. Remember that there are three factors:

- Alternatives

- Variables

- Reactions

And then there are seven steps to take:

1. Check to be sure the situation requires only one decision to be made at a single point in time. Be sure it doesn't require a sequence of decisions over an extended period. For that, you'll need a decision tree, a method I'll cover next.

2. List the alternatives available.

3. Specify all the variables that could result from these alternatives.

4. Construct a table by assigning and labeling a column for each alternative, each variable, and each possible reaction.

5. For each alternative, decide the financial reward or penalty for each possible reaction. Start a weeding-out process, by first eliminating any alternatives that would have an insignificant effect on the reaction. In the example, we determined the bank would consider three senior programmers adequate, and that offering four would not significantly affect its reaction to the proposal.

6. Check for and eliminate variables that would have an insignificant effect on the reaction. This step applies to the decision made when the low-bid figure wouldn't generate enough gross profit to make the job feasible, so we eliminated the low bid from consideration.

7. Quantify the reactions: How likely are they to happen? From this, choose the optimum alternative. The key here is how accurately you can predict the reactions to the variables.

## CONQUER MULTISTAGE DECISIONS WITH DECISION TREES.

Reaction tables work well with one-stage decisions, when you make a careful choice and it either works or it doesn't. When the first stage of a decision leads you only to the next stage and another decision must be made, you need a more involved process. Decision trees are the best method to use for multiple-choice decisions where the outcome of each choice is uncertain and multistage decisions are necessary.

Multistage decision making means that you'll make an initial decision and then have to make further decisions based on what happens next. An obvious example of a multistage decision is a military invasion. You don't know how the enemy will react, so you must plan for every eventuality. For example, when you've made a counterresponse, you have to plan for every possible reaction the enemy might make to your response. That's the kind of decision that requires a decision tree.

Decision trees become very valuable when we must juggle more than seven alternatives in our minds. Remember the process of chunking information in the chapter on intuition? Our minds can only hold seven pieces of information at once. After that, we mentally bog down. That's why golf and chess are such challenging games; they require us to juggle more than seven possibilities at a time. That's why phone numbers and license plates don't have more than seven digits. If the decision requires us to juggle more than seven possibilities, our minds blow a fuse. The result of this is that one moment you'll think of a decision and feel good about going ahead. Half an hour later, you think about it again, and it seems like a dumb idea. Your mind is vacillating from one possibility to another because it's overloading.

What's the answer? Break down the components into fewer than seven alternatives with a decision tree.

To illustrate this, let me tell you about a decision with which I've been wrestling. I can't decide whether or not to build a house on some land I own in the state of Washington, a state for which I have a lot of affection. From 1968 to 1970, I lived in Yakima, Washington, and my youngest son, John, was born there. It was there, at White Pass, that I learned to ski. I also climbed my first mountain there, Mount Adams; and in 1970 I first climbed Mount Rainier. Ever since then, I've dreamed of owning some land in Washington with a view of Mount Rainier. On it I'd build a retirement home, and spend the twilight of my life in my log cabin, gazing out at the mountain.

Fast-forward through the script of my life eighteen years, to 1988. My daughter, Julia, who was seven when we left Washington, becomes interested in climbing. She hikes up Mount Whitney, the highest point in California, with a friend. She's so fascinated by the sport that she wants me to take her to the top of Mount Rainier. I think it's a terrific idea and start getting back into training.

Since I'm still dreaming of the log cabin with a view of the mountain, I call some local real estate agents, looking for land with a view of the mountain. My vision has now expanded from a log cabin on a small lot to a house on five acres. I end up talking to Marge Winebrenner at Eatonville Realty, telling her that after climbing the mountain, I'd like to look at parcels of land. Julia and I successfully climb the mountain and meet Marge, who shows us some parcels of land. Nothing clicks for us. None of the parcels have any pizzazz; they don't match my dream. We drive back to Marge's office. I ask her, "Don't you have anything with a great view of Mount Rainier?"

She tells me, "I do have one great piece of land, but it's far more than you're looking for. It's one hundred acres."

"May we look at it?" I ask.

"Sure," she says. "Follow me." She walks us out of the office, around the corner, and points up at the hill just outside town.

"Where's the piece that's for sale?"

"That's it! The entire hillside," she says. "It has a terrific view of Mount Rainier, and a sweeping view of Puget Sound and the Olympic Peninsula." My head immediately swims with visions of the Dawson empire that I could create up on the hill. Within an hour, I walk the land and make an offer the seller accepts.

Now we get to the decision part, building the house, which involves many multistage procedures. This is a classic case of a decision that can be solved with a decision tree. The decision tree looks like a family tree. Have you seen one of those? At the top you might have your great, great-great-great-grandparents. Then, going down to the bottom, are all the generations of children, each of them having a different number of children themselves. This all fans out into a huge number of boxes at the bottom. A big difference is that between every generation on a decision tree, there's a circle. In the circle, you write the possibility of each event happening. If you're lost, take a look at the chart, and you'll see what I mean.

Building a house on the land will involve a lot of different decisions. Every one of these decisions involves me making an additional branch on the decision tree. At each point, I must consider all the options and calculate the chances of each one happening. Then I have to consider, do I go ahead, or do I kill the plan; or now that this has happened, do I need to modify my plan? So in this decision tree, I have three boxes at the top, the three variables:

1. Build the house.

2. Don't build the house.

3. Build the house later but not now.

The boxes that lead down from the "build now" box, include all the possibilities:

- I go broke.

- I fall in love with someone who thinks Washington is awful.

- I die before finishing the house.

- I love the house and live happily every after.

From each of these boxes are drawn other boxes, which show every further variable.

From the "don't build" box are boxes that list all the variables:

- The land goes up in value.

- The land goes down in value.

- The land value stays the same, and property taxes eat me alive.

# TABLE III.   DECISION TREE

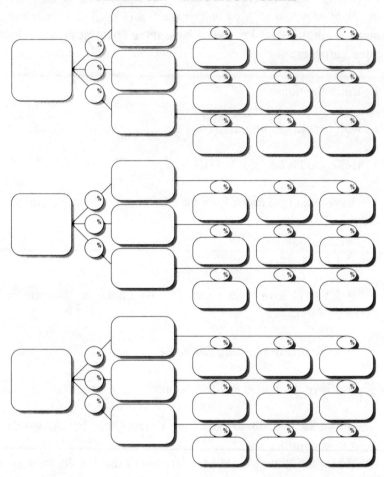

From the "build later" box, the alternatives really spread out. They include:

- Interest rates go up.

- Interest rates go down.

- I can't get financing later.

- The cost of building goes up.

- The cost of building goes down.

- The building restrictions get more restrictive.

- The building restrictions loosen up.

- I come up with a better idea for a different style of house.

- I marry someone who has twelve children, and we need a bigger house.

Having put all the possibilities onto the decision tree, I now must rate the probability of any of these things happening. See the circle that's on every line leading to a square? In the circle, you put the likelihood of each event happening. To do that accurately, you need to know something about odds-making, and later I'll teach you about the science of probabilities.

First I have to negotiate with the holders of the underlying financing to release the twenty acres of the land on which I want to build. This creates a "yes" branch, which I judge has a 70 percent chance of happening, and a "no" branch, which has a 30 percent chance. Then there are subbranches of "yes," meaning they will show the various amounts they might charge me to do this, with the odds of them accepting each amount shown. The subbranches of "no," meaning they won't release just the twenty acres, include either killing the whole plan, refinancing the entire hundred acres, or paying off all the underlying financing myself.

Then I have to find water and drill a well, and I have to get septic-tank approval. Each of these creates a subtree. Will I find water or won't I? Should I invest thousands of dollars in test holes or not? Will I get approval for a septic field, or will I have to go with a more expensive above-ground system? Also, electricity and telephone lines have to be run to the land. I'm taking these one step at a time, in no particular hurry to move ahead.

Meanwhile, two other events take place that affect my decision. I get a chance to buy another twenty-three acres next to my land. I put another branch on the tree. How much should I offer? What are the odds of the seller accepting at each of these levels? The land has some valuable lumber on it, and he's asking $150,000. If I pay that much, I'll have to put my house plans on hold for a long time. Another branch of the tree considers the possibility of him selling to someone else, with the new owners building something that would ruin my view of the mountain.

At this point, I start to go through the ten Creative Synthesis steps I talked about in Chapter Six until I come up with a creative answer:

**STEP ONE: VISUALIZE THE OPPOSITE OF THE SITUATION.** I work on this for a while, but it doesn't produce any ideas.

**STEP TWO: EXAMINE THE ENVIRONMENT IN WHICH THE PROBLEM EXISTS.** I work at this one, too, but it doesn't help.

**STEP THREE: VISUALIZE FINDING THE PERFECT AN-
SWER.** Pondering this produces some interesting flights of fantasy, but none of them seems realistic. Perhaps I would find gold
or oil on the land, or a mysterious stranger would endow the
project, but it doesn't seem likely.

**STEP FOUR: IMAGINE ALL THE ASSUMPTIONS THAT
HAVE BEEN MADE ARE WRONG.** This starts me thinking.
I assume the seller wants to sell the land for $150,000, and it's
worth so much because the lumber is valuable. I reversed that
premise: What if he doesn't want to sell the land? No, that
doesn't make sense. Then what if he doesn't want to sell
the timber? No, that's crazy, he can't sell the land and keep
the timber. But this step triggers something in the back of my
mind.

**STEP FIVE: IMAGINE WHAT I'D DO IF I KNEW I
COULDN'T FAIL.** This encourages me, but it doesn't produce
a creative solution.

**STEP SIX: RUN THE DECISION BY A SERIES OF ROLE
MODELS.** The problem with that is, my role models don't know
anything more about buying land than I do.

**STEP SEVEN: THINK BACKWARD FROM THE SOLU-
TION TO THE PROBLEM.** Okay, I do that. My desired
solution is to have a beautiful two-story home sitting on the
top of the hill, surrounded on all sides by beautiful mountain
meadows. Everywhere I look, there's a wonderful carpet of
wildflowers. Snowcapped Mount Rainier fills the horizon. Every evening, I sit in my hot tub watching the mountain turn
bright red as the setting sun sinks over the Olympic Peninsula.
I love it! Now let's retreat in time from that point. How did

this come together? I can't build the house if I spend $150,000 for the land. To create the view of the mountain, and the lush mountain meadows, I need to log the land and landscape it with a bulldozer. Wait a minute, those trees are valuable. I don't want them, but the present owner of the land does. Suddenly, the answer pops into my mind. I'll buy the land, but not the trees. I offer the owner thirty thousand dollars for the land, with me paying seventy-five hundred dollars cash down, and him carrying back the financing at 10 percent. He gets a five-year right to log the timber on it. Perfect! I don't have to put up a lot of cash, and he can play the timber market, waiting for the perfect time to sell the trees.

I put another branch on my decision tree to consider all the possibilities, and they all look good. I make the offer, and the seller accepts it. Then I get an offer for twenty of my original hundred acres and put another branch on my decision tree. Accepting the offer doesn't solve any problems or create any opportunities, so I turn it down.

Then I get a chance to sell sixty of the first hundred acres, for more than I paid for the whole hundred. This decision-tree branch produces some interesting possibilities. The cash generated will pay off the underlying financing on the twenty acres on which I want to build. The payments on the financing I would carry back on the land I'd sell would pay the mortgage on the new house. I'm left with only forty acres, not one hundred, but the high point of the land—where I want to build—is right in the middle.

I decide to sell and immediately regret it, wishing I'd kept it all. The buyer of the sixty is having trouble finding water on his land and a place for septic drainage fields. He can back out of buying the land, but instead we go through the ten creative steps together and come up with a perfect win-win decision. He'll run electricity, water, and telephone to my house location if I'll let him drill a well and put a septic field on my land. We both run a decision tree on this solution and agree it's perfect. We both get a perfect system of utilities. I get it free, and he gets it much cheaper than if he had to do expensive engineering work on his land.

The point I'm making here is that if I'd tried to make all these decisions at once, it would have been a mind-blower. When the decisions are made one by one, they fall into place. I complete the sale of the sixty acres and use the funds to pay off the underlying loan on the land on which I might build. I decide on the house I want, a two-story Victorian, and negotiate the price with a builder. I get the bank to approve my construction loan, and I'm ready to roll. The payments coming in from the sale of the sixty acres will pay the house payments, and I've already got all the utilities run to the site.

Then the wheels come off. The economy suddenly takes a nosedive. This calls for a brand-new decision tree. I'm a full-time professional speaker who gives about one hundred talks a year to corporations and at association conventions. If the economy gets much worse, it will dramatically affect my speaking business. Companies will cancel their meetings to save money, and associations won't be able to get their members to attend their conventions. Should I go ahead with the house or not?

Soon my new decision tree, the one I did when the economy went south, has sprouted many branches, and it's full of possibilities. But the further I go with it, the best decision becomes clear. I should wait out the recession. When the downturn ends, I will see how it affects building costs and interest rates. The moment they begin to move up, I can jump quickly to lock in the price with the builder and the loan with the lender.

Decision trees enable you to break down decisions so that you can manage uncertainty more effectively. As you develop your tree of options, you need to accurately predict the likelihood of something happening or not happening. That's where the science of probabilities comes into play.

## THE SCIENCE OF PROBABILITIES

Remember that on every branch of the decision tree, there's a circle showing the likelihood of any possibility happening. The success of your decision tree depends on how well you judge the odds. So you need to learn about the science of probabilities. The best way to understand odds-making is to look at how bookmakers make odds for a horse race. If only two horses are running in a horse race, and one horse carries odds of 10-to-1, the other horse must carry odds of 1-to-10. In that way, if you bet one hundred dollars on horse A and ten dollars on horse B, you'd come out even. If horse A wins, you win ten dollars and lose ten dollars. If horse B wins, you win one hundred dollars and lose one hundred dollars. If the odds deviated from this in your favor, you could bet on both horses and win money regardless of which horse won.

In the world of high finance, looking for a discrepancy like that is called *arbitrage*. In the old days, fortunes could be made in arbitraging currencies. By buying one currency and converting it into another, and sometimes through several currency exchanges, the trader could be assured of a profit. In today's computer world, the possibilities of these errors being made are remote, and when it happens, traders can spot it and act in a matter of seconds, which quickly removes the opportunity.

In the wholesale-grocery arena, this is called *diverting*, and the companies that specialize in it are called *diverters*. If a manufacturer offers a special price in one part of the country in order to stimulate sales, diverters will pick up on this and offer this price to other regions in the country, which undermines the manufacturer's sales in that area. The goods do not physically move; everything is done electronically.

For the purpose of a decision tree, think of a certainty as one hundred and a "no possibility" as zero. Express levels of possibilities as 50 percent for a toss-up, 67 percent as a 2-to-1 chance, and so on. Don't narrow it down to closer than a 5 percent possibility. For example, on the decision tree for building the house, the chance of my marrying a woman with twelve children might be 5 percent. And the chance of my not doing so would have to be 95 percent. The chances of building codes becoming more restrictive might be 70 percent, and the chances of them loosening up must then be 30 percent.

Be sure you carefully include all possibilities. For example, interest rates wouldn't be dichotomous. Here there are three possibilities. They go up, they go down, or they stay the same. Since the total must add up to 100 percent, I might judge the possibility of an increase as 70 percent, a decrease as 10 percent, and staying the same as 20 percent.

You can use probability in a workplace situation as well. Here's a simple and effective way of getting accurate projections from your employees. Managers are plagued by employees who either budget sales projections conservatively, because they want to look good, or are wildly optimistic and are always making their projections too high. You can solve that problem with this simple technique:

*Ask the person how he or she would bet on the outcome.*

If you ask someone if he'd bet money on it, it brings the problem into his personal realm of profit or gain. Let's say you ask your salesperson, "What do you think you can sell this month?"

And she tells you, "Twenty thousand dollars."

Then you say, "If you could bet one thousand dollars at even money that your sales would be more or less than twenty thousand dollars, on which side would you bet?"

She says, "Less than."

You continue, "At what point would you feel comfortable betting that you'd exceed the figure?"

"Oh, I'm sure it'll be higher than fifteen thousand dollars."

"At sixteen thousand, five hundred dollars, would you bet high or low?"

Finally, she says, "I'd have a tough time at that figure, I'd be willing to bet either way." In that manner, you determine that sixteen thousand, five hundred dollars is the most likely figure for her sales that month. Try that, and I think its accuracy will amaze you.

## USING FAULT TREES TO PREDICT THE FUTURE

Now let's look at fault trees, which are decision trees in reverse. With these, you list first the worst-possible outcome of the decision you make and then work backward to see how you arrived at the problem.

To see how they work, let's apply one to a business opportunity that came up near where I live in La Habra Heights, California. A couple of miles away from me is a very successful locally owned pizza parlor. It started as a walk-up, a take-out hole in the wall. Then the owner added a few benches inside and finally expanded to a smart sidewalk café on the outside. His overhead was low, and his volume was high, and over the years he became very successful. Now he has the ambition to move on to something more grand. He wants to open another Italian restaurant a few miles away, but this one will be an upscale trattoria.

Let's use a fault tree to figure out if there's a compelling reason for him not to go ahead. We'll head up the fault tree with the obvious reason a business would fail—not enough profit. That goes in a box at the top of the page. Then you break that down into two subboxes: not enough gross sales and overhead that's too high. Next you list reasons for each category. Under "not enough gross sales," you might list:

- Poor location

- Poor food

- Poor employees

- Too expensive

- Too much competition

- Poor atmosphere

- Location too small

- Changing customer tastes, etc.

Under "overhead too high," you list things like:

- Changing food costs

- High waste

- High theft

- Expensive help

- Long hours of opening

- High cost of financing

- Poor restaurant design

- Too much overtime, etc.

For each of these elements, you draw a branch of the fault tree that further breaks down the reasons for each fault. For example, one reason you listed for low sales was poor food. That might get broken down into:

- Failure to hire the right chef

- Inadequate suppliers

- Poor storage facilities

- Delay in getting food to the table and so on

Each of these might then have subcategories.

You rack your brains for everything that might go wrong, and believe me, that's hard to do. It's almost like proofreading a large brochure before giving the final go-ahead to the printer. Unless you're ten times more thorough than you think you need to be, a mistake will always slip by.

Having created a chart of every possible thing that could go wrong, you start working on responses. Could you adequately react to each of these problems? For most of them, you probably could, but there may be one killer that simply creates unacceptable risk and causes you to kill the project.

This may all sound very negative to you, but it's very smart business. An effective fault tree could have avoided Union Carbide's disaster in Bhopal, India. It could have prevented the tragic oil spill in Alaska. And it could have prevented many of the major bankruptcies that plagued the 1980s.

Astronaut Edgar Mitchell made a strong case for fault trees when he said, ''We spent ten percent of our training time studying plans for our mission to the moon, and ninety percent of our time learning how to react to all the 'what ifs.' ''

By the way, the new Italian restaurant is doing fine—in spite of some equipment breakdowns during the first week, an initial loss of business at the owner's first location, and a direct competitor opening up down the street. By anticipating these problems, the owner has now created a very successful new business.

So now I've taught you three more ways to handle decisions when there are several choices available. You'll see that those are now added to the following Categorizing the Decision chart.

Note that both decision trees and fault trees incorporate a very fundamental element in major decision making. That's the willingness to break big problems down into small portions. If you're faced with a very big decision, it's easy to become overwhelmed by it. This creates two responses, and both could lead to problems. The first is overestimating the challenge—''This is so overwhelming I won't even attempt it.'' The second is underestimating the challenge—''Sure it's a big project, but I feel good about it, my intuition tells me to take a chance. I can handle any problems that come up.''

Fault trees enable you to break down decisions into more manageable pieces, so that you can better anticipate problems and overcome them.

At the start of Chapter Seven, I talked about how appealing it is to think of intuition alone as the answer to decision making. However, the bigger trap we're likely to fall into these days is feeling that all decisions can be made with logic alone. As we've seen earlier, that won't work, either. What it takes to become a Confident Decision Maker is knowing when to use logic and when to use intuition. Techniques that help you to handle dichotomous decisions, multiple-choice decisions, or decisions involving sev-

# Categorizing the Decision 3

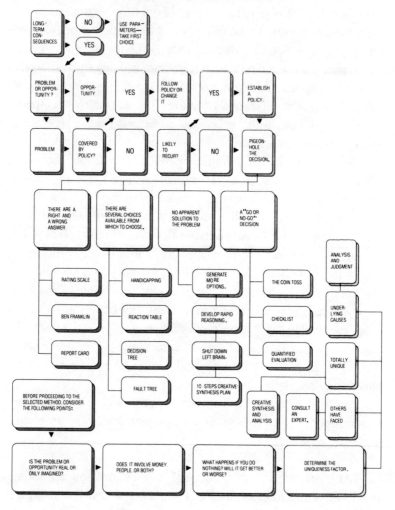

eral unknown factors include methods such as coin tosses, handicapping, reaction tables, and fault trees. Let these be your starting point. However, when it comes to making the final choice, integrating the accuracy of logic with the magic of intuition is what will give you the best-possible outcome.

# CHAPTER NINE

# Huddling

## Huddling Is the Key to Group Decision Making.

Have you ever noticed the blurry-eyed executives who populate the breakfast coffee shops at business hotels? They're trying to jump-start their brains with black coffee because they have been up half the night agonizing over this dilemma:

"Should I go ahead and make the decision myself, or should I get other people involved in this? If I go ahead and make the decision myself, and I'm as right as I think I am," their vacillating minds reason, "where could it lead? Perhaps I'm at the high tide of my career, which as Shakespeare said, 'taken at the flood, leads on to fortune.' If I'm right, everyone might hail me as a courageous genius, a bold innovator, a captain of industry.

"On the other hand, what if I'm wrong? Then I might really be in trouble; I'll be made an example of. Decades from now, they'll hold business classes on campuses across the nation on the foolishness of my decision.

"Or worse yet, I could be right; but then everyone in the organization might gang up and teach me a lesson because I didn't get them involved in the decision. Then they'll give lip service to the whole project, and I'll be left twisting slowly in the breeze. Should I get other people involved in the huddle or shouldn't I?"

Huddling is my word for group decision making. Any time a decision involves a group of people, it can be daunting. But sometimes you're better off getting other people involved in a decision, rather than being a dynamic leader who goes it alone. Then again, there are some decisions that are better made autocratically. How do you know when to take a decision to a huddle? What are the advantages of Huddling? How do you set up a huddle? And finally, when does Huddling create more problems than it solves? I'll teach you in this chapter.

## How to Know When It's Right to Huddle

There are five conditions when you should opt for a huddle rather than make the decision on your own:

1. When you think that Huddling will generate more options;

2. When outside expertise would be helpful;

3. When you want to raise the ethical standards of the decision;

4. When you need the support of the huddle to follow through on the decision; and

5. When you're afraid the huddle will turn down your idea.

   Let's take a look at these conditions more closely:

### WHEN YOU THINK THAT HUDDLING WILL GENERATE MORE OPTIONS.

Sometimes, when you've done everything you can to gather all the information, and you still don't think you have enough, Huddling gets you over the hump. That's because talking about a decision with others stimulates creative thought and helps to broaden your view of the decision. When you're stuck, huddlers can sometimes help you to become unstuck.

## WHEN OUTSIDE EXPERTISE WOULD BE HELPFUL.

When you huddle with a group of other professionals, such as an outside board of directors, you may have an expert on transportation, international law, or someone who has handled strikes in Argentina among the group. It's the kind of expertise you simply don't have available to you in your company, and you'd be foolish not to take advantage of it.

## WHEN YOU WANT TO RAISE THE ETHICAL STANDARDS OF THE DECISION.

Have you ever wondered why a hospital has a surgeon's review *board* instead of just one administrator? It's because, in theory, boards keep people honest. While one or two people might be willing to cover up malpractice, a large group is more likely to maintain high standards.

Government is structured like this for the same reason, although when we look at our government bodies, we can see that huddles don't always produce the most ethical decisions. Huddles can sometimes result in decisions that are clearly wrong in retrospect. That's because the opinion of the majority often sways the opinion of the other huddlers. Although a group of people should have higher ethical standards than an individual, there's also a danger that Huddle Rot—where majority opinion dominates—could set in.

The classic example of Huddle Rot is the Bay of Pigs decision. Individually, the people in power knew it was a mistake to use U.S. troops to support an invasion of Cuba. But they all got swept up with the desire to be team players. Arthur Schlesinger had stated in writing that he considered the proposed invasion of Cuba immoral. But then Robert Kennedy took him aside and said, "You may be right or you may be wrong, but . . . don't push any further." That's Huddle Rot. And the outcome of this type of peer pressure is that it leads people to go along with a decision that individually they would reject because it doesn't meet their ethical standards.

## WHEN YOU NEED THE SUPPORT OF THE HUDDLE TO FOLLOW THROUGH ON THE DECISION

Unless you just got here from Communist China, you're well aware of the value of getting the group involved in a decision. People will simply support decisions with more enthusiasm when they help make the decision. However, there are certain techniques that are important to remember so that you don't wind up manipulating the group. When I was in my twenties and just getting started up the corporate ladder, I was very much an autocratic decision maker. I knew what was right for the organization, and I didn't see any reason to waste a lot of time getting other people involved in the decision-making process. My boss at the time, Don Rainwater, was much smarter than I. He told me that if I wanted the support of the organization, I had to let them make the decision.

Still, I was young and foolish enough to think I could work my way around that with no problem. I typed up the six things I wanted to get approved and ran off enough copies for the group but kept them hidden. Then I led them into a discussion on the problem we were having. But I led the discussion so skillfully, they ended up deciding on the same six things. With a flourish,

I produced my prepared sheet of paper and distributed it to the group, saying, "I believe this is what we all agreed upon." They were generous enough to see the humor in this situation, but Don Rainwater called me on that one and taught me a lesson I won't forget—be persuasive in leading the group to the right decision, but avoid being manipulative. Do it right, and accept input from the rest of the huddlers.

## WHEN YOU'RE AFRAID THE HUDDLE WILL TURN DOWN YOUR IDEA.

Any time you're concerned that the group might reject your proposal, you must take it to the huddle. Does that seem like a contradiction? Not really. If you fear the group might turn down your idea, then your instincts are telling you your idea has problems. When we fall in love with something, we become blind to its faults. Ideas are no exception.

Let's say you think you can take the Australian market by storm with a new high-tech fly deterrent. It works on batteries, is rechargeable, and will scare off flies within a one-hundred-foot radius. You figure you can get exclusive distribution rights and manufacture it in Bangkok for a price lower than anywhere else in the world. With the swarms of flies in Australia, there's no way it's going to fail. However, if you take it to the executive committee for approval, you are worried that those people are such "stick-in-the-muds," they'll never agree to it.

Hey, wait a minute, who are you trying to kid? If you can't convince the ten people on your executive committee, what chance do you have of convincing the two thousand people in your organization that it's a good idea? What chance do you have of convincing the 16 million people in Australia that it's great? See what I mean? If you don't want to take it to a huddle because you're afraid the huddlers will turn it down, that's exactly why you should be Huddling.

## The Advantages of Huddling

When you're not sure whether to take on the responsibility for a decision yourself or huddle with your team, consider these benefits:

**HUDDLES USUALLY OUTPERFORM INDIVIDUALS, BECAUSE THE PARTICIPANTS ARE ABLE TO COR-RECT ONE ANOTHER'S MISTAKES.** Try this problem: A man buys a watch in a store for sixty-five dollars. The watch costs the merchant thirty dollars. The customer pays with a hundred-dollar money order and gets thirty five dollars cash back. The money order turns out to be stolen, and the merchant can't redeem it. How much is the merchant out?

It's a mind-bender, isn't it? Individuals get confused on this kind of problem, whereas huddlers can handle it better because they can more objectively point out the mistakes of the others.

If you're still working on it, the answer is this: The merchant's out sixty-five dollars—thirty dollars for the cost of the watch plus the thirty-five dollars cash he gave back to the man.

**HUDDLING FORCES ACTION ON PROBLEMS.** Let's face it, everybody in an organization has his or her own problems. Unless the new computer assembly plant in São Paulo directly affects an individual, he or she's not going to worry about it too much. But when you announce that the following week there will be a meeting to discuss whether to go ahead with the plant, suddenly everyone gets involved in the project. They start accumulating information and brainstorming so they can give intelligent input. Huddling forces people to get involved in a project they might otherwise ignore.

**HUDDLING INCREASES TRUST IN THE ORGANIZATION.** When people feel the organization is involving them in decisions, they trust the organization more. Job satisfaction goes up, along with motivation and morale.

**INFORMATION IS OF BETTER QUALITY, BECAUSE THE HUDDLE WILL REJECT ERRONEOUS INFORMATION.** Somebody might come to the Huddle with a proposal to buy a distribution warehouse in Mobile, Alabama. If the person could have made the decision alone, he or she would have done it by now. Yet when he or she presents it to the Huddle, somebody who knows that part of the world says, "Wait a minute. Have you checked the union environment in Mobile? That's one of the worst union towns in the country. Don't go ahead before you find out exactly what you're getting into." So Huddling allows others to scrutinize your information and may give you new information.

**WITH MORE PEOPLE GIVING INPUT, YOU'LL GET MORE INFORMATION WITH WHICH TO WORK.** That's obvious, but it isn't always good news. You can easily get bogged down in too much information. Be careful that inputting too much information doesn't lead to indecisiveness. As a leader, you have to be willing to say, "We know enough about the problem, now let's make a decision."

**THE INFORMATION PRESENTED AT A HUDDLE TENDS TO BE MORE THOROUGH AND THE SUMMATIONS MORE CLEAR.** In plain language, that means that one-on-one, people might try to feed you a load of garbage. But when they have to make a presentation to a huddle, they're going to be much more thorough in their research and draw conclusions more carefully.

## Solo Huddles Are Good for Decision Hurdles.

I'm sure you've been a part of the more familiar formal and semiformal huddles such as the committee meeting, the executive committee, and the board of directors. However, there are three other structured methods of Huddling that you may not have experienced. They're more involved, but they may be very helpful when you're faced with a complicated or obscure decision.

The first is called Solo Huddling. That seems like an oxymoron, doesn't it? Sort of like jumbo shrimp, postal service, and normal teenager. However, it can be a great decision-making tool. Here's how it works:

First, take fifteen minutes to write down every possibility that occurs to you. Think of yourself as a photographer who takes hundreds of pictures and later selects the one that's just right. The threshold theory says: The more you have to choose from, the better the quality. Then wait until that afternoon or the next morning and go at it again. Meanwhile, your subconscious mind will have been at work on the problem. Being able to do this over two separate sessions is a big advantage over Group Huddling, which logistically needs to be done at one session. In the meantime, mention the decision to others and get their input.

Next separate your list into an A list and a B list. Don't be too selective. Include anything that might work on your A list, and put only the things you *know* won't work on to the B list. Then rate the ideas on your A list from 1 to 10. Try pairing the three best ideas on your list with all the other ideas. And, finally, take the best idea on your B list and pair it with all the other ideas. By keeping yourself open to all the various possibilities and combinations, you may find that this random association generates new possibilities.

## Analogy Huddling—Seeing the Decision in a New Light

Analogy Huddling is a fascinating way of looking at a problem from new directions, rather than stimulating numerous creative options. There are a number of phases to go through, and the first three are common to all decision-making processes.

1.  Present a detailed statement of the problem to the group. You develop this statement by Categorizing and Blueprinting, as I taught you in Chapters Two and Three.

2.  Overload the huddle with information about the problem. This brings hidden aspects of the problem into the open.

3.  Be sure every member of the group thoroughly understands the problem by asking each of them to restate it in his or her own words. This is important, because in a corporate environment, it's very hard for some people to admit they don't understand something. They sit and listen to what's going on, hoping all the pieces will drop into place for them. To be sure they understand, you might say to the group, "Okay, as we go around the table, I want each of you to give me a quick statement. Why do you think we're opening up a computer-assembly plant in São Paulo? Each of you should offer a new reason. Don't repeat something that someone's already said."

The first person might say, "Because we can make computers cheaper there than anywhere else."

The second person might add, "Well, I thought the major reason is the subsidy the Brazilian government will give us."

Then the third person might say, "Well, isn't the improved access to the South American market a key consideration, too?" As you go around the table, everybody gets a clearer understanding of the problem you're facing.

The last phase is to develop analogies, for a better understanding of the problem. An analogy is a figure of speech that attempts to make something clear by comparing it with something else. "As exciting as watching grass grow," is an analogy. So is Tallulah Bankhead's description of herself: "As pure as driven slush." Analogies are effective in problem solving because they cause the mind to make a great leap in thinking.

There are four types of analogies:

• Direct Analogies

• Personal Analogies

• Fantasy Analogies

• Symbolic Analogies

How do they work? Let's say a group of executives is discussing a new car at an automobile company. Then the rule is that they need to express their preference as an analogy. One executive might start with a direct analogy by saying, "The lines should be as smooth as Bailey's Irish Cream." Another might respond with a personal analogy, "I want it to be as exciting as my first toboggan run." Then somebody chimes in with a fantasy analogy: "It should sparkle like Cinderella's glass slippers."

And someone else might contribute the symbolic analogy, "The acceleration should explode."

Analogies are effective in problem solving because they cause the mind to make a great leap in thought. Thomas Edison used an analogy when he said, "I'm experimenting upon an instrument that does for the eye what the phonograph does for the ear." The analogy helped him to apply what he had learned from inventing the phonograph to his invention of the motion-picture projector.

Most inventions that result from dreams are the product of analogies. Friedrich Kekule von Stradonitz, the German chemist, discovered the structure of the benzene ring in a dream. He dreamed of the atoms he'd been studying, and they appeared to him as a snake. Suddenly, one of the snakes bit its own tail. He woke up with a start and knew the answer to the problem he'd been pondering for weeks—that organic compounds such as benzene have atoms structured in closed rings, not open lines.

Elias Howe couldn't make the sewing machine work. He was experimenting with a needle that had the hole halfway down. Then he dreamed of savages with spears that had holes near the tips. He remembered this analogy when he woke up, and it was the key to his invention.

## Successful Analogy Huddles Make the Familiar Seem Strange.

Ask everybody in the group to come up with an analogy relating to the decision you're making, and watch what happens. They don't have to apply all the different kinds of analogies, but I'll do that here to illustrate them clearly.

Somebody might start with a direct analogy about the computer-assembly plant in Brazil. This person might say, "Well, the operation should flow like oil through a pipeline."

Somebody else might jokingly respond, "Well, that's a better analogy than sending it on the *Exxon Valdez.*" Then this might trigger a discussion of pipelines of supplies through Central America if a civil war broke out. Or shipping problems that might exist. The word "pipeline" might even trigger talk of sabotage and a discussion about security precautions at the plant.

Then somebody might use a personal analogy. "The unemployment is so bad there, that for the Brazilians, going to work will be as exciting as going to Disneyland for the first time."

Somebody else might respond, "Well, that's an interesting thought, because we are importing a new type of technology to the country. It's similar to when Disneyland opened up in Tokyo and Europe. They faced all kinds of cultural considerations that were strange to them."

"I know a consultant who worked with them on Euro Disney," somebody else might say. "Let me give her a call and see if she knows anything about the problems we're facing."

Next a fantasy analogy may be used. "This is going to seem so strange to the workers. It will seem like *Star Wars* to them."

Somebody might say, "If only we could program them to do the work the way R2-D2 programmed itself." Then this might trigger a thought about program systems and employee orientation and training.

Finally, somebody might use a symbolic analogy, such as, "This should push our profits through the roof." Everybody then suddenly visualizes the roof of the plant, and somebody says, "Have we considered putting a helicopter pad on the roof of that plant? We have a corporate helicopter at our Rio location, don't we? Wouldn't it make sense to do that?" In this way, the conversation bounces around the room.

Can you think of a few analogies for a decision you are

presently faced with? Use the chart below to help you sort out your ideas.

| Direct | Personal | Fantasy | Symbolic |
|--------|----------|---------|----------|
|        |          |         |          |
|        |          |         |          |
|        |          |         |          |
|        |          |         |          |

Analogy Huddles are small, and the people who participate are better qualified to come up with solutions. The value of Analogy Huddling is this: It makes the familiar seem strange. Through the analogies, you see the problem in a different way. Just beware of reading too much into analogies. As Sigmund Freud once said, "Sometimes a cigar is just a cigar."

## Computer Huddling

The third and final method of Structured Huddling is called Computer Huddling. This method allows for feedback from individual contributors, the objective assessment of input, opportunities to revise previously stated views, and anonymity to the participants.

Computer Huddling, which uses computer surveys so that respondents never meet face-to-face, is comprised of five stages. Stage 1 is *exploration*. In this stage, you ask each participant to contribute information to the survey. For example, you may run a chain of nationwide fast-food restaurants, and during your last annual meeting in Acapulco the question of adding doughnuts to the line came up. There appeared to be popular support for this, so you'd like to get some more input on it. In the exploration stage, you might send out a memo on your computer network that says, "At the Acapulco meeting, there was support for adding doughnuts to the line. We'd like to get some feedback. Please give me three reasons why you think this is a good idea and three reasons why you think this is a bad idea."

Stage 2, or the *interpretation* stage, is when a group of data-processing experts at the head office attempts to understand how the participants view the problem—where they agree and where they disagree. It's possible, at this stage, that you'll get such overwhelming support for the program that you'll want to run with it. Or you could get such overwhelming condemnation that you want to drop the idea. If you have significant disagreement, though, you can move on to the next stage, which is *reconciliation*.

In the *reconciliation* stage, the head-office team eliminates the more extreme responses. It ignores the 10 percent who loved the plan and the 10 percent that hated it. Then, from among the more moderate supporters of the plan, it reaches for agreement. For example, a follow-up letter might go back out with questions such as, "How would you feel if we offered doughnuts only during the morning?" Or, "What if we offered doughnuts only on a take-out basis?" The response to this questionnaire uncovers the reasons for the difference of opinion.

Stage 4 is called the *evaluation* stage. During this stage, you analyze all the information and condense it into options for a management decision. The head-office team may report, "There's very little support for carrying doughnuts throughout the day. The feeling is it would cut into lunch and dinner sales. However, 82 percent of the managers like the idea for the morning hours. They're less in agreement on whether the doughnuts should be take-out items only. Fifty-seven percent think they should be available only at the drive-up. Forty-three percent think it would increase add-on sales if the doughnuts were also available inside.''

The final stage is *summarization*. Here you feed the information back to the participants in a summarized form. This gives them a better idea of why management arrived at the final decision. It draws the support of people who may have opposed it or favored a different version of the same basic decision, or even people who may have favored a less modified version of the original decision.

It may seem like a drawn-out process, but there are many advantages of Computer Huddling. Among them:

- You can involve more people than is practical in a face-to-face huddle.

- It's cheaper than getting them together.

- Severe disagreement can be more easily resolved, because of the anonymity of the people involved in the survey.

- Dominant personalities can't sway the opinions of the other huddlers.

Like the other forms of the structured huddle, this process can be very useful when you have a complicated decision and you've come to a roadblock along the road of possibilities.

## How Many People Should Huddle?

Having made the decision that one way or another you're going to huddle, the next decision you have to face is how many people should you get involved in this? How big should your huddle be? The upside of larger huddles is that getting more people involved increases the amount of information that's going to be inputted. Because of that, you'll probably get more options. Also, a higher level of synergistic creativity comes out of larger huddles, so they generate more information.

The downside of larger huddles is that, while you'll get more options, you'll probably have a tougher time reaching agreement. And, as the size of the huddle increases, participation by the less active members drops dramatically. Studies have shown that huddles of more than eight people generate factions that act independently, and become counterproductive to the huddle.

So what's the best size for a huddle? Well, the size of the huddle probably should be based on the type of decision. Smaller huddles are better for concrete problems, but larger huddles are better for abstract opportunities. Problem solving is easier with a large huddle, but decision making is harder. All too often, committees are dark alleys down which good ideas are lured and quietly strangled. Try using a larger huddle to debate the problem, and then appoint a subcommittee to come up with a short list of optimum solutions.

Obviously a larger huddle is going to be considerably more expensive in terms of person-hours. It's going to be much harder to control. And it ties up a lot of administrative effort just to stage the event. However, the time and effort may be worth it if you're making a delicate decision that will require a lot of enthusiastic support.

Congress probably knows the optimum size for committees. It sets up subcommittees in the Senate with five people for action taking, and fourteen for nonaction taking. The fourteen generate many options, and the five narrow down the list and implement the decision.

Huddles function best if they contain people with similar status. If you put trainees in with vice presidents, a lot of things go on in that room other than decision making. The trainees are trying to impress the executives and the executives become more conservative in front of their employees.

## Creativity and the Brainstorming Huddle

I'm sure you've all experienced the most popular form of structured huddles known as *brainstorming*. But perhaps you don't know where brainstorming originated. Alex Osborn was a partner in an advertising agency, Batten, Barton, Durstine and Osborn, or BBDO, when he decided to declare war on left-brain thinking. He developed the process of brainstorming at his agency to stimulate ideas, and it soon spread to other companies. In 1953, his landmark book *Applied Imagination* was published. Then, in 1964, he started the Creative Education Foundation in Buffalo, New York, which still receives royalties from his book. He died in 1966, and while he didn't win the war, he had the satisfaction of knowing he had taken a few million people hostage to the process of brainstorming.

When you're planning a brainstorming huddle, the optimum number of people to include is twelve, although it could range from four to two hundred. There are four rules to remember:

1. Don't permit any judgment, evaluation, or criticism in the huddle. Don't allow anyone to say anything positive, either, such as, "That's a great idea," because if someone presents an idea that isn't responded to positively, or that is met with silence, it might be construed as criticism. Nor is a speaker allowed to use such qualifiers as "This may not work, but . . ."

2. Don't consider any idea too wild or too absurd.

3. Stress the quantity of the ideas, not the quality. Get the huddle to throw out as many ideas as you possibly can in a short period. A good brainstorming session generates excitement. As I've said earlier, high arousal often shuts down the left brain and makes the right brain dominate. People become more creative in this kind of environment.

4. Encourage a combination of ideas or improvements. Everybody in the group can pick up on somebody else's idea and suggest an improvement, although they mustn't criticize the original idea. People can also combine ideas. Someone at a cereal company might say, "Why don't we take Joe's idea of packaging cereal in smaller packages and combine it with Anne's idea of a big-ticket item and put together a sampling pack? We'll shrink-pack twelve tiny individual servings of cereals and sell them as one large package."

One problem with brainstorming is that it can become so much fun, the huddle never wants to break up. There are several ways to decide when to end a huddle. The first is when you've used up the allocated time. You might decide to devote thirty minutes to brainstorming and see what you can come up with. While this sounds like a very logical, left-brain thing to do, it forces the pace of the discussion.

Another way to know when to end is when the enthusiasm of the huddle runs out. Similarly, if the time between insights becomes too great, the energy of the huddle might be drained. When the input begins to die down, it might signal that it's time to wrap things up. Finally, you can decide in advance how many alternatives you want to reach. Then, when you've reached your set number of options, you can stop. I prefer this method because it forces you to pass up the first option that seems right and continue looking for other answers.

Another problem with brainstorming is that it's so much fun

to do, you fall in love with the process and start making all your decisions this way. However, as with the other forms of Huddling, brainstorming is more a problem-solving process than a decision-making process. It merely generates alternatives that can later be screened and evaluated by someone who wasn't part of the original huddle.

If you're dealing with a conventional decision where you already know all the options, brainstorming isn't a good idea because it wastes time. If twelve people meet for an hour in a brainstorming session, it consumes twelve person-hours of effort. What you get out of it is a list of ideas and no decisions at all. Two or three professionals can produce better solutions in less time. So remember to keep away from brainstorming as a substitute for systematic reasoning or as a way to arrive at an optimal solution to a complicated problem.

## When Huddling Creates More Problems Than It Solves

Now that I've shown you some advantages to Huddling, you might wonder why those business executives in the hotel coffee shop are so reluctant to do it. As great as it sounds, Huddling is not always the best way to make a decision.

First of all, Huddling is time-consuming. A typical CEO attends an average of eight meetings a day, and middle-level managers in a corporation may spend 80 percent of their time in some kind of huddle. No wonder people don't like meetings and are often contemptuous of them.

And don't assume that a huddle decision is always better than a solo one. Huddles usually perform better, but not always. The quality of decisions is usually raised or lowered by the average qualifications in the group. And it's very easy for peer-group pressure to turn into Huddle Rot. If enough members of the huddle are telling us something, we tend to believe it, even when we know it's not true.

Remember the famous Asch experiment? Researcher Solomon Asch designed a chart with four lines on it, a test line at the top and then three other lines underneath it. Line A was longer than the test line. Line B was the same length, and line C was much shorter. He asked the subjects to tell him which line was the same length as the test line.

Test Line _____
Line A     _____
Line B     _____
Line C     _____

Over 99 percent picked line B, of course. Then he arranged a new group of test subjects and coached the people at the front of the group to select line A. Although it was clearly longer, he found that if someone had three people nearby who all picked line A, then there was a 33 percent chance the fourth person would also pick line A. When he told the entire group they would be rewarded if they all got it right, an astounding 47 percent of the people picked the longer line, although it was obvious they must be wrong. The Asch experiment was a classic example of Huddle Rot.

High on the list of bad Huddles would have to be Coca-Cola's decision in 1985 to drop the regular Coca-Cola formula that had made billions in profits. Coca-Cola researchers had two hundred thousand people taste-test the new Coke formula over a three-year period. The company invested $400 million on the study. It was the most exhaustive and expensive research program in Coke's history. However, there were three glaring errors in the study that must have been apparent to any member of the executive committee. Yet nobody spoke up against management, which was behind the move.

What were the three errors? First, the Coke people didn't put any large quantities into customers' homes to see if customers still preferred it over an extended period of time. Second, they didn't do any test marketing. They didn't pick a city and try substituting New Coke for old Coke, which would be a standard market-research technique. And third, in blind taste tests, they didn't tell the participants that voting for New Coke would be a vote to kill the old Coke. The new product lasted only ninety days. The only way Coca-Cola's management averted a complete disaster was by boldly admitting the mistake quickly.

Another problem with Huddling is that members rally around the opinions of the leader—particularly when their leader is the boss. The classic example is the naming of the Edsel automobile, a word that subsequently became synonymous with "loser." An advertising agency spent a year coming up with eighteen thousand ideas, but the executive committee couldn't agree. Finally, in exasperation, board chairman E. R. Breech said, "Why don't we just call it Edsel, in honor of the founder's son?"

A combination of boredom, frustration, and the need to please the boss caused them all to applaud the decision. When an executive went to tell Edsel Ford's widow, she slammed the door in his face, horrified that they wanted to immortalize her husband with such an ugly car. Her three sons agreed. When researchers asked people what they thought of the name "Edsel," most people thought it sounded like pretzel or weasel. But the committee decision held.

Sometimes the whole purpose of Huddling is defeated if the board of directors tends to rubber-stamp decisions. Particularly when the chief executive officer selects and grooms the company's board members. Then it isn't hard for a savvy CEO to develop a board that will support almost anything. Al Neuharth, former CEO at Gannett Newspaper Company, raised this process to an art form. Karl Eller owned $362 million worth of Gannett stock, but when he tried to take control, he failed miserably. Al Neuharth had manipulated the board so well that Eller couldn't even get it to a vote. And when Neuharth wanted to launch *USA Today*, he had such control the final vote was 12 to 0.

Then there's the difficulty involved with removing a rebel member of the huddle. It can happen, but it can be costly. Take, for example, Ross Perot at General Motors. Perot, the founder of Electronic Data Systems, sold the company to General Motors for $2 billion. He then got a seat on the board of GM and was anxious to introduce his entrepreneurial ideas to GM and get the company out of the mess it was in. At the time, GM was dramatically losing its market share to the Japanese and to Ford. Unfortunately, Perot became an irritant to GM chairman Roger Smith. Finally, GM paid $700 million over the market value of the GM stock Perot owned to buy it back—just because he didn't fit in with the bureaucracy.

The dynamics of having a dissenter in a group have an influence on the fate of a rebel. If the huddle is right and the rebel is wrong, the rebel is merely an irritant who's tolerated. If the huddle is wrong and the rebel is right, the rebel either agrees with the huddle or gets kicked out. And either way, the company loses.

## The Major Problem with Huddles: Illusions of Unanimity

Huddles have a tendency to compromise. That's because huddlers develop illusions of unanimity. Remember the Bay of Pigs example? The huddle members were so cohesive they didn't bring up what they knew: The lack of ground support for the invaders would doom the plan. They didn't want to challenge the others for fear of being seen as disloyal. Some of the brightest brains in the world planned the Bay of Pigs invasion. George Bundy, Allen

Dulles, Robert Kennedy, Robert McNamara, Dean Rusk, and Arthur Schlesinger all contributed to a major blunder.

The group that made this bad decision had fallen victim to illusions of unanimity. This exerts two major pressures on the group: (1) Any lone voices that oppose majority decisions may feel they're being disloyal, and (2) when the team is too cohesive, they see themselves too much as one team, as the Kennedy team did, rather than individuals brought in for their expertise. Both of these pressures stop individual huddle members from speaking up. Fortunately, there are some warning signs that tell you when your team is becoming too cohesive, such as when the huddle doesn't want to consult with outside experts for fear of offending the experts within the huddle or when there is a strong feeling within the huddle that it should appear united. Or when it fails to challenge weak assertions of a member.

If these signs appear and you're worried about a huddle becoming too agreeable, then take some steps to break up the opinion gridlock. Better yet, if you take the following precautions, you can protect the huddle from cohesive thinking:

1. Don't let the leader of the huddle reveal his or her decision up front, because everyone is tempted to rally around it. Japanese huddlers have a rule that the lowest-ranking person must speak first, and so on up to the leader. They don't place anyone in the unacceptable position of having to disagree with his supervisor.

2. Try to avoid the huddle becoming a top secret matter because it makes the huddle coagulate. If Ford Motors hadn't been so intent on keeping the Edsel secret, it probably wouldn't have made the mistake in the first place. If Coca-Cola was less obsessed with keeping its "New Coke" decision a secret its executives would have avoided making such a decision.

3. Appoint a devil's advocate who will always present a challenging viewpoint. Don't let the same person play this role each time, or he'll become typecast and ignored.

4. Require each huddler to present two different viewpoints on the decision.

5. Encourage the huddle members to call each other after the meeting. Doubts will very often be expressed one-on-one that won't be raised in front of the entire huddle.

6. Have a PR person present to tell you how this would all play in Peoria. In other words, make sure the ideas are sensible enough to win the approval of the public.

7. If the huddle is reporting to a key decision maker, be sure they present all acceptable alternatives and not just the one they chose. Henry Kissinger was proud of his ability to present all options to President Nixon and avoid revealing his viewpoint unless he was asked.

8. Rotate new members into the huddle so it doesn't turn into a clique. Don't give new members too much power by introducing them as experts, or too little power because they're outsiders.

A. P. Sloan, former chairman of General Motors, was well aware of the danger of illusions of unanimity. When chairing a meeting, he once said, "Gentlemen, I take it we are all in complete agreement. So I propose that we postpone further discussion of this matter until our next meeting, to give ourselves time to develop disagreement and perhaps gain some un-

derstanding of what the decision is all about.'' Now that's smart
thinking!

## In Japan, Huddling Means Defining Problems.

Since the Japanese have such a different style of decision making,
I think it's important to examine how they make decisions. Not
only might it prepare you for working with their culture, should
you have the opportunity, but it just might spark a few ideas for
your own decision making.

Remember I told you about how much the Japanese love to
huddle? Well, when they huddle, everybody is expected to come
to the group without preconceived opinions. The purpose of each
person being there is to listen, not to give opinions. The lowest-
ranking person must speak first, and so on up to the leader. Each
person inputs any relevant information he may have, but there is
no debate. When enough information is on the table, the decision
becomes obvious. The Japanese operate in an environment that
doesn't question the idea that the more information you have, the
better the decision will be. Defining the problem is far more
important to the Japanese than searching for answers. There are
two things that they consider crucial to find out—whether there
is a need for a decision, and how to blueprint the problem accurately.

Once this is done, very often the answer is obvious to them.
They may be slower than Americans in making decisions, but
once they decide, they're fully committed to the decision because
they involved everyone. If you're used to dealing with Americans, this will come as a delightful surprise. In America, we sell
our product or service to an executive at a company, knowing
full well that somebody further up the corporate ladder may over-
rule them. In Japan, it may take longer to get a decision, but once

it's made, you know that it's been approved by everyone who needs to be involved. Defining the problem is far more important to the Japanese than searching for the right answer.

If you're doing business with the Japanese, you'll have already encountered this frustration: It isn't clear who is making the decision in Japanese companies. They encourage overlapping managerial jobs and collective authority. American companies want to be able to hold peoples' feet to the fire and prefer clear lines of authority and distinct areas of responsibility. This gives Americans the impression the Japanese have trouble making decisions, but that's really not so. Whereas American executives are eager to assert or gain power by making unilateral decisions, the Japanese are afraid to do this. They don't want to be held accountable. The Japanese executive sees his responsibility as being the catalyst of innovative ideas, unlike the American executive, who thinks he or she is obligated to come up with innovative ideas. So the Japanese executive puts a premium on ideas generated by others in the group, not himself. He constantly asks questions; he creates an atmosphere conducive to innovation by encouraging eccentricity; and he understands it takes fifty or sixty good ideas to generate one winner.

American companies operate decision making like a courtroom drama. Executives, like attorneys, present their arguments to the boss who acts like a judge. They present evidence as supporting data; a verdict is made, and sentence is passed down. American executives tend to approach this process with trepidation, with fear of punishment rather than hope of reward, and this often stifles innovation.

Americans who work for Japanese companies are very often at a disadvantage because Japanese firms don't see Americans as making a lifetime commitment to the company. So they tend to be left out of the decision-making loop. Shigem Okada, head of Japan's largest department store, Mitsukoshi, may have put his finger on the difference between American decision making and

Japanese decision making when he said, "Our success was due to our adoption of the West's pragmatic management combined with the spiritual aspects of the East."

## The Advantages and Disadvantages of Huddling

Huddling can be a valuable way to solve problems. It can add new information, perspective, and vision. If the huddle will be responsible for following through with the decision, it generates support. Group decision making usually reduces the chance of making glaring mistakes.

On the other hand Huddling is better at problem solving than it is at decision making. It's also very time-consuming, and huddle decisions tend to be less bold than autocratic decisions. If you learn to manage a huddle well, and avoid the pitfalls I've taught you, then Huddling can be a very valuable method of finding the right decision. If you are afraid of Huddle Rot, illusions of unanimity, or a huddle dissenter, consider making the decision on your own. Ultimately, the real art in decision making comes when you know how to balance the advice of others with the knowledge that you already possess.

# CHAPTER TEN

# Barriers to Confident Decisions

## Avoiding the Potholes on the Decision-Making Path

Now that I've shown you how to improve your decision-making ability, I've got some bad news for you. There are several barriers that can stop you from becoming a Confident Decision Maker.

**DON'T . . .**

- Act too quickly

- Act too slowly

- Misjudge the urgency factor

- Be unwilling to admit your mistakes

- Be too autocratic

Before you memorize these five rules of warning, let's examine each one individually.

## DON'T ACT TOO QUICKLY: OR THE CASE OF THE SURPLUS SKIS

The first barrier, acting too quickly, probably causes more bad decisions than anything else. Generally, this occurs because you are forced to make a decision under time pressure. To see how this can create horrendous problems, let's examine a hypothetical business situation and see what can go wrong when time pressure is added to the decision-making process.

You're the president of a 140-store chain of sporting-good stores, most of them west of the Mississippi and in the Northeast. Although it's a competitive business, it's going well. You're in the middle of a large expansion program, business is good, and you're feeling great. Suddenly, your luck turns sour. Your VP of finance comes to you and says, "We've got a real cash-flow problem. It's February the fifteenth, and we've just had the worst ski season of the last twenty-five years. Hardly any resort in the country opened up before Christmas, and with so little snow, it's been a disaster all across the nation. We've got a ten-million-dollar excess inventory in ski equipment. We can't make the interest payment on the fifty-million-dollar expansion loan that's due tomorrow, and the bank won't extend it. What are you going to do?"

If the last words a pilot always says before his plane crashes are "Oh, no!" then the last words a company president speaks before his company crashes must be, "Why wasn't I told?"

This started out as a little problem that just kept on growing, until it became a monstrous problem. Your ski buyer, who is one of the best in the industry, cleverly inserted a weasel clause into all his contracts, so he could cancel or renegotiate in the event of poor snow. Because of the bad snow conditions, he had planned to take advantage of it. However, the night before he was going to cancel the orders, he got arrested for drunk driving and called in with the flu. Preoccupied with his problems, he missed the deadline to cancel. Because he was covering up his arrest, he didn't tell anybody. He lit candles in every church he passed, though he wasn't Catholic, and wore his knees out praying for late snow to bail him out. It never came. Now it's so late in the season that a clearance sale wouldn't generate enough cash to pay for the advertising.

You tell the CFO, "I need time to think about it."

He says, "You don't have time! You've got to do something now! If we don't make the three-million-dollar loan payment tomorrow, the bank will call the loan into default. The financial papers will pick it up on the first-quarter projections, and our stock is going to drop in half. Let me remind you, that would mean a personal loss in net worth to you of over fifteen million dollars."

That's the kind of real-world situation they don't prepare you for in business school. Namely, the major decision that has to be made under time pressure, when you've pushed all the chips into the middle of the table. Under this kind of time pressure, any reaction to this situation may have dismal consequences.

Now with the added burden of time pressure, trying to make a good decision is like trying to stay dry in a swamp.

*Under time pressure, you attempt to speed decisions by getting less input.*

You rush to accounts receivable to see what cash you can bring in fast. However, you're in such a hurry, you don't check the accounts payable.

There, you'd find the company hadn't yet paid for $3 million worth of the ski equipment. They cut the check and charged it against the books, but didn't mail it yet.

That information might be all you need to solve the problem. But you're under too much pressure to realize it.

*Under time pressure, you analyze information less thoroughly.*

You might assume the ski inventory is scattered around the country, in your stores. That's where it's supposed to be, on February 15. Given more time, you'd have found most of it sitting in a warehouse in Oakland.

That information would expand your options. You could ship it to New Zealand in time for their ski season, or have a clearance sale at the warehouse. In one location, the advertising costs would be much less.

*Under time pressure, you overlook important information.*

You may forget the drawing for a ski trip to Argentina that your company held last spring. That gave you a data base of five thousand Bay-area ski customers. Within forty-eight hours, you could mail out a sale notice to them.

*Under time pressure, you tend to slim down the list of possible alternatives.*

One option may be renegotiating the lease payments of the stores to improve cash flow. If the bank saw you were doing that, it might renegotiate the loan. However, under time pressure, you dismiss it. "We've got one hundred forty different landlords," you say. "We don't have time to go to them all."

*Under time pressure, you tend to consult with fewer experts.*

You may know that Charlie over at Universal Sports had this happen to him once. If you could get him on the phone, he may be a big help to you. However, Charlie is scuba diving in Belize and can't be reached. So you dismiss that possibility. If you had more time, you'd track Charlie down, or find somebody else at his company who knew how the problem was resolved.

*Under time pressure, you tend to get fewer people involved in the decision-making process.*

We don't have time for an executive committee meeting, you're thinking. I've got to earn my pay and make a bold decision now. With more time, you might get some very valuable insights by getting the regional managers involved in a conference call.

*Under time pressure, you tend to jump at the first decision that looks right.*

Now it's 11:00 P.M., and everybody's beat. Your office is a sea of computer printouts and dirty ashtrays. Your executive vice-president is saying, "I hate to do this, but it looks as though we're going to have to close a bunch of stores. Here's what we should do. Call a press conference in the morning and announce that we're closing the forty least productive stores. With that, the bank will renegotiate the loan. The stock analysts will love it, and our stock probably will go up ten dollars a share overnight."

You say, "But that would be a debacle, half our top store managers would jump ship in the panic. You know they've been approached by headhunters as it is. Besides, we'd ruin the relationships we worked so hard to build with our suppliers!"

"Would you rather file a Chapter Eleven? That would hold off the creditors and give us some breathing room."

"I'll never do that," you sigh. "Let's call the press conference. Which stores are we going to close?"

Because you made the decision under time pressure, it was a bad decision. If you'd have spent more time, you'd have done better. You'd have learned about the negotiating leverage that existed because you hadn't yet paid the ski suppliers. You could have gone to the supplier and negotiated a deal where he'd cancel the $3 million invoice, rebilling you on September 1. Then you could arrange a massive preseason ski sale at the San Francisco

Convention Center, for Labor Day weekend. You would move the merchandise into a separate corporation that you set up, which gives you collateral against which to borrow and frees up the pressure on your existing inventory.

And since this is a fantasy, we may as well make it a good one! The Labor Day sale is such a huge success, the following year you hold preseason clearance sales in convention centers across the nation. You promote the event on cable TV, with the show hosted by the nation's top ski racers. It becomes the most successful event in sporting-goods history.

That's the way it should have gone, but instead it all went down the tubes because you made the decision under time pressure. So don't be overzealous. Have the patience to understand that making the right decision may take time. Examine the possibility of going with a temporary solution, rather than committing to a long-term answer.

What would give you breathing room?

If you are forced to make a rash decision, be sure that when the pressure's off, you take another look at the problem. See if there aren't additional solutions.

My golfing buddy Phil Branson, who's the brilliant founder and CEO of First American Home Warranty Company, tells me this: "When you're forced to make a decision under time pressure, you're usually better off to defer the decision until you feel comfortable making it—despite how much pressure you're under. It isn't always the right thing to do, but it's the right thing to do enough of the time to make it a good rule."

## BEWARE OF AN EMOTIONAL BIAS WHEN MAKING DECISIONS.

Another catalyst that might cause you to make decisions too quickly is your emotional state. If you're angry, depressed, or not feeling well, you're liable to make a decision that could cause you significant damage. An example of this is the time I drove down to my office boiling over with anger at a secretary. I couldn't believe she made a mistake for the tenth time, and I felt like storming in there and reading her the riot act until she quit. Then I remembered I wasn't feeling well that day. Perhaps I was coming down with something, or maybe I was tired because I'd just come off a long speaking tour. I backed off and said to myself, "I'll take another look at this tomorrow, and see if I still feel the same way." I've never regretted being cautious when dealing with people.

The same rule applies when you're overly enthusiastic about something. Feeling too good can be as great a detriment as feeling lousy. At my company, we have a standard line when we've made a bad decision. We say, "Wow, you must have been feeling good when you made that decision." Enthusiasm can blind you— if it feels too good to be true, it probably is. The time for enthusiasm is after you've made the decision, not before. Once you've made the decision, then your enthusiasm can sometimes make even a weak decision work. But being enthusiastic before you make a decision is inviting disaster.

## DELAYING A DECISION IS EQUALLY DETRIMENTAL: DON'T ACT TOO SLOWLY.

The second barrier to good decisions, acting too slowly, can be just as much of a problem as moving too quickly. There are six reasons why we sometimes delay a decision past the critical point.

1. Defensive Avoidance

I believe psychologists when they say that everyone has a built-in defensive avoidance of problems. In layman's lan-

guage, that means we avoid problems and move toward opportunities. In decision making, this psychological desire to move
away from problems causes certain attitudes that slow the
decision-making process:

- *It can't happen to me.* The reasoning behind the first attitude is that while ten restaurants have gone out of business
  at this location, they weren't doing what I'm going to do.
  I'm not going to let the same thing happen to me.

- *I can take care of it later.* Rather than recognizing we have
  a problem that needs a decision, we tend to think, I have
  lots of other things to do, and this can wait. It doesn't
  occur to us that we're procrastinating because the other
  things are much more fun.

- *Let somebody else worry about it.* If you're the president
  of your company, that's a disastrous attitude to take and
  one you must resist. When you're running the company,
  the responsibility lies with you. Unless you're actively
  making things happen, the inertia that's built into any
  organization will take over.

2. A "Don't Fix It Unless It's Broke" Attitude
    The second reason for acting too slowly is being satisfied
with what you've got. This attitude can sink you. In today's
fast-moving business environment, you must anticipate that
it's going to break, which translates into the attitude that it
isn't always going to be a best-seller, so improve it before its
sales peak.
    Gillette was riding high in 1990. It was the market leader
in both disposable and cartridge razors by a 3-to-1 margin.

Even so, the Gillette Company spent $200 million to develop the Sensor razor and an additional $175 million to advertise it. That's well over all the company's profits from the previous year. Gillette had every justification for saying, "Let's not fix it, because it isn't broken." But they know you can't get away with that attitude for very long in today's business environment. Never become satisfied with what you've got.

3. Obsession with Huddling

The third reason for acting too slowly on a decision is an obsessive desire to involve other people. Huddling can be a very valuable aid to good decision making, but don't let it delay the decision too much. If a decision must be made, set a deadline for making it. Get as many people involved as you can, but again, not if it will hold back the decision too much. Unless something significant comes up to make you change the deadline, go for it. If you still can't get a consensus, and the deadline is near, let the manager closest to the problem make the decision.

4. Gathering Too Much Information

Too much information is a real threat in today's world. We have access to so much information, we easily become confused. It acts as a mental noise that blocks intuitive thinking. Secretary of Defense Donald Rumsfeld once said, "[Trying to find out what's going on at the Pentagon] is like trying to drink out of a fire hose, there's such a flood of information."

On a ski trip to Lake Tahoe, I met a man whose company specialized in creating paperless environments. He'd go into a company and set up its computer systems to eliminate every scrap of paper. That's a tough concept for most companies to accept! With his system, if you wanted to ask somebody to lunch, instead of writing a note, you'd leave a message on his or her computer mail. The highlight of this man's career came when the Pentagon hired him to do a study to see whether he could do the same thing with its operation. It would have meant millions to him in consulting fees. After thirty days, he walked out of there, shaking his head. "That place is so confused," he told me, "no one will ever straighten it out."

5. Attempting to Predict the Future

The fifth reason for slow decision making is time wasted in attempts to predict the future. Even economists can't predict the future. If you laid all the economists in the world end to end, you still couldn't get a consensus!

At a banquet in New Orleans, I sat next to a man known as an expert in economics. He subsequently became chairman of the Federal Reserve Board. It was a wonderful opportunity to ask him why I'd lost $2 million in the early years of the Reagan administration. When Reagan was running for president, his program was to dramatically increase military spending and also give huge tax cuts. A surefire formula for massive inflation, according to all the experts. I was so convinced that Reagan's policies would create hyperinflation, I bought every piece of real estate into which I could possibly leverage myself. Instead of going into a period of great inflation, we went into a brief but very deep recession, and I lost it all. I didn't have to file bankruptcy and I didn't lose my home, but I lost my entire portfolio of investment real estate.

So I asked this expert, "What happened? We had a president with a surefire formula for generating hyperinflation. You were even warning us about it, but it didn't happen. What happened to all your predictions?"

Well, he launched into a long, convoluted explanation. As best I could figure out, he was saying they'd overlooked one fact—that while all this was going on, American business was finally facing up to the severity of competition from abroad. American companies simply started doing a better job of being more competitive, and this stopped us from going into an inflationary spiral. He was about ten minutes into this explanation when it suddenly dawned on me. This man, who probably knew as much about economics as anybody in the nation—if not the world—was full of it!

Economists fail in their predictions because they won't accept that people are well-informed, rational creatures who'll always do what's in their best interest. Every other business runs on that assumption, but economists refuse to factor it in. My conclusion about all this? Futurism is fascinating but rarely accurate.

How relevant are predictions to your business anyway? *Ninety percent of your future is determined not by what happens to you, but by how you react to what happens to you.* It's far better to monitor what's going on and react to it than waste time trying to predict what might happen.

6. Fear of Failure

The sixth reason for making decisions too slowly is an obvious one, fear of failure. Keep reminding yourself that you can't win if you're afraid of losing. The best way I know to avoid the fear of losing is to figure out the worst-case scenario. What's the worst thing that could happen if you make a wrong decision? It's probably not as bad as you fear. Remember, the only person qualified to tell you that something won't work is a person who has tried it and found it didn't work. There are a million people out there running around telling you that things won't work, but when you check their expertise, they don't have much. They're telling you it won't work, and yet they've never attempted it themselves. So, my rule is:

Nobody's entitled to tell me I can't do something unless he or she has done it and failed.

**Now for a Recap . . .**
The six reasons why we might make a decision too slowly are:

1. Defensive avoidance. We have built in a psychological mechanism that encourages us to avoid problems.

2. A "Don't fix it unless it's broke" attitude. Anticipating that what you're doing now won't always be the best thing to do keeps you one step ahead of the competition.

3. Obsession with Huddling. Participative involvement is great, but not if it delays the decision too much. Set a deadline, and when it comes, go with the best available solution.

4. Gathering too much information. Don't let it bury you.

5. Wasting time trying to predict the future.

6. Fear of failure.


## DON'T MISJUDGE THE URGENCY FACTOR.

How quickly should you make a decision? Sometimes the urgent need to make a decision overrides all the rules about how to make the decision. When that happens, you have to go with the best input you've got, from the best minds available at that time. But understanding the urgency factor, rather than taking the time to make a more perfect decision, is a fine art. There are certain urgency factors that tell you how quickly you have to move.

**URGENCY FACTOR #1: WHAT'S THE COMPETITION DOING?** In business, knowing what the competition is doing is essential if you're to know how fast to move. If you have an exclusive patent on a new genetically engineered drug, you may have months or years in which to make a decision. You can take the time to get everything just right before you move. In the computer business, you may have only hours to make a move. The Syntel company was the first one to make a 256K computer chip. Syntel managed it when everyone else sold 16K chips and thought the next upgrade would be 64K chips. Syntel got to market with its chip only sixteen weeks ahead of its competition, but what a sixteen weeks it was! In that short period, Syntel made a profit of over $130 million.

Knowing the competition is the key, but how do you get information on the competition? First, don't be afraid to call. Unless it violates fair-trade rules, just pick up the phone and ask. Now your question may not be answered, but a good reporter knows there are many more reasons to ask a question other than the hope the person might give you an answer. Consider when Sam Donaldson was interviewing General Norman Schwarzkopf during the Persian Gulf War. He asked, "Well, General, when are you going to start the ground war?"

Did he really think the general was going to say, "Sam, I promised the president I wouldn't tell the other five hundred reporters here, but since you asked, I'll tell you. Monday morning at four o'clock."

Of course not. He knew perfectly well he wasn't going to get an answer. Still, you can learn a lot by studying the way people respond. Sam Donaldson wanted to know how the general would refuse to answer the question and how he would react to being asked. So ask, and you still gather information, even if you don't get an answer.

I was once the dinner speaker at the annual meeting of a large packaging company. At dinner I was sitting between the president of the packaging company and the vice-president of its biggest customer, a Fortune 100 company. I said to the president of the packaging company on my left, "How much of these people's business do you get?"

He told me, "We don't know—they wouldn't tell us that. We just know they don't like to give all their packaging business to one company."

A few minutes later, I turned to the vice-president, who was the packager's biggest customer, and said, "How much of your packaging business do these people get?"

To my astonishment, he told me, "Twenty-seven-point-eight percent."

I said, "I suppose you like to spread your business around?"

He said, "Well, that used to be our policy, but we recently changed that. Now if we find a supplier that's willing to get into bed with us, we're prepared to give them all our business."

Here was valuable information the man on my left would've loved to have and could have had. But he didn't ask, because he didn't think his question would be answered. The moral of the story? Ask the question even if you don't think it'll be answered.

When you talk to a competitor, if you want to get, you've got to give. Be ready to horse-trade information. Sometimes it's best to volunteer the information first, which obligates the other side to reciprocate.

"But that doesn't make sense," you say. "I don't want to give my competition any information." Well, I can see where that may be so. Just be smart about the way you do it. Don't call or go to see the competition yourself. Send somebody who doesn't know your secrets. Then, when your representative is asked for information you don't want to give away, he or she can honestly say, "I'm sorry, I just don't know. I'd tell you if I did, but I don't." In that way, you only have to trade the information you want to trade.

**URGENCY FACTOR #2: THE LIFE CYCLE OF THE DE-CISION.** Sometimes, if you wait too long, it's too late—however good the decision. The classic example of this is the Edsel automobile. In 1954, there really was an opening in the marketplace for a high-quality but medium-priced car. But the people at Ford got so excited about it, they wanted to make it perfect, and the delay was fatal. When they finally got the Edsel to showrooms in 1958, the market had changed. Consumers were moving away from the big, heavy automobile toward more compact automobiles. *Time* magazine described it as the "classic case of the wrong car for the wrong market, at the wrong time." The only good news Ford's PR people could come up with was that in the first year, only one Edsel was reported stolen!

So, if your decision has a short life cycle, you need to make a decision faster. What business people all over the country are telling me is that in today's speeded-up economy, decisions need to be made faster, because their life cycle is so much shorter.

**URGENCY FACTOR #3: HOW REVERSIBLE IS THE DE-CISION?** Which means, if you goof, how easily can you get out of trouble? Perhaps your banker has called you and said, "I can't believe the real estate opportunity we have for you. We've just foreclosed on an office building that would be an ideal headquarters for your company. If you can make a decision by noon tomorrow, you can get it for fifty percent of the true market value, and we'll finance it one hundred percent."

If you're a Confident Decision Maker, the question isn't, "Would this make a good main office for us?" That might take you weeks to decide. Rather, the question is, "If I go ahead, how reversible is the decision?" If you truly can buy it for 50 percent of the market value, and the bank will finance it 100 percent, you can't lose. Even if you never move into the building, you can sell it and probably make a very good profit. To me, that's a decision that shouldn't take more than five minutes to make, even if it's a multimillion-dollar investment. Provided, of course, you know enough about the current real estate market. And your corporate-mission statement supports such a move.

## URGENCY FACTOR #4: HOW BIG IS THE DOWNSIDE?

What's the loss potential if you make the wrong decision? We all fall into this trap. We agonize over which video to rent. We should be saying, ''Why am I spending time on this? The downside is only three dollars. I'll get this one, too. If I decide not to watch it, I've lost three dollars. That's tipping money, so it's no big deal.''

I remember very clearly standing in the streets of Pamplona, Spain, with my son, who wanted to run with the bulls. His motto is, ''It's better to be gored than bored.'' I wanted to run with the bulls, too—mainly because it would make a terrific story for my talks! But if I got tossed by a bull, my speaker friends would never let me get over it. When a speaker gets tossed by a bull, it's like a man biting a dog—it's headline news!

So, when I evaluated the upside versus the downside, the risk didn't make sense. The upside was very small, and the downside huge. I wouldn't have to be tossed by a bull for it to be a disaster, either. After we left Spain, we were going to the Alps to climb Mont Blanc and the Matterhorn. Just a twisted ankle would bring that plan to a screeching halt. My son was twenty-one. If worse came to worst, he has a couple of decades left to climb those mountains. I was fifty, so I didn't have many years left when I could throw myself at the Matterhorn and have a chance of getting to the top. That's what we call a small upside and a huge downside!

## DON'T BE UNWILLING TO ADMIT YOUR MISTAKES.

Some of the smartest businesspeople I know have fallen into the trap of being unwilling to pull the plug on a decision to which they're committed. For fourteen years, Lockheed kept pouring money into its failing L-1011 Tristar Jumbo Jet project. In 1983, after losing $2.5 billion, Lockheed finally pulled the plug.

Over at Federal Express, Fred Smith was a lot smarter. He decided the next stage in communications, after overnight packaging, was an electronic-mail delivery service. He launched it under the name ZapMail. It ran into many early technical difficulties. He finally got it right just when we all had to have a new toy in our offices called a fax machine. We could do what Fred Smith wanted us to without having to call Fred Smith. Although he had been glorified for his incredible success in creating Federal Express, he didn't have a moment's hesitation in zapping ZapMail.

One of the reasons we hesitate to admit our mistakes is the feeling that pulling the plug will be harmful to the image of the company. As a nation, we crucified ourselves in Vietnam because we thought to pull out would send the wrong signal to the Soviets. In fact, by staying in as long as we did, we played right into Soviet hands.

The other reason we're reluctant to admit mistakes is that we decide up front that some things are unthinkable. It was unthinkable that we'd pull out of Vietnam, and 47,355 of our troops died in combat. The Soviets didn't feel it was at all unthinkable to pull out of Afghanistan. A smart businessperson doesn't feel that filing Chapter 11 bankruptcy is unthinkable, if it's the only way he or she can save the company.

The all-time classic example of failing to admit your mistakes was Saddam Hussein's unwillingness to admit that invading Kuwait wasn't his smartest move. His stubborn refusal to back down almost cost him everything.

A smart decision maker learns to deal with what's happening right now. Being upset and angry with people who have let you down doesn't solve problems. Accepting the realism of the moment and moving forward from there is what solves problems. Let's say you're climbing a mountain and the rope breaks. You find yourself stranded on a narrow ledge with a broken ankle. It's okay to curse the manufacturer of the rope—but only for a while. After a few minutes, it becomes counterproductive behavior. The sooner you get past that and start dealing with the existing situation, the better off you'll be.

Don't get too personally committed to your plan. You can ride that plan into oblivion if you're not careful. Sure, you've made a good decision, and you want to get behind it all the way. Yet to be 100 percent committed to making it work is deadly. In other words, you may be riding the horse in the right direction, but if it drops dead, get off as quickly as you possibly can.

In the same vein, if someone in your organization initiated a project, don't let that person have the final say on pulling the plug. He or she may be too emotionally involved with the decision to be objective. If the initiator is reluctant to pull the plug, move the decision to someone who isn't emotionally involved. Remember how Roger Smith became emotionally committed to absorbing Ross Perot and EDS? So committed that it cost General Motors $2 billion to buy the company, and another $700 million to get Perot off the board.

Overcommitting to the solution contributed to the *Challenger* shuttle disaster. There were three strong pressures at work there—wide publicity for the "Teacher in Space" program; pressure to generate additional funding for the shuttle program; and a strong desire to avoid the extra expense of more engineering work on the solid rocket boosters. With all this, the decision makers overrode the advice they were getting from experts to pull the plug on that particular launch.

Sure it's wonderful to say to yourself, "I'm going to make

this decision work even if it kills me.'' Just don't *let* it kill you. Be realistic enough to realize that you've made a mistake. Correct the decision and get back on track as quickly as you can.


## DON'T BE TOO AUTOCRATIC.

The moment you set up an environment in your organization where people don't feel comfortable challenging you, you've created an enormous barrier to decision making. Don't be the kind of person who thinks "team effort" is getting everybody doing what you want them to do. Unless we let people challenge our beliefs, they become more deeply ingrained. Take Jimmy Hoffa, for example, who said, "I may have my faults, but being wrong ain't one of them."

Some pretty smart people have made some pretty dumb pronouncements because people quit challenging them. For example, in 1899 the director of the U.S. Patent Office said, "Everything that can be invented has been invented."

Frank Whittle's engineering professor at Cambridge University said, "Very interesting, Whittle, but it will never work," when Whittle showed him his plan for the jet engine.

Newton Baker, United States secretary of war, said, "That idea is so damned nonsensical and impossible that I'm willing to stand on the bridge of a battleship while that nitwit Billy Mitchell tries to hit it from the air." He was responding to General Mitchell's suggestion that battleships could be sunk by planes dropping bombs on them.

The Consumer Product Safety Commission of Washington once printed eighty-thousand buttons with the words FOR KIDS' SAKE, THINK TOY SAFETY. They all had to be withdrawn because of dangerously sharp edges, parts that could be swallowed by children, and paint with a poisonous lead content.

What about this quotation? ''The Olympic Games could no

more have a deficit than a man could have a baby.'' That was Mayor Jean Drapeau of Montreal three weeks before the 1976 Olympics ran up a deficit of $1 billion.

Lord Kelvin, president of the Royal Society of London, made a career of such pronouncements. Included were, ''Radio has no future.'' ''X rays will prove to be a hoax.'' And ''Heavier-than-air flying machines are impossible.''

So be sure you've established a climate in your organization where people feel comfortable challenging you, because misguided beliefs can be embarrassing and detrimental.

You also appear autocratic if you limit the number of people with whom you confer because you fear leaks. Fix the leaks, don't change the system of decision making. That was President Kennedy's conclusion, after the disastrous Bay of Pigs invasion. Yet it seems every president since then has forgotten that lesson. Nixon lost his presidency partly because of his paranoia of people leaking information outside the government. There was even talk of impeaching President Bush because he didn't consult with Congress before sending an additional two hundred thousand troops to Saudi Arabia before the Persian Gulf War.

Every businessman knows the seed of failure is sowed during times of great success. If you're on a roll, be very careful that you don't become a victim of the omnipotence syndrome. I personally know two businesspeople who lost millions when this happened to them. Although they don't even know each other, their stories are remarkably similar. They were both doing so well in their businesses that they got involved in developing real estate outside their geographic territory. In both instances, people in their companies were telling them they were making a mistake. However, they were psychologically on such a roll that their attitude was, ''I can't lose, I can't do a thing wrong.'' They both lost millions of dollars because they were operating too far from their core business. Watch out for that.

Golfers lose tournaments because of the omnipotence syndrome. Arnold Palmer was once seven shots ahead with nine holes to play in the U.S. Open at the Olympic Club in San Francisco. He could have played it safe and easily won the tournament. But he was playing so well, the omnipotence syndrome overcame him. He decided to go for a U.S. Open record score, and attempted some shots that even he couldn't make. Billy Casper caught up to him and won the tournament in a play-off.

## How to Turn Barriers into Building Blocks

Now that I've warned you about all the problems you might encounter on the way to making a confident decision, I'd like to build your confidence back up. Remember the five don'ts? To remind you, here's that list again.

**Don't . . .**

- Act too quickly

- Act too slowly

- Misjudge the urgency factor

- Be unwilling to admit your mistakes

- Be too autocratic

Notice that each barrier is a mirror image of what makes you a Confident Decision Maker.

Confident Decision Makers can act quickly and decisively, but they don't let people force them into making decisions under time pressure.

Confident Decision Makers understand the need to gather

information and work through the decision making process. But if speed is essential, they're willing to move with less than all the facts they'd like to have.

Confident Decision Makers commit to their decisions, and yet they're always willing to pull the plug if it turns out they made a mistake.

Confident Decision Makers are bold and courageous in their decisions, but know they must not be too autocratic.

Because every barrier to good decision making mirrors the characteristics of a Confident Decision Maker, balancing these elements is an art that comes with experience.

# CHAPTER ELEVEN

# Styles of
# Decision Making

## The Importance of Decision-Making Styles

Everyone has a different approach to decision making. If you've ever chaired, or been part of, a decision-making committee, you know how fascinating it is to observe people's different decision-making styles. As you listen to the people around the table, it's hard to believe they're all talking about the same thing, because they're all taking such different approaches to the decision.

Once you become aware of the different styles of decision making, you'll not only be able to assess your own style, but you'll also be able to analyze instantly the decision-making styles of other people. You'll know when and how they're going to decide. If you're a salesperson, that's invaluable information! If you're a manager, you'll know what it takes to persuade your employees. If you're an employee, you'll know exactly how and when your boss is going to decide on your raise in pay or your promotion.

To help you learn how to recognize these four styles, let's look at the following hypothetical business situation.

You're the chairman and CEO of Gudenhot Saunas. Your father immigrated from Sweden and founded the company in Minneapolis in 1912. He built the first few saunas himself and gradually expanded, bringing in skilled craftsmen from the old country. By the time he retired in 1951, he had built Gudenhot into the largest sauna manufacturer in the country. Athletic clubs, resort hotels, and fine private homes all over North America were proud to own a Gudenhot sauna.

At first, corporate salespeople did all the selling. Then, after you took over for your father in the 1950s, you began to build a network of independent dealers. This dramatically expanded your business and enabled you to reduce head-office overhead. Throughout the seventies, your business continued to grow and expand. Every year was better than the year before in both sales and earnings. You built a reputation for high quality, but your saunas were the highest-priced in the country.

The years 1981 and 1982 were banner years for you. The fitness craze took over, and business was so good you were running two shifts at your manufacturing plants. Then, in 1983, trouble started to loom. Tip-Top Saunas, a subsidiary of a huge conglomerate, got into the business and started undercutting your prices by 40 percent and sometimes 50 percent. The quality of its saunas wasn't as good as yours, but it was hard for the consumer to see the difference. By 1985, your son Karl, who was vice-president in charge of manufacturing, was putting pressure on you. He wanted to be president, because he felt he could turn the company around with aggressive marketing techniques.

So even though you were only sixty, you relinquished the presidency and became chairman and CEO. You didn't approve of everything your son Karl did, but you let him have control. He introduced two lines of lower-priced models and a sauna kit you sold in discount hardware stores nationwide. Then he hired an aggressive corporate-marketing team that worked trade shows and county fairgrounds to generate leads.

Now, three years later, the company has had its best year ever, although profit margins were slimmer than in the good old days. Your plants are working at maximum capacity again, although the cost of the overtime is eating into your profits. Clearly, this aggressive marketing has given Tip-Top Saunas trouble. Forced to reduce its prices more and more to match your new lines, it's started losing substantial amounts of money, and last month it almost threw in the towel.

When a vice-president of the conglomerate that owns Tip-Top calls and asks you to fly to New York to discuss a buyout, you're curious. In a suite at the Plaza Hotel, he makes you a terrific offer. You could have Tip-Top Saunas, your major competitor, for one dollar. All you have to do is assume $2.5 million in long-term debt, and it's yours. To further sweeten the deal, the vice-president has already arranged financing with his bankers. All they'd need would be your corporate guarantee. It appears to be an irresistible offer. For $2.5 million, which is only 5 percent of your corporate profits from the previous year, you can buy out your major competitor. Tip-Top has a manufacturing plant in Atlanta that will dovetail perfectly with your operation. You also get a well-known brand name and a network of dealers around the country.

Tempted to shake hands right there in the Plaza Hotel, you remind yourself you are no longer the president of the company. You ought to go back and let the executive committee make the decision.

A few days later, you're staring down the long table at your executive committee. Your son Karl, the president, is there, along with Harry King, the sales manager, Jeannie Hampshire, the human-affairs vice-president, and Andrea Mills, the controller. They've been analyzing the data on this decision for several days, and it's finally time to bring it to a vote.

As you listen to each one speak, you can't believe what you're hearing. Your son Karl wants to renegotiate the deal. He wants to go back to Tip-Top's creditors and get a 20 percent reduction in the debt. If the Tip-Top people don't go along with it, he'll threaten to force the company into bankruptcy. He also

plans to go on a whirlwind tour of Tip-Top's facilities and renegotiate the leases on all their company manufacturing facilities and
sales offices. In Seattle, Dallas, and Orlando, where Gudenhot
already has branch offices, he wants to get the leases completely
canceled. He also wants to fire 80 percent of Tip-Top's personnel
at those locations, before completing the acquisition. But you've
assured the sellers that Tip-Top's company executives would all
be merged into your management staff. Nobody would lose his
or her job. Karl doesn't agree with that and wants resignation
letters from them before making the deal.

Harry King, your sales manager, is excited about the opportunity and can't wait to move on it. He's saying, "Let's do it,
and we'll straighten out any problems it creates afterward. I've
been at conventions with the salespeople from Tip-Top Saunas.
They're great people. With both of our companies working as a
team, we can double our sales."

Jeannie Hampshire, the human-affairs vice-president,
doesn't want to touch the deal. She's saying, "We've spent over
thirty years building up a loyal network of distributors. They've
been aggressively battling this competitor, and now we're inviting
Tip-Top into our family with open arms. I don't think it's fair to
our people."

Andrea Miller, your controller, is very suspicious of the
whole thing. She doesn't understand why it all has to be done
so fast. The conglomerate must be covering up some serious
deficiencies for it to move that quickly and decisively. She favors
hiring a Big Six accounting company to do a thorough study of
Tip-Top before moving ahead. You tell her the opportunity won't
wait. She says, "Well, perhaps it's better to miss this one than
to take a chance of moving before we have all the information
we need."

What's going on here? Why is it that you can't get the others
to go along with your recommendations? The reason is that you're
dealing with four very distinctive styles of decision making. Each

person is coming up with a different conclusion. This happens because either they have a different method of inputting the information you've given them, or they have a different way of processing that information into a decision.

Those two dimensions create four distinct decision-making styles that I call:

- The Bull

- The Eagle

- The Bee

- The Bloodhound

Bulls relentlessly attack a problem until it gives in. Eagles take great soaring passes at a problem. Bees buzz around looking for a consensus. Bloodhounds nose around for a solution until they come up with it.

These titles seem whimsical, but there's a lot of sound scientific thought that has gone into this analysis. Your son Karl is the Bull. Harry King, your sales manager, is the Eagle. Jeannie Hampshire, your human-affairs manager, is the Bee. And Andrea Miller, your controller, is the Bloodhound.

As a decision maker, you fall into one of these four styles also. As I go over each of the four decision-making styles, pick the one that describes you the most.

Let's start by putting those four styles on a chart. Starting in the top left corner and going around clockwise: The Bull is in the top left, the Eagle is in the top right, the Bee is in the bottom right, and the Bloodhound is in the bottom left. The chart compares how we gathered information about the decision (the

**Decision Process**

|  | | Conscious | Unconscious |
|---|---|---|---|
| Knowing | Process | The Bull | The Eagle |
| Observing | Input | The Bloodhound | The Bee |

input process) to what we're doing about making the decision (the decision process).

Let's look first at the top-to-bottom aspect. The vertical line of the chart is the type of input you use to make decisions. You react either to what you know or what you observe. In colloquial terms, I might call that inflexibility at the top and flexibility at the bottom.

So the Bull and the Eagle, at the top of the chart, have pretty much made up their minds before they go into the decision-making arena. Karl and Harry had a fairly good idea how they were going to react to the Tip-Top Sauna buyout before they heard all the details.

On the bottom of the chart, the Bloodhound and the Bee are much more open to new input. Jeannie and Andrea wanted to get all the facts before they decided.

So, the vertical line is labeled "Input Process," with "knowing" on the top and "observing" on the bottom. "Knowing" means arriving at what we know based on what we already believe to be true. "Observing" means the flexibility to change our mind based on what we learn, not preconceived notions.

Now let's examine the left-to-right aspect. The horizontal

line is the way people process the decision. You process information based on either conscious or unconscious thought. So the horizontal line is labeled "Decision Process," with "conscious" thought on the left, and "unconscious" thought on the right. Conscious thought is gathered by the five senses. Primarily in decision making, that's what we see and hear. The other three senses—taste, touch, and smell—are less important. Karl and Andrea, the controller, made their decisions based on the facts they got about Tip-Top Sauna. Unconscious thought, on the right, is awareness of things without being conscious of them. Harry just knows he can take care of any problems that come up. Ask him what problems he's considered, and how he would handle them, and he probably couldn't tell you. Jeannie knows in her heart the right way to treat people who work at her company. Ask her why she feels the way she does, and she won't be able to say. She just does.

Now that we have the four styles placed on the chart, let's take another look at them.


## HOW THE BULL MAKES DECISIONS

The Bull in the top left-hand corner, that's Karl, perceives the problem with conscious thought, rather than instinctively understanding it. He'll make a decision based on what he observes rather than preestablished emotions. He's for the buyout because it's a chance to kill a competitor and put money on Gudenhot's bottom line. Lyndon Johnson was a Bull, and so is Lee Iacocca.

The Bull wants to do it now. He doesn't want to chance getting consensus and opinion, because they might nix a good idea. Team effort to him is a group of people doing things his way. It's more important to get something under way than to waste time planning. We can make course corrections later, he thinks.

The Bull is always wondering, "Why is this taking so long? Is someone trying to sabotage this?" The Bull wants to be personally involved and has a high disposition to action. His mottos are, "Strike while the iron is hot; crush the opposition; crawl over or tunnel under anyone who gets in the way." To him, motivating people is simple—give everybody a piece of the action, and of course they'll get behind it.

His decision making is gut feel, or a decision tree with gut feel about probabilities. Karl the Bull thinks:

• Harry the Eagle is naive.

• Jeannie the Bee is too controlled by others.

• Andrea the Bloodhound has limited imagination.

## HOW THE EAGLE MAKES DECISIONS

Harry, the Eagle sales manager, in the top right, differs from Karl the Bull in the way he sees the problem. Rather than laboriously having to figure out what the problem is, he understands it instinctively. But the Eagle's method of making the decision is the same as the Bull's method. That is, they both objectively decide. Ronald Reagan is an Eagle, as was Walt Disney.

Harry the Eagle makes the decision because it sounds like fun. "We can get the people excited about this. It'll be terrific PR for the company. It'll look great when we've done it, let's run with it." He has terrible follow-through and will lose interest quickly if it isn't rolling along. He knows the upside potential is enormous, and anyone who even wants to talk about a downside is just a negative thinker.

The eagle has a high disposition to action. His favorite decision-making process is the informal bull session. "See if we can sell the people on it, and then let's do it." Harry the Eagle thinks:

- Karl the Bull is devious.

- Jeannie the Bee pampers people instead of pursuing company goals.

- Andrea the Bloodhound is frozen in inactivity, because analysis leads to paralysis.

## HOW THE BEE MAKES DECISIONS

Jeannie the Bee, in the bottom right-hand corner, is the opposite of Karl the Bull. She operates almost entirely on feelings, not facts. She recognizes the problem instinctively and then makes a decision based on preconceived beliefs rather than observation. Jimmy Carter is a Bee, and so is George Bush.

Jeannie the Bee says, "Will we be comfortable with it? How will the people react? Let's be sure everyone is behind us on this. If it's going to cause friction, let's not do it." She has a low disposition to action. "Let's not rock the boat. We just got everybody settled down from the last wild idea we had." Her favorite decision-making method is small decision groups with everyone having the power of veto.

Jeannie the Bee knows that only people will make it happen and thinks:

- Karl the Bull is ruthless and often unethical, although she's too polite to say it.

- Harry the Eagle takes foolish risks.

- Andrea the Bloodhound sees only projections and statistics.

## HOW THE BLOODHOUND MAKES DECISIONS

Andrea the Bloodhound, in the bottom left, is the opposite of Harry the Eagle. She operates almost totally on facts. She blueprints the problem based on conscious thought or analysis, then makes decisions based on already established beliefs. Gerald Ford is a Bloodhound, as is Harold Geneen, the brilliant former head of ITT.

The Bloodhound says, "Let's not jump into this, we need far more input. Let's hire an outside consultant and do a study. Let's measure twice and cut once. The upside is far smaller than the downside." She uses analysis to prove it will work and has a low disposition to action. "We need far more information than this before we can begin to decide." Her favorite decision process is evaluation, research, and cost-benefit analysis.

Andrea the Bloodhound thinks:

- Karl the Bull takes unnecessary risks.

- Harry the Eagle is unwilling to temper his wild ideas to reality.

- Jeannie the Bee is so set in her ways that she won't listen to reason.

## HOW TO HANDLE THE DIFFERENT
## DECISION-MAKING STYLES

How do you, as CEO of Gudenhot Saunas, work with all these styles? Over the years, you've come to recognize them in the people you've managed, mainly because at different times in your career you've been like them yourself. When you first took over the company, you were like Harry and would do anything to make a sale, without worrying about whether it made fiscal good sense. When the company got into financial trouble, you became more like Karl, and made tough decisions that hurt people without realizing the impact it was having on company morale. When the company went through an attempt to go public, you even became like Andrea the controller, and saw the company only as numbers on financial statements. As you got older, you became very compassionate in your approach to people and like Jeannie, hated to fire anyone. In each case, you retreated from these positions and took a more moderate stand. Now, you see a time for each of these approaches, but have learned to take each person's decision-making style into account when chairing your executive committee meetings.

First you realize that this decision needs to be made fast, and it's basically a "go or no go" decision. Either you buy or you don't. A quick reaction table tells you that it's an excellent move. The assets clearly outweigh the investment. Simple projections tell you that with a minimum loss of cash flow, you can get Tip-Top Saunas back into a profitable position.

But each member of your executive committee is bringing up reasonable concerns. So you say, "I don't want to endanger this company, and I don't want to hurt any of our people. Andrea, go to our bankers, and get them to put up the $2.5 million to replace the existing debt. Get them to secure it with only Tip-Top's manufacturing plant in Atlanta. I don't want to give a corporate guarantee. That way, if it's a disaster, we can't lose. Jeannie, I want you to offer early retirement to any Tip-Top people who would overlap our people. Offer them Tip-Top stock. It isn't worth anything now, but it'll be worth a lot in a few years. Harry, I want you to get on a plane and see every one of our distributors. Sell them into folding Tip-Top's distributors into their system, but don't ram it down their throats. And, Son, from now on, you're the CEO, because I'm going fishing. I'll see you at the next board of directors meeting.''

## Can You Identify Your Decision-Making Style?

Most people are a blend of decision-making styles. However, you'll probably find that there is one style, of the four I've illustrated, that predominates over the others when making decisions. So let's first identify your decision-making style. Look at how each describes the way he or she makes decisions, and then pick the one you relate to the most.

*The Bull.* That's the son, Karl. He says, ''The key to good decision making is cutting through the clutter and getting at the facts. I won't make a decision until I'm sure all the facts are in, but when they are, I move fast and decisively.

''I make fewer bad decisions because I don't let people snow me. I can't stand people who treat this place like a country club, more concerned with the size of their office than whether we're making money. I don't like clutter. My written and spoken communications are clear.

''People tell me I dress too conservatively. They tell me I need to update my wardrobe, get some Italian suits and brighter ties, and so on. But this is an office, not a nightclub. Brooks Brothers makes a perfect suit for business, and I don't see any reason to get anything snazzier.

''They're always on me to fix up my office, but why should I spend a lot of money on a decorator when the style might be different next year. Sure my office looks a little plain, but I've organized it well, and there are no distractions.

''My hero is Lee Iacocca. There's a man who can cut right

through to the heart of the problem and make tough decisions based on the facts.''

As you read about Karl, the Bull, did any of his characteristics remind you of yourself? He's all business, eager to cut the best possible deal for Tip-Top Sauna regardless of whose feelings get hurt. He's a wonderful father and cares about his place of worship and community—but when he's at work, it's time to get serious.

*The Eagle.* If you don't see yourself as a Bull, perhaps you're an Eagle, like sales manager Harry King. Harry says, ''I love decision making—it's like going to one of those murder-mystery weekends. You watch, you observe, you gather information, and suddenly the answer pops into your head. New ideas fascinate me.

''I like to know what people are thinking, and I also like to know why they're thinking it. I take an organized, systematic approach to decision making, but I'm open to what other people have to say. I enjoy debating the decision with them. Sometimes I like to play devil's advocate, because it's fascinating to put yourself in the other person's shoes for a while.

''Sometimes I upset people because I'm too abrupt, but I don't have time to write a two-page letter when a brief note will get the point across. Sometimes people want to wander into my office just to talk things over. I don't have the patience for that. Let's find out what the problem is, kick it around to see if we can come up with something creative, and then run with the best answer. I agree with Malcolm Forbes, who said, 'Men who never get carried away, should be.'

''People tell me my office is a mess; that's true, and it bothers me sometimes. But I'm just involved in so many exciting things, I never get around to straightening them out.

''My hero is Walt Disney. He was always fascinated by new

ideas. He was thorough in the way he put together business decisions, but he always listened to his intuition. Of course, he didn't have to put up with people like Andrea the controller. Without her dragging us down, we'd really make some money around here.''

As you read how Harry the Eagle thinks, did you see yourself? Do you think the way he does?

*The Bee.* Perhaps you're more like Jeannie Hampshire, the human-affairs vice-president, who's a Bee. "This is the way I feel about decision making. I think all the research and analysis is fine, but long term I always end up doing what feels right to me.

"Before I make a decision, I want to be sure that it's going to be agreeable to the troops. They're the ones who really count. I do research by walking around. I talk to dozens of people and get their feelings. It's amazing how often they'll think of a great idea, one that a dozen committees wouldn't have thought of.

"People say that sometimes I'm too nice for my own good, that I let people take advantage of me. Maybe that's true, but that's the way I am, and it's what works best for me.

"They think my office is one big mess, and perhaps it is cluttered. But I've lived there for a long time, and I feel comfortable with it. Besides, I usually know where everything is. I've got a lot of personal mementos in my office, too.

"People are always after me because I don't get things done on schedule. They say I get too bogged down because I take on too many things, but I hate to say no to people. They say I dress too casually, but I work better when I feel comfortable. Why wear heels if flats are so much more comfortable?

"My hero is George Bush—no, maybe Barbara Bush— they're both good people with good values. They care about other people. I like the way he sends out those little notes—even a president should find time to do that.''

*The Bloodhound.* Well, if you can't identify with any of these people, you must be a Bloodhound, like Andrea Miller, the controller. She says, ''I love decision trees and payoff tables. Nobody should be making decisions by shooting from the hip. As we used to say at Lockheed, 'When the weight of the paperwork equals the weight of the aircraft, you're ready to start building—not before.'

''I think that intuition is a myth. In today's world, you've got to work at decisions. First you decide what process you're going to use to describe the problem. That's before you even start thinking about the problem.

''People are fallible, and we ought to realize that. One day we'll have computers that can make perfect decisions every time. Until then, we'll just work to eliminate as many errors as we can.

''Harry in Sales says I never want to take chances. I say, he's always going off half-cocked. He says he can't understand my memos because they're too technical. He calls me a number cruncher, and probably a bean counter, behind my back.

''My hero? Harold Geneen, hands down. He said, 'Facts are the highest form of professional management.' And I believe it. Every time I see a business getting into trouble, I know it's because management lost control of what was going on out there.''

## Why You Should Understand Decision-Making Styles

Before you read on, I want you to pick the decision-making style you relate to the most: The Bull, the Eagle, the Bee, or the

Bloodhound. That's going to help you understand why people are different in the way they make decisions. It's a really valuable decision-making tool in two areas.

First, knowing whether you're a Bull, an Eagle, a Bee, or a Bloodhound will dramatically affect your willingness to work with the decision-making processes I've taught you. If you're an Eagle or a Bee, you love intuitive and creative thought. If you're a Bull or a Bloodhound, you're much more impressed with the logical approaches I've discussed. What I'd like to see you do is expand your decision-making capabilities so that you're matching your approach *to the problem* rather than matching it to your style as a decision maker.

Second, it'll work wonders for you in knowing how other people make decisions. If you're a salesperson, you're probably plagued by two frustrating situations. First the person who says he wants to think it over. Second, the buyer who refers the decision to a higher authority, such as a committee or boss. The Confident Decision Maker knows why the buyer wants to think it over, and how he's going to think it over. The Confident Decision Maker knows why the buyer wants to delay the decision by referring it to a higher authority. If you're a supervisor, you'll know how people are going to react to a proposal before you make it. You'll know which of your people are going to give you trouble with your plan. And you'll know how to make them decide to support you. If you're an employee, you'll know exactly how your boss decides to approve or disapprove your proposals. You'll know how your raise in pay is decided and your promotion. All this useful information can help you get the decision outcome you want.

# How to Apply the Right
# Decision-Making Style

So let's take another look at the chart on page 232 and use it to understand how others make decisions. People make decisions in three stages:

• They take in information about the decision;

• They process that information; and

• They decide.

The top-to-bottom dimension on the chart analyzes how people take in information. At the top, you have people who already know, or think they do. At the bottom, you have people who want to learn.

When somebody with a clipboard knocks on the door at home and says, "Hi, I'm from XYZ Company, and we're taking a survey," the person at the top of the chart, the Bull or the Eagle, is immediately going to think, No, you're not, you're selling something. The person at the bottom of the chart, the Bloodhound or the Bee, is going to think, Maybe you're selling something, or maybe you're really taking a survey. I'll watch what happens and then decide.

Relate that to a big-ticket selling situation. For instance, you're selling point-of-purchase display programs to manufacturers. As you start to make your presentation, you observe how your prospects are inputting what you're telling them. Do they seem to have set ideas about how they want it done, or are they open to suggestions?

Now back to the survey-taker example. The next dimension, the left-to-right dimension on the chart, is how people process the information they get. Conscious thought on the left, unconscious thought on the right. On the left, the Bull or the Bloodhound will think through his or her reaction to standing at the door answering questions. The inflexible Bull may think, This is a waste of time, but maybe he'll give me a free sample of something that'll make it worth my while. The more flexible Bloodhound may think, This is interesting, I wonder what kind of questions he'll ask? If this person is really selling something, how is he going to make the transition from survey taker to salesperson?

On the right, the unconscious thinking Eagle or Bee will be reacting with feelings, rather than thought. The inflexible Eagle will say, "This is interesting. I thought they quit selling like this years ago. I'll give it a couple of minutes and see how I feel about it." The more flexible Bee will say, "This seems like a nice person. I bet this is a tough way to make a living. Unless I start to feel uncomfortable, I'll go along with it."

Let's apply that dimension to the big-ticket sale. You approach one of the auto manufacturers as a point-of-purchase display-program salesman. You want to sell him high-tech computer screens for his dealer showrooms. This will enable customers to see and select the various car options. You've already observed the level of flexibility in the way he inputs information. The inflexible Bull or the Eagle may already have formed an opinion about your program. The Bull is thinking, This is nonsense. The last thing we want to do is give the customer a million choices at the point of sale. The dealers could never move the cars they're already flooring. The Eagle is reacting emotionally, but still has a firm opinion: Sounds great, but we could never sell it to the dealers. They have enough trouble explaining work schedules to their salespeople. This approach is too high-tech.

The more flexible Bloodhound or Bee has a more open mind. The "conscious" Bloodhound may think, The dealers won't like it because they want to steer the buyers to what they have in stock. But why couldn't we program the computer to offer only what's on the lot? That would make it work. We could have the computer show what the option would cost in pennies per day. The salesperson would say, "Let's look at the power-windows option." The customer touches the screen, gets a visual of the power windows in action, and a little box that says: The investment for this option is 11 cents a day. Then he could touch the screen again to approve the add-on.

The Bee is thinking, I like this. At our annual dealer convention in Dallas, I really got the feeling the dealers are getting more conscious of meeting the customers' needs, rather than high-pressure selling. I like it, and I think our people will, too.

# How to Approach Each Decision-Making Style

In order to assess decision-making styles, first you observe how flexible people are in their thinking. This is how people input the decision-making information. Then you'll know whether they're Bulls or Eagles at the top of the chart; or Bloodhounds or Bees at the bottom of the chart.

Next observe the way they react to the information. By applying the second dimension, you'll know which of the four decision-making styles they're using.

With Bulls, be direct and straightforward. If you have to disagree with their assumptions, be careful not to butt heads with them. Agree, and then turn it around gently. "I understand exactly how you feel about that. Most people would share your concern. However, this is what we've found. . . ." They're opinionated but will listen to bottom-line facts. Don't try to snow them, because they're really turned off by flashy selling techniques.

With Eagles, you again have to be careful to overcome their preconceptions, but you convert them with enthusiasm and flair.

You can get them excited about new ideas, and they'll make a fast decision if they like what you have to say.

Bees are open-minded people, but they're skeptical. A hard sell will turn them off. Work on building a relationship and closing gently when they feel comfortable with you.

Bloodhounds are the ones who have the hardest time making a decision. They're very open-minded, but very fact-oriented, so they don't have any preconceived notions on which to make a decision. Their natural tendency to make decisions based on facts, not feelings, makes it worse. It's hard to feed them enough facts for them to make a decision.

## Adapt Your Style to the Problem

The smart thing for you to do is adapt your decision-making style to the type of decision with which you're faced. When you're faced with a decision that calls for bold, fast choices, you should be a Bull.

When choices aren't obvious, and a bold creative choice is called for, you should be an Eagle.

If there aren't obvious choices, and you're going to have to slowly build consensus around the decision, you need to be more of a Bee.

If there are all kinds of choices available to you, and your problem is picking the right one, you should be a Bloodhound.

## Can You Guess Which Style Will Cause the Most Trouble?

When you use this technique to understand how other people make decisions, you should realize that you'll have the most difficulty with the decision-making style in the opposite corner to yours on the chart.

If you tend to be a Bull, you'll have the most trouble working with the Bee. You're ready to make a move while the Bee's still getting comfortable with the situation.

If you're an Eagle, you'll have the most trouble understanding how the Bloodhound decides. You're all excited and ready to run with the decision, while Bloodhounds think there are weeks of research that need to be done yet.

If you're a Bee, you don't understand how the Bull can be so callous and uncaring.

And if you're a Bloodhound, you can't believe the Eagle wants to run with the first decision that feels good. To understand this even further, let's see how the personality styles that I talked about in Chapter Five fit into the different decision-making styles.

| Left-Brained | Right-Brained |
|---|---|
| Pragmatic | Extrovert |
| (A Bull) | (An Eagle) |
| Unemotional | Emotional |
| Assertive | Assertive |
| Analytical | Amiable |
| (A Bloodhound) | (A Bee) |
| Unemotional | Emotional |
| Nonassertive | Nonassertive |

I arrived at those four styles by evaluating temperament, not decision-making styles. However, the Pragmatic probably has a Bull decision-making style. The Extrovert will decide like an Eagle. The Analytical will be a Bloodhound as a decision maker. And the Amiable will make choices like a Bee.

Carl Jung first came up with these decision-making styles, early in the twentieth century. They've stood the test of time. They're not easy to understand when you first read them, but it's well worth your time to keep rereading this chapter until you're familiar with them. It will make you a confident Decision Maker!

# CHAPTER TWELVE

# The Nine Traits of Great Decision Makers

In this final chapter, I'm going to teach you the traits that make you a great decision maker. Add these traits to the techniques I've taught you and you'll make the right choice every time.

I've narrowed the list down to nine traits, beyond all the technicalities of decision making, that make great decision makers. They are:

1. Having a high tolerance for ambiguity

2. Having a well-ordered sense of priorities

3. Being a good listener

4. Always building consensus around a decision

5. Avoiding stereotypes

6. Always remaining resilient

7. Being comfortable with both soft and hard input

8. Being realistic about cost and difficulty

9. Avoiding decision minefields

And while you may not be born with these traits, that doesn't mean you can't learn to adopt them the next time you are forced to make a decision.

If we take a look at each of these traits separately, you'll understand why they provide an invaluable foundation for any decision maker.

# Trait #1: Have a High Tolerance for Ambiguity.

Confident Decision Makers have a high tolerance for ambiguity. They don't have to have everything laid out in black-and-white for them. They don't have to know every little detail that's going on. They may be aware there are problems in the plant in Bangkok, but they're comfortable with the framework they've set up. They know somehow it'll get taken care of, because they don't have to be there for problems to get resolved. Most of us either feel comfortable with this kind of ambiguity or we don't.

To illustrate this, let me tell you about a trip I once took. Every six months, I take off a month or so, and go traveling. I've been to ninety-two different countries and am a provisional member of the Century Club in Los Angeles. I hope to be a full member within a couple of years, which means I'll have visited one hundred countries. Because I'm a professional speaker, I want to make my last speech quotable. I want to be able to say on my deathbed, "Did I see it all?" I don't want to end up like Pancho Villa, the Mexican revolutionary, whose dying words in 1923 were, "Don't let it end like this. Tell them I said something."

For this trip, I simply bought an around-the-world air ticket, and took off for five weeks, following the sunset. I could go anywhere I wanted, as long as I kept going west and never backtracked. Without any plans or hotel reservations, I went to Tahiti, New Zealand, Australia, Singapore, and Thailand. Then I flew to Frankfurt, Germany, where I rented a car and drove around Europe for a couple of weeks. I finally picked up a flight in Paris for the trip back across the Atlantic. It was the most exciting, enriching vacation I've ever taken.

I don't have a problem with taking a trip like that, where nothing is planned ahead. Had I spent a month planning the trip, I'd have run into less frustration and maybe seen more. But would it have been as much fun? I don't think so.

I thought it was such a great idea that when my youngest son, John, graduated from college, I gave him a similar trip. I went with him on the first three weeks. We rented a car and drove around Japan for ten days and nearly reached the top of Mount Fuji, even though it wasn't the climbing season and we didn't have our climbing gear with us. Then we flew to Seoul, Korea. Next we rented a car in Taipei and drove around the island of Taiwan for a week, with a side trip to do some white-water rafting. Finally, we flew to Hong Kong, where I left John and returned to California.

He continued on around the world, trying to stretch his limited amount of spending money as far as he could. He stayed with friends in New Delhi, and then flew down to the Maldives for some scuba diving. Next he flew to the south of France and ended up spending several weeks with friends in Paris. Then he decided to spend some time with his mother's relatives in Iceland, and I flew there to be with him. Finally, he completed his round-the-world pilgrimage, having been gone for over four months. Not once on this trip had he prebooked a hotel room. Sure, for the same amount of money I could have bought him a car, or put a down payment on a home, but where's the fun in that? Not only did he have a great time, but he learned a wonderful lesson, the ability to live with ambiguity.

Some people wouldn't dream of doing something like that, because they have a low tolerance for ambiguity. They want to have everything planned in advance; they don't want to leave anything to chance. That's a very good characteristic to have when you're in the Categorizing and Blueprinting stages of decision making. It's a terrible characteristic to have when the crunch is on and you have to make a fast decision. You probably bought this book because I promised that you'd learn to make the right choice every time. *But the right choice isn't always the perfect solution.* In a lifetime, you're only going to run into a perfect solution once or twice, three or four times at most. Almost invariably, you'll have to go ahead with something that only has a good chance of succeeding, with no guarantees. If you've a low tolerance for ambiguity, this will drive you crazy.

Remember the decision-making styles we talked about in our last chapter? The Eagles and the Bees feel comfortable with ambiguity. The Bulls and the Bloodhounds hate it.

## Trait #2: Have a Well-Ordered Sense of Priorities.

A well-ordered sense of priorities is the framework within which you make the decision. It isn't the decision itself; it's the arena in which you operate. You define your priorities by your virtues. Here are five virtues that will make you a better decision maker:

- Having long-term vision

- Being able to see the big picture

- Acting without the need for others' approval

• Thinking independently of others

• A strong sense of inner values

The *first virtue*, long-term vision, means being able to see through the decision to all its future implications. Often it's very easy to seize a decision and run with it, and that's okay on a short-term basis. But it's better to see through the immediate decision and look at the long-term implications.

How does this apply to problem solving, and how does it apply to opportunity seizing?

If you solve a problem with a quick fix, you don't get to its heart. You treat the symptom, but you don't treat the cause, and the problem keeps coming back.

If you're the master of the quick fix on opportunities, you may be very good at seizing an opportunity before anybody else. But other people will do better, because their long-term vision takes fuller advantage of the opportunity.

The *second virtue* is the ability to see the large picture. Don't confuse this with the virtue we were just talking about, which was long-term vision. Long-term vision examines what happens in the future after the decision has been make. Looking at the large picture trains you to see the effect of the decision on a much wider scale.

First, be sure you're paying attention to the right problem. We talked earlier about BART, the Bay Area Rapid Transit System, where the county spent hundreds of millions of dollars on a new subway system. Then it devoted all its concern on how to build the best, most modern subway. It had forgotten the reason for building the subway in the first place: to reduce surface traffic congestion. The situation in San Francisco was no less ludicrous than the scenario in *The Bridge on the River Kwai*, where a crazed British officer permitted his men, as Japanese prisoners of war, to work on the bridge as therapy. He completely lost sight of why he let them build the bridge in the first place and became obsessed with building the best bridge in the world.

The answer to this problem is to be willing to remove yourself from the problem. You can't see the big picture when you're standing in the middle of it. As the saying goes, "When you're up to your elbows in alligators, it's hard to remember that your initial objective was to drain the swamp." If people would see the value of moving away from the problem in their personal lives, they would become big believers in it when it came to corporate decision making. Some people stay in unhappy marriages for year after year after year. They never have the courage to say, "I need to move away from this in order to view it objectively. It doesn't really matter where I go, but I want to move away from this situation and take another look at it from somewhere else." It's amazing how often when you gain distance, the situation isn't nearly as hopeless as when you were in the middle of it. You really do have a lot more options than you think you do.

Another key to seeing the big picture is to be sure you're not focusing too closely on what it is you do, instead of why it is you're there. We all know of industries that lost their creativity because they didn't understand their broad mission and remained too focused on a product or service. The story that you always hear about is how railroads went broke because they didn't understand that they were in the transportation business. You hear all the time that they should have made the move into airlines, but they were too focused. That's just not true. The railroads saw the opportunity, but the federal government, God bless it, wouldn't allow them to diversify.

In another example, the Bell System understood its business was transmitting information, not selling telephone systems. But the federal government did everything it could to stop them from branching out.

To give you a current example, I see Federal Express as

being in real trouble unless it accepts that it has to expand from its core business of transmitting documents. In my company, we do a lot of express transmission of documents, so we were a good customer for Federal Express. But I realized the truth just a couple of years ago when I was down in Australia. There, I found that just about everybody has a fax machine in his or her home. If you ask for somebody's home phone number, the person will produce what looks to us like a business card. It has both a telephone number and a fax number on it.

This was when fax machines were new in the United States. An Australian businessman was telling me he was talking to an American corporation, and he told the Americans he'd fax them some information. One of the Americans responded, "Well, when will you be faxing it?" and the Australian said, "Sometime in the next day or so, why do you need to know?" The American said, "I need to know when to switch on our fax machine." This astounded the Australian, who was so used to sending and receiving facsimiles that he left his machine on all the time.

I came back from that Australian tour and said to the president of my company, "I really don't know what a fax machine is, but I think we probably need one. Why don't you shop around and make a decision on it?" Within six months, we were in a position of not knowing how we could operate our business without a fax machine. Remember, we're not General Motors, we're a very small company, but we're perfectly comfortable now sending information by fax or by modem. I have a fax and a modem in my home also. We probably use Federal Express 80 percent less than we did a year ago. A year from now, we probably won't even need a fax machine, because we will transmit documents from computer to computer.

The point is to be sure you're seeing a big enough picture to understand what your business is. If you're totally focused on just one aspect of the business, you can easily become obsolete in this fast-moving, high-technology age.

The *third virtue* is being able to act without needing other people's approval. You're sunk if you're always wondering, "What will my boss think of this?" Use your decision-making skills to make the right decision, and use your persuasion skills to sell it to your boss.

That's the difference between the Vietnam War and the Persian Gulf War. The generals in the Vietnam War constantly had to please the administration. The administration constantly had to please public opinion. In the Persian Gulf War, President Bush was smart enough to realize that he was the one giving the order to attack. Beyond that, it would be the generals who'd make all the fighting decisions. It makes all the difference in war, and it makes a huge difference in business.

A Vietnam vet once said, "I was watching the Gulf War on television and saw thousands of Iraqi soldiers waving their surrender leaflets." And I thought to myself, We could have won that war with *both* hands tied behind our backs.

The *fourth virtue* is the ability to think independently of others. What happens when everyone else is pushing you to change your mind on a decision? Can you still hold firm? If you felt confident that you made the right decision, you will.

The *fifth virtue* is to have a strong sense of inner values. As the ancient Chinese philosopher Mencius said, "Men must be decided on what they will not do; and then they are able to act with vigor, in what they ought to do." That means your inner values won't be seduced, despite the temptation.

You can see the value of this virtue when you consider an amazing piece of absurdity that took place in Los Angeles. Voters, concerned about the lack of ethics in city government, passed a proposition in November 1990. It insisted the city council hire an ethics chief to keep watch on it. The council hired a very qualified applicant, Walter Zelman, who for twelve years had been the executive director of California Common Cause. They agreed on a salary of $90,000 a year. On the day before he was to report to work, the council met and slashed his salary from $90,000 to $76,254. And this was for the executive officer in charge of ethics! He stood on his principles and told the council to forget it.

Before you make a final decision, you should ask yourself, "Could I survive a *60 Minutes* investigation of what I plan to do?" The ranks of the bankrupt and unemployed have recently swelled with people who said to themselves, "We probably can get away with it; but if anybody does ask, we can cover it up." That's not smart thinking. If you can't survive a *60 Minutes* investigation, I suggest you rethink your plans.

Apart from the obvious issue of morality, shallow ethical values drain away the energy of the organization that must implement the plan. Better to go with a plan that isn't as promising than to go with one that will be questioned by the people who have to implement it because they won't give it their full support.

## Trait #3: Be a Good Listener.

I can guarantee you that if you take two business executives and one is a good listener and one is a bad listener, the one who's a good listener will always be the better decision maker. It's especially critical in this day and age when we're bombarded with information. A top executive may spend 80 percent of his or her time in meetings listening to discussions. This is a very frustrating, often very boring process, and unless you're an expert listener, you won't get from the discussion what you need to make a Confident Decision. So, let's talk about improving listening skills in different areas.

*Increasing your concentration during a speech.* Our minds quickly wander when the speaker is boring, but our reactions can encourage a more interesting presentation. Here're some positive things you can do for the speaker:

- Lean forward.

- Tilt your head a little to show you're paying attention.

- Ask questions.

- Give feedback.

- Mirror what he or she said.

If you think of listening as an interactive process, you will do much better.

Avoid boredom by playing mind games. Concentrate on what the speaker is saying, not the style of delivery. You can do this by picking the longest word in a sentence or rephrasing what has just been said. Because you can listen four times faster than the speaker can speak, you need to do something or your mind will wander.

You can raise your alertness level by changing your breathing pattern. If you want to become more alert, breathe in more than you breathe out. This feeds oxygen to the brain. Breathe in to a six count and out to a three count. It might sound silly, but it works. It also works in reverse to relieve stress. When I first started out as a speaker and was panic-stricken before each speech, I'd breathe in to a three count and out to a six count. It's amazing how this relaxes you.

*Increasing your comprehension of what's being said.* First, take notes right from the start of the conversation. Whether you're listening one-on-one, in a committee meeting, or in the audience at a large meeting, take a large pad of paper with you. Head it up with the date and the topic and start to keep brief notes on what's being said. Paper is cheaper than the time it takes to go back and get details. Perhaps you take notes like this, but there's no reason for any follow-up, so you throw them away. But chances are, if you file them somewhere, they will become a very valuable resource for you. Also, of course, note taking communicates to the other person that you care about what he or she is saying. An additional bonus is that when people see you're writing things down, they tend to be a lot more accurate in what they're telling you.

Defer making judgments about the speaker until he or she is through. If you immediately analyze someone as phony or manipulative or self-serving, you tend to shut the person out and quit listening to him or her. So just hold off, and wait until the speaker's through, before you evaluate.

Know in advance what you're listening for. When I'm writing, I might read thirty or forty books on the topic during my research. I find I can read a book very quickly, perhaps a two-hundred-page book in an hour, if I know why I'm reading it in the first place. If you sit in an audience and just listen to a speaker, there's a very good chance your mind will wander during much of the talk, unless he's a particularly skilled speaker. However, if you go to the talk saying to yourself, "I want to learn what this man has to say about a particular issue," you'll be much more focused in what you bring away from it.

Recognize which side of the brain is dominating. If you feel angry or excited by something you hear, which is a right-brain reaction, switch to the left brain by concentrating on facts and figures. If you feel bored or impatient by what's said, which is left-brain thinking, switch to the right brain by putting yourself in the shoes of the speaker and empathizing with his or her feelings.

This is going to sound wacky to you, but there's a lot of scientific research that shows you can change your ability to listen well by changing the ear through which you listen. Stay with me; this isn't as wild as it sounds. It's particularly valuable if you're listening on the telephone, where you can control which ear you use. The right brain is fed by the left ear, so it's particularly receptive to emotion. The left brain is fed by the right ear, so its forte is facts and figures. Don't expect anything too spectacular here, but try it and see if it helps. If you're talking to someone you love, the conversation may be enhanced if you hold the phone to your left ear. If you're having trouble concentrating on a complicated set of facts, hold the phone to your right ear, so you can feed the left side of the brain.

*Using facts to improve listening when you're taking directions.* I'm sure you've asked someone for directions and because it sounded so simple you thought, I can't go wrong. Yet you made a couple of turns, and suddenly you became confused and lost. This happens because you're visualizing when you listen to the directions. For example, let's say you're in a hospital, and you're asking for directions to the X-ray department. You're told, "Turn down the large hallway, go past the glass doors, and turn left at the nurses' station." This is very much a visual description. If the scene you encounter doesn't reflect the visuals you've created in your mind, you'll get lost. When you heard "glass doors," you may have visualized the kind of heavy clear doors that you might find in an expensive attorney's office. But in the hospital, you might see wooden doors that have opaque glass inserts in them, and you become confused. "Did she say glass doors? Is this a glass door?" you wonder.

So when taking directions, don't use visuals. It's better to get directions that are factual, such as "Turn left at the third hallway, go past the glass doors that say Intensive Care, and turn left at the next hallway."

*Improving your ability to evaluate what's said.* For one-on-one conversations, here's a rule that's so valuable for increased evaluation that once you start using it, you'll wonder why you ever did it any other way. Ask the other person to present his conclusions first. Then, if you don't agree with him completely, ask him to support his conclusions. But of course you should keep an open mind until he finishes.

I learned this technique from years of handling complaints for a major department-store chain. People would come storming into my office and say, "This washing machine, television, or stereo [or whatever the product might be] hasn't worked since we bought it."

I don't know who first originated that phrase, but it's something that everybody who ever complains to a retail store always says: "This hasn't worked since we got it!" This is clearly a "terminological inexactitude," as Winston Churchill was fond of saying. It simply can't be true. Nobody has a washing machine or television or stereo for two years that hasn't worked at all since it was purchased. Eventually, we'd get around to the second phrase that every customer who ever complains to a retail store says, and that's, "What are you going to do about it?"

You feel like saying, "I've been listening to you now for half an hour, and I've come to the conclusion I don't like you very much. What I want to do about it is the very least you'll let me get away with." But that's not appropriate.

Then I found out you're a lot better off asking what the person wants you to do first. When customers come storming into your office, obviously upset, and they want some action, calm them down. Then say, "Please understand, I want to resolve this problem. I'm on your side, so would you first please tell me what it is you'd like me to do?"

Usually, they will start up again and say, "But first I want to tell you all the suffering I've gone through since I've bought this from you."

But then you respond with, "Yes, I understand that, and I want to help you. But, first, I'd like you to tell me what it is you want me to do. I might just do it." As I gradually learned this skill, I could get people to tell me what they wanted me to do first. Then, if I needed more information, I'd ask for it. If we still couldn't agree, we'd discuss what we would and wouldn't do.

Once I realized this, everything started to drop into place for me. I didn't know I'd stumbled upon some fundamental rules of negotiating terrorist situations, but I had. If you're negotiating a terrorist situation, first you get the other side committed to a position. What do the terrorists want? Then, if you don't reach agreement, you seek information. Finally, if you still don't have agreement, you start to reach for compromise. When you do it that way, everything drops into place for you, and life becomes so much simpler.

The second thing that improves your ability to evaluate what they're saying is to be aware of your personal biases. Be conscious of how they're coloring your reactions. For example, if you're aware that you don't like attorneys, notice that this causes you to distrust the attorney who's talking to you. You can evaluate information much more clearly when you're aware of your biases. The same holds true in a sales situation if you're a person who can't stand people trying to hype you. You might automatically resist what the salesperson has to say whether it's right or wrong. Be aware of that. It improves your ability to evaluate what the salesperson's saying.

Don't let your enthusiasm for a concept carry you away. Sometimes you start to listen to people, and it sounds so great, you can't wait to implement it. You're usually better off to train yourself to listen to all the facts before you jump on the bandwagon. Not only may a fact come to light that cools you on the idea, a fact may appear that makes you even more enthusiastic, because it triggers a thought that would improve the concept.

Finally, learn to take notes with a divided notepad, one with a line down the middle. On the left, list the facts as they were presented; on the right, note your evaluation of what was said. That way you can study the information later, form a more objective viewpoint, and see how accurate your evaluations were.

## Trait #4: Always Build Consensus Around a Decision.

Great decision makers make a decision they know will have the support of the people in their organization, and follow through to be sure they get that support.

Remember the dog-food story that has been circulating in business for years? A major company spent years researching a new line of dog food. They spent millions of dollars on an advertising campaign, but the dog food didn't sell. The president of the company called in all the salespeople and said, "Why aren't you doing your job? What's gone wrong here? We spent millions on market research. We spent millions on advertising. Why can't you sell it?" Somebody in the back of the room said, "You forgot to ask the dogs if they liked it!"

Be sure you're asking the dogs before you go ahead and make a final decision!

The other aspect of building consensus around a decision is to be sure you have the support of the people who must implement the program. While you're probably such a brilliant motivator that you can get anybody to do anything, it might be a lot easier to go with the flow. However tempting the decision may be, if you don't have the enthusiastic support of the people who must implement it, say no.

Some smart people have made this very mistake. I remember talking to a Wall Street financier who'd just purchased one of the smaller national real estate franchises. "Have you ever been involved in real estate brokerage before?'' I asked him. He hadn't, so my next question was "Then why are you doing this?'' It turned out he was already into insurance and mortgage banking. Now he was drooling at the thought of thousands of loyal real estate agents, who'd obediently send him insurance and mortgage business. There was a major flaw in the plan. He hadn't asked these agents how they felt about doing that for the owner of the franchise. The answer was that real estate agents wouldn't get excited about it. They weren't interested. His plan was a disaster, and two years later he was out of the business, having just unintentionally taken a multimillion-dollar ''seminar'' in decision making.

## Trait #5: Avoid Stereotypes.

We're all guilty of assumptions, which is a nicer word than prejudice, but it means the same thing. I don't think I have to hammer this point home, but it is important to avoid visual stereotyping. Not all men with long hair are hippies. Not all people who wear pocket protectors are nerds. Not all football players are freewheeling in their lifestyle. Not all accountants are boring. Stereotyping happens because the mind always seeks the shortest route to a decision, the path of least resistance. It's easier to assume that a person or situation fits the mold of your previous experience than to evaluate each person or situation on its merits.

We stereotype in areas we dislike or that disinterest us. I don't like foreign cars, so I tend to lump them together as difficult and expensive to fix. I'm not interested in basketball, so I lump all teams and all players together in my mind.

Stereotyping from people who are close to an industry may be the reason so many inventions come from outsiders. The inventor of the pneumatic tire, John Dunlop, was a veterinarian. The inventor of the safety razor, King Gillette, was a cork salesman. George Eastman, who founded Kodak, was a bookkeeper.

Stereotyping can be valuable because it enables us to draw conclusions even when we have incomplete information. However, it stops us from seeing new combinations of elements in the problem.

Did you ever hear the old riddle about the young man brought unconscious to the hospital emergency room? The doctor sees his name on the chart and says, "I can't treat him, he's my son." But the young man's father had been killed in an accident several years earlier. Who is the doctor? Stereotyping prevents us from seeing that the doctor may, in fact, be a woman, not a man. The answer is that the doctor is the young man's mother.

However, worse than any of these stereotypes is an assumption that you can make about yourself, which is, "I am the way I am." Most people at some point in their life stop changing. With some people, it's at ten years of age, with other people it's at one hundred, but at some point in our lives, we arrive at a point from which we'll never change. Edward R. Murrow said, "Some people haven't had a new thought in years. They've simply been having the same thought over and over." Don't freeze. *You can change the way you are.* I know this is true because every month I talk to dozens of people who validate this. Simply by reading this book and applying some of its methods, you can change. While stereotyping other people is disgraceful, stereotyping yourself is tragic.

Stereotyping is the dark side of chunking information. We become more intuitive decision makers if we can chunk information. As I've told you, the mind can juggle only about seven things at once. If those seven things are major chunks of information, our minds can much more quickly seek out and join unrelated facts. That gives us the illusion of intuition. But the dark side of chunking information is stereotyping, where we close our minds to the possibilities. Confident Decision Makers avoid that.

## Trait #6: Always Remain Resilient.

There are three points I'd like to cover in regard to resiliency.

First, be a little firmer than flexible but a little more yielding than rigid. In other words, be firm in the way you make decisions, but be prepared to bend the rules if it will produce a better decision for you. Developing a method of making decisions and then never deviating from that procedure is fatal. Decision making should be an art, not a science. Varying your methods produces more creative solutions.

That's why I stressed in Chapter Two the importance of Categorizing the problem before you go ahead. If you use Analysis when a decision calls for Synthesis, you're not going to come up with the right answer. If you think you're dealing with a dichotomy when you're dealing with a multiple-option situation, you're in trouble. The same is true with policy versus nonpolicy decisions. The first key to resiliency, then, is to realize that it's a mistake to develop one favorite way of making a decision. You should Categorize the decision and then apply the optimum method of arriving at the right answer.

Second, resiliency gives you the ability to move with a less than perfect decision if you have to. Not moving ahead can kill even a good decision. Howard Stein, chairman of the Dreyfus Investment Fund, says, "By the time you get a program approved and people are committed to it, things change, and it doesn't work. Make the decision, and move forward; but don't feel wedded to what you're doing."

The third point about resiliency in decision making is that you should always be willing to abort. "Go or no go" is a decision that's always on the table. In large corporations, because the board chairman may be enthusiastic, the board gives its approval to go ahead. Then management plows ahead, assuming it has an irreversible mandate to proceed. It makes all the right decisions within that parameter, but excludes the possibility of going back to the board with a recommendation to abort. The problem is, management is worried that canceling the program would be an admission of failure. It is afraid the board will say, "Well, it's still a good idea. We're still enthusiastic about it. The problem is, we obviously picked the wrong people to get the job done."

A classic example of this was Rayonier's decision to invest in a paper pulp mill in Quebec. The company was part of ITT, a huge conglomerate that owned 350 businesses in eighty countries. At one of their board meetings, Harold Geneen, the CEO of ITT, approved an $85 million expansion of its Georgia plant. Feeling good, he leaned back in his chair and said, "What else have you got?" Russ Erickson, the head of Rayonier, told him the government of Quebec was offering timber rights on fifty-two-thousand square miles for a token amount, to stimulate industry. They could build a pulp plant there and corner the world market on cellulose, from which rayon is produced. Geneen said, "Sounds great, let's do it."

The project was plagued from the start. Everything that could go wrong did go wrong. At a dozen points along the way, the project should have been killed. Why wasn't it? Because everybody involved was under the impression Geneen was enthusiastically behind the plan. They thought heads would roll if they admitted failure. Eight years later, they finally canceled the project, taking an immediate write-off of $320 million. The CEO was understandably furious. "Why wasn't I told?" he asked. No one knew about the "go or no go" rule. In business, you never pass the point of no return.

# Trait #7: Be Comfortable with Both Soft and Hard Input.

What do I mean by that? Hard input is statistics, reports, analysis. Japanese business leaders have an amazing ability to absorb a huge amount of hard input. Soft input is feedback from customers and employees, the willingness to pay attention to the casual reaction of potential customers. It requires you to listen instead of talk.

A good example of soft input is the story I told you about Tomomasa Matsui, the North American president of Canon Cameras. Remember? He spent the first few months on the job going around the country to the dealers, asking them why they weren't buying Canon cameras. Tom Peters calls it management by walking around. Confident Decision Makers know you need a balance of both hard and soft input.

Flight attendants often ask me to fill out questionnaires, but I never do. Not that I don't see the value of hard input like that. The problem is, I don't see airlines making any effort to collect soft input. I've flown the equivalent of twenty times around the world on the major airlines, American, United, and Delta. As a professional speaker, I spend anywhere from five thousand dollars to ten thousand dollars a month on airline tickets just for myself. Never has anybody from one of those companies called me up to say, "Mr. Dawson, would you mind telling us why you pick one airline over another?" That's soft input. Since they don't care enough to do that occasionally, I really don't see any reason for me to be taking my valuable time filling out the surveys.

Confident Decision Makers know how to balance soft and hard input. They also know how to avoid confusing the two. Auto executives who hang around car lots can become a real pain—if they treat soft input as if it were hard input. Problems will arise if, when they talk to two shoppers on a car lot, they both happen to be whistling gophers. That's someone who kicks the tire and asks, "What does this one go-fer?" The salesperson tells the person, and that person whistles in surprise. The executive then treats this information like hard input, and thinks the cars are overpriced, as though he'd just had input from ten thousand informed consumers.

## Trait #8: Be Realistic About the Cost and Difficulty.

This is particularly true when other people are bringing you the idea, asking for your approval. In that situation, most people are overoptimistic. They're enthusiastic about the plan and concerned you might say no. So they're not realistic about the time and money it's going to take.

Here's my advice, gleaned from starting up some half-dozen different companies. It will cost you at least 20 percent more than you think; and probably twice as much. Also, it will take you at least 20 percent longer than you think; and maybe twice as long. Say to yourself, "What if this costs me twice as much as I've budgeted and takes twice as long to get into the black as I think? Is it still a good idea?" If you can answer positively to that, you've probably got an excellent idea on your hands.

Hold everything if your response is a resounding, "No way would I go ahead if it's going to take twice as long and cost twice as much!" You need to take another look at the decision and be more cautious.

Next, be realistic enough to avoid blind trust. Before you go ahead with the decision, say to yourself, "Can I adequately supervise the person who'll implement the plan? Or will he be out there somewhere doing whatever he wants?" It's unfortunate that anyone will steal if the temptation is great enough. Go ahead and hate me for saying that if you want. But, as an employer, you have the obligation to remove the temptation. You can eliminate 90 percent of the temptation by being sure that two or more people have to collaborate to steal from you. In this area, it really is true that an ounce of prevention is worth a pound of cure. Have a system in place that keeps track of the progress of the project. Don't set up systems to observe people stealing if you can stop them from stealing in the first place.

The jury at the John DeLorean trial evidently agreed with me. Remember John DeLorean? Clearly, the jury was disgusted that law enforcement was spending a lot of time and money encouraging him to commit a crime, instead of making an effort to prevent the crime in the first place. The same thing happened at Washington mayor Marion Barry's trial.

A way to avoid blind trust is to be sure the person running the plan has just as much to lose as you do. Say to yourself, "A year from now, if this thing has gone down the tubes, what will I have lost?" Compare this to what the person who's pushing this plan will have lost. This doesn't mean he or she has to put cash into the plan. Perhaps the individual would have worked for a year without pay, or for substantially less than he or she could have earned otherwise. Then, he or she would also have suffered, so it reduces the risk of the decision. Don't go along with a decision where you'd have lost everything and the other person would have lost nothing. He or she would have had a good job for a year, plus a shot at greatness. All you've done is expose yourself to serious risk.

## Trait #9: Avoid Decision Minefields.

Decision minefields are those areas into which you walk, where you have to say to yourself, "I'm walking through a serious minefield here. It may not blow me up, but I need to be very alert.'' There are five common minefields that you really need to watch out for.

*1. "If Donald Trump made an offer, it must be a bargain."* When Donald Trump made an offer to buy the Eastern Airlines shuttle, other people immediately started coming out of the woodwork to make offers, too. Just because a shrewd businessperson is going ahead, it doesn't follow that it would be a good idea for you also. Allen Bond, the Australian, is a very shrewd businessperson, in spite of his current problems. What if you'd have been at the auction where he paid $53.9 million for Vincent van Gogh's "Irises"? Would you make the assumption that because a smart businessman like this paid $53.9 million, it would also be a good buy at $54 million? I hope not! Smart businesspeople make big mistakes, too. But even more important, you and they are probably in completely different situations. It may be a terrific idea for them, and a lousy idea for you. You're walking through a minefield when you make decisions based on what other people do, however smart they may be.

*2. If they're advertising it, it must be selling.* Every so often, I see an ad for a new product and say to myself, ''They'll never make money selling that. The advertising-cost ratio is far too high.'' So I watch for the ad to see if it continues to run. Common sense would tell you that if the ad isn't effective, the company would quit running the ad. Well, that's usually true, but not always. Sometimes management doesn't know any better. Sometimes it's locked into a one-year advertising contract. Sometimes it's got such an excess inventory of the product, it's better off losing money to get rid of it, instead of letting it sit in a warehouse. There are all kinds of different situations. So don't assume that just because somebody else is advertising it, it must be selling. That's a minefield.

*3. If the Japanese are doing it, it must be right.* Why have we become so enamored of the Japanese? Why assume everything they do is right? Japanese productivity is good because they have a low-paid, overworked, highly captive work force. Americans wouldn't want to work in that environment for very long. So don't walk into that minefield.

4. *If the person pushing the idea seems enthusiastic, he must be convinced he can make it work.* Robert Bernstein, former chairman of Random House, Inc., says, "Beware of the articulate incompetent. Particularly in a business that depends on people and not machinery. Only intuition can protect you from this most dangerous individual of all."

If the person making the proposal is enthusiastic, it colors the decision-making process. Paul Schoemaker did a study with his students at the University of Chicago Graduate Business School. He presented a business situation and a possible solution to two groups. He told one group the idea had an 80 percent chance of success. He told the other group it had a 20 percent chance of failure. The first group rallied behind the plan. The second group vetoed it.

In the formative days of Mary Kay Cosmetics, Mary Kay Ash had agreed to hire a man who had a terrific plan to get the company off the ground. She tells this story: "I stood talking to the man outside my office. I suddenly changed my mind. I had no reason, just intuition. Six months later, I read in the newspaper that he had been indicted on a felony." So, remember, just because the person pushing the plan is enthusiastic doesn't mean he can make it work.

5. *If experts tell you, it must be true.* Experts can be wrong and very frequently are. Twenty-one publishers rejected the book *M\*A\*S\*H*. It became an incredible best-seller and was turned into a blockbuster movie, followed by a television series that ran for years.

Eighteen publishers rejected *Jonathan Livingston Seagull*, a book that became the third best-selling book ever written. The Munich Technical Institute rejected Albert Einstein, because he showed, as they said, "no promise." And Darryl F. Zanuck wouldn't sign Clark Gable because his ears were too big.

So you're walking through a minefield when the experts say it won't work. But you may also be in a minefield when the experts say they're sure it will work.

Jonas Salk wouldn't have discovered the cure for polio if he hadn't questioned the experts who said the only way you become immune to a virus is to be infected by it. He had the courage to question this belief, and produced the cure for polio, a disease so dreaded that not being inoculated for it had seemed unthinkable. Most great discoveries in science occur when somebody has the courage to challenge the experts.

And finally, my favorite "experts say they're sure" story. In 1906, astronomer Percival Lowell charted the red canals of the planet Mars so accurately that they were published in maps and school books throughout the world. Later we found out there are no red canals on Mars. Percival Lowell was suffering from a rare eye disease that caused him to see the veins in his own eyes! But don't worry, he didn't sink into oblivion. The disease is now known throughout the world as Lowell's syndrome.

Now that I've explained them to you, study once more the nine traits that make you a Confident Decision Maker. As you read through the list, see how many of them you can already incorporate into your daily decisions.

1. Having a high tolerance for ambiguity

2. Having a well-ordered sense of priorities

3. Being a good listener

4. Always building consensus around a decision

5. Avoiding stereotypes

6. Always remaining resilient

7. Being comfortable with both soft and hard input

8. Being realistic about the cost and difficulty, and

9. Avoiding decision minefields

Being alert to the characteristics of Confident Decision Makers will make you more effective.

## Some Final Thoughts and a Bit of Unsolicited Advice

Well, we've come a long way in the time that we've spent together. I've told you how decision making shapes your life and defines who you are. Decisions are the building blocks of life. I've shown you how to categorize and blueprint the decision, and how to use intuition and Creative Synthesis to expand your options. You've learned how to use reaction tables and decision trees. I've shown you how to huddle, and covered the barriers to good decisions and the four different styles of decision making. In this last chapter, I've told you what makes you a great decision maker. So now you're ready to graduate as a Confident Decision Maker!

Let me leave you with this thought. Tom Monaghan, who was raised in an orphanage and started Domino's Pizza with five hundred dollars and turned it into a $480 million fortune, has lived the American dream. His is one of the great success stories of this century. Recently, he said a very interesting thing, "Material things don't mean a thing to me anymore. They did when I was younger. Now I've got everything I ever dreamed about . . . and it's not that big a deal.''

Tom Monaghan now refers to the second half of his life as "The Main Event.'' He's discovered what we all must learn before this adventure we call life is over. That we're on a journey together, which one day will end. The destination doesn't matter. It really doesn't matter if you end your journey with $480 million dollars or stumble through the gates of heaven struggling for financial survival. What matters is how much joy and satisfaction you derived from the journey. And what a journey it is! Would you ever, in your wildest dreams, have scripted your life the way it has gone so far? What an exciting adventure!

Learning to make confident decisions will make you a lot of money, but don't use it just to make money. Use Confident Decision Making to see how good you can get at doing whatever it is you do. If you take this approach, I promise you that you won't have to worry about money anymore, because it will flow to you as a by-product of what you do.

Don't just use this book to build a fortune. Use Confident Decision Making to build a better life.

# The 21-Day Plan
# for Confident
# Decision Makers

Now that you've read *The Confident Decision Maker*, you probably have all the answers you need to change the way you make decisions. However, you still might not be ready to apply what you've learned to your daily life. I've given you a lot of information, but without a little practice, you could very easily forget what you have just read.

That's why I've created this *21-Day Plan* that will help to flex your thinking muscles and exercise your decision-making abilities. All you need is some paper and a pen. Then, every day, try to tackle a new page of this plan. At the end of three weeks, you will return to the first day and compare what you have learned with what you already knew. My hope is that you will see a change not just in the decisions you have made, but also in the way you think about making decisions. Remember, decision making is a process, and the more you practice changing the method you use to make decisions, the less you will worry about making the right decisions.

After you have finished the 21-Day Plan, hold on to your notes. Then, a month later, take out these exercises and redo the plan once more. Remember, these are exercises, and the more you use them, the stronger your decision-making ability becomes. You will know when you have mastered these techniques by seeing the positive results of your decisions.

So pick up your pen and get ready to start. And remember, the following techniques to Confident Decision Making won't automatically provide you with all the answers. But you will have gained a systematic approach to tackling your problems, the ones you encounter on a day-to-day basis. Mastering these problems will give you the confidence you need to handle the larger issues in your life.

## DAY ONE

To begin, I want you to think of some decision that you have faced lately. It might be a problem that occurs daily or it might be a decision you've put off for a while.

- Grab a piece of paper and a pen and write down the decision you've been thinking of.

- Write down the steps you would normally take to make this decision. Would you ask for advice? Would you decide on the spur of the moment? Would you make a list of choices? Try to break down this process into as many stages as you can.

## DAY TWO

Many times personality is an important function in the decision-making process.

- Choose four adjectives from the following list that you think best describe your personality. Write them down.

Assertive, Passive, Introvert, Extrovert, Amiable, Analytical, Pragmatic, Impatient, Factual, Detail-oriented, Social, Emotional, Unemotional, Slow, Quick, People-oriented

- Take a look again at the decision-making process you recorded yesterday. Which of the adjectives you've just chosen play an important part in the way you make decisions? Study those adjectives.

- Choose four adjectives that are the opposite of the four adjectives you've chosen to describe yourself. Now apply those to your decision-making process and notice the changes. How might your decision have been different?

## DAY THREE

Every decision comes with built-in clues about how it should be handled. That is, every decision can be slotted into a specific category, and each category has its own set of decision-making techniques.

- Think of a simple decision that you make daily, such as whether you're willing to meet with a salesperson who calls to try to make an appointment. This type of decision would fall under your *parameters category*. How many minutes does it take you to make this decision? If the answer is more than a few, you have not established for yourself the minimum criteria needed to help you make this decision.

- Choose one simple daily decision you make that takes

longer than a few minutes to resolve. Now write down exactly what determines this decision; in the case of the salesperson, it may be if they're offering an opportunity or a solution to a problem. The next time you're faced with this decision, see if you are able to answer it more quickly now that you have defined your criteria. Practice this technique with a new decision daily, until you have exhausted the number of simple decisions with which you are faced in your life.

## DAY FOUR

Remember when you were a kid? When you did something wrong, your parents would punish you. And your parents probably tried to make the punishment fit the crime. Pulling your sibling's hair might mean no television for an hour, or when you stayed out too late, perhaps you were forced to spend a weekend indoors. How did you know what punishment to expect? Generally, a spoken or unspoken *policy* was instituted in your family.

- Many times decisions that are more complex require you to examine existing policy. Naturally, these decisions would fall under the *policy category*. Think of three moral dilemmas you have faced in the last week—dilemmas such as whether or not to take on a new client for a service your company never before has provided.

- Next to each dilemma write a *P* for policy or an *NP* for no policy to indicate whether each problem is covered by existing company policy. For every *NP*, think about whether you should institute a new policy. This might be something to discuss with others in your company.

## DAY FIVE

Many times we are faced with a problem, and because of the time involved, we are forced to make a decision in a hurry. Usually, however, that means we are lacking one of the most important ingredients necessary for all decision making: information. It is only after you've gathered all the information you need to make a decision that you can begin to put all the pieces of the puzzle together. I call this information-gathering process *Blueprinting*.

- Think of a decision that requires you to choose between two options. This might be a situation that you've only recently encountered, one to which you haven't given much thought. Based on your gut instinct, choose which answer you think is the most logical choice.

- Now research and list five things you have found out about this problem that you didn't know before. Make sure that all your factual information is fully relevant, not extraneous. Take a look again at your two choices. Would your gut instinct point you to the same conclusion as before? If it did, congratulations, you probably have what I call a "golden gut," or maybe you're just lucky. Either way, remember that by fully *Blueprinting* a problem before deciding about it, chances are your decision will be a better one.

## DAY SIX

The best decision often comes from daydreaming, because it means you're using your imagination. Many times a problem will not have a logical or rational answer, or even any answer. In these cases, it's important to practice using "right brain" thinking, that is, using the creative part of your brain.

- Think of something you want, but for which you're afraid to ask. Possibly a raise, job promotion, or perhaps new responsibilities.

- Now try using your imagination to see what would happen if you did the opposite of the obvious thing to do. What if you didn't ask for it? What if you didn't try to persuade others to see things your way? What if you tried to convince them not to see things your way? How might things be different? By imagining the opposite of a situation, sometimes you are able to understand it more clearly or come up with a better alternative.

- Take that same situation and pretend you're a child. How would you have asked for what you wanted? Would you have been less afraid to say a few things? More direct in your statements? Would your childlike imagination have allowed you to come up with new alternatives, stronger empathy, more resilience? Sometimes, when we look at something with childlike innocence, we can cut through the clutter and get to the heart of a problem.

## DAY SEVEN

Sometimes using your imagination helps you generate ideas and information about a decision you are trying to make. Other times, decisions require logical decision-making techniques.

The *report-card method* works for a decision that involves two likely possibilities, such as choosing between two suppliers for a company project. Think of a problem that requires you to choose between two comparable alternatives.

- First, list the ten most important criteria you have in making this decision.

- Next to this list, make two columns, one for the first vendor and one for the second. Then, using a rating scale from 1 to 10, make a numerical evaluation of how well each supplier fulfills each item on your list of criteria.

- Now total both columns separately, and compare the two numbers to determine your answer.

## DAY EIGHT

*Handicapping* is a more complicated method for decision making. It is used for multiple-choice options, such as choosing to which city you should relocate. Pick a decision that requires you to choose between three or more options. For our purposes, this might have been a decision you've already made.

- Make a list of the ten most important factors that will influence your decision.

- Rate each factor in terms of its importance, on a scale from 1 to 10.

- In the next column, write one of the choices you have. For example, let's say you're relocating to New York. Then, going down your list of factors, rate how well New York meets each criteria.

- Finally, in the last column, multiply your two columns of numbers. The total of this column is the one at which you should look. Do this for your other two choices and compare your total results.

## DAY NINE

What do you do when faced with a decision that has an unpredictable outcome? Plant a tree—a decision tree, that is. Those life-determining situations such as choosing between three different career paths often fall under this category. Decision trees are diagrammed like family trees, with each branch sprouting several smaller branches.

- Think of a decision in your life that forces you to choose between three unpredictable options. Again, this can be something that already occurred, or something with which you're faced. Form three circles, one spaced under another, and write your choices in the circles. Refer to the following decision-tree chart.

- Next to each circle, draw three smaller circles and connect them to the larger circle with lines. Then, next to the three smaller circles, draw three large circles, spaced apart as you did the first time, and connect these to the smaller circles with a line. You can see how one choice spawns three other choices. The small circles in the middle are to be used to calculate a percentage based on the likelihood of each choice happening.

    *For example, let's say you have to choose between: traveling overseas for a year, taking a position as a marketing director for a hospital, or presiding over the family busi-*

*ness. Each circle would list one of these choices. Then, next to the first choice, you might list learning a foreign language, broadening your life experience, opening up job possibilities overseas, as the three opportunities that might occur from this choice. In the small circles, you might put 60 percent for language, 80 percent for life experience, and 30 percent for job opportunities. Then you would do the same for the other two choices that start your tree.*

- If they're needed, you can continue to add branches from the tree you've created, until you've exhausted your possibilities. When you are through, you will have created a logical estimate of the outcome of your choices. (For a more in-depth description of decision trees, see pages 160–172.)

## DAY TEN

So far, you have learned creative visualization, Blueprinting, the report-card method, Handicapping, and decision trees. But how do you know which technique to use when? Below are some different kinds of problems that require decisions. Next to each scenario, write the steps you would take to help you make a decision. Some decisions may require a combination of techniques. When you are done, go back over the previous exercises to check your answers. For those techniques that were not correct, or that you forgot, you might want to review them a few more times.

- Your company needs to add a computer in its public-relations area, but you don't want to spend much money. Your managers have finally narrowed the list down to an

## DECISION TREE

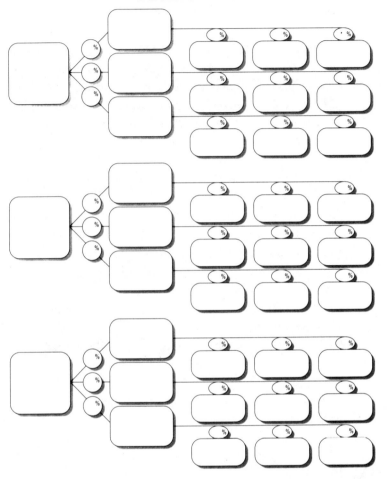

IBM clone or a good deal on a used Macintosh. What technique would you use to make the final choice?

- A friend calls you on the phone and has a hot stock-market tip to share with you. He persuades you to invest in some stocks that are rumored to sell at a high rate and warns you to act fast. You pick up the phone and call your broker, who insists you are making a mistake. Where do you go from here?

- As the development director for a small telemarketing firm, you've managed to secure two new accounts. You have four hungry account executives who all complain they don't have enough work to keep them busy. Two of the four have six years' telemarketing experience. One of the four, who has only two years' experience, has worked for several months in the same industry as one of your new accounts. The other account, which might be a more complicated project, has a marketing manager who you know has a special bias for working with college graduates. While you have several college graduates on staff, the only one who isn't busy is a recent graduate who still has to undergo training. How would you decide to whom you should give the accounts?

## DAY ELEVEN

Sometimes, instead of trying to make a decision on our own, we need the input of a group. *Huddling* is the term I use to describe what happens when you consult with others about your decisions.

- Try to think of an idea you presented at a meeting recently that was not accepted. Did you discuss this idea with anyone else before you went to the meeting? Did you discuss it with anyone after the meeting, to see what went wrong?

- If you didn't discuss the idea with anyone, choose two logical people in your field who might have information on this subject. Ask to meet with them in private and write down the feedback they give you concerning your idea. If you have already discussed your idea with someone, see if you can recall what you were told.

- Take the information you have received about your idea and try to generate more options for the idea. Sometimes huddling allows you to gather more pertinent information and reject your own erroneous information.

- Did you find that the second time you explained your idea, you were able to describe it more clearly? Huddling can also serve to help you sharpen your ideas, making them as concise and understandable as possible.

## DAY TWELVE

When you're faced with a fairly complicated decision, but you've run out of ideas, you might try an analogy huddle. While these huddles are more fun to practice with others, if you can't find anyone with whom to practice, try them on your own. They will help get some of your thinking unstuck. Use the same idea with which you worked on Day 11 and see if these analogies give you some fresh ideas.

- A *direct analogy* is an analogy that compares one idea directly with another. For example, someone could say,

"This infomercial should be as entertaining as a clown on stilts." This might remind you of a circus master you once saw who might make a perfect announcer. See if you or someone in your huddle can come up with a good direct analogy.

- A *personal analogy* allows you to use something from your personal experience. Using the infomercial example, you or someone else might say, "The actor who plays the grandmother should be as warm and old-fashioned as my grandmother in Idaho who grew up on a farm." This might remind you of an actual farm in Idaho that would be perfect for the shoot. Now try a personal analogy.

- If you're using a *fantasy analogy,* you might say something a little far out, such as, "The shot of the car driving down the highway should make people think of flying into a distant galaxy." This might trigger an idea of using an overhead shot taken by helicopter, instead of the camera that might normally follow the car in the back of a van. Brainstorm a fantasy analogy.

- Finally, a *symbolic analogy*, such as, "The response from this project ought to make our competition see red." This might trigger an idea for the literal use of that color, when working on the accompanying print campaign. See if you can determine a symbolic analogy.

## DAY THIRTEEN

One more method of Huddling that might be useful when you need to generate more options is Solo Huddling. With Solo Huddling, you can get fresh ideas without relying on the help of others. Try the following exercises with a decision that has no obvious solution.

- List the characteristics of your problem across the top of the page. Under each characteristic, list an alternative. When you have listed alternatives for each characteristic, begin matching up the alternatives from one column with alternatives from another column. Each time you create a new pairing, see what creative ideas this triggers for you. The method may produce hundreds of options.

- Idea clustering consists of writing down your problem and drawing a circle around it. Every time you think of a possible solution, draw a line from the circle, write down the solution, and draw another circle around your solution. If your solution triggers another idea, draw a line from the solution and continue the process. Sometimes seeing your ideas diagrammed in front of you triggers more creative connections.

- Sometimes the best way to stop set thinking about problems is to use random stimuli. Using a dictionary, for example, to offer you new words at random, might trigger different connections and ideas. Or try looking up a few words in a thesaurus. Sometimes if you express a problem using a different vocabulary, you might see a solution more clearly. See if you can come up with any other ways to gain a fresh view of your situation.

## DAY FOURTEEN

When we go from making a decision on our own to making a decision with the input of others, we usually benefit, but it can result in Huddle Rot. Similarly, making a decision on our own can either be more efficient or a mistake. Examine the pitfalls of making solo decisions and of Huddling.

## What's Wrong with Solo Decisions:

You might get too personally committed to your decision and not be able to see your mistakes.

You might discourage people from challenging you.

If you are paranoid about leaks and don't ask for enough advice, you might make the wrong decision.

If you feel omnipotent about your decision making, your self-confidence could cause you to wander astray.

## What's Wrong with Huddles:

Illusions of unanimity; huddles have a tendency to compromise and stop individuals from speaking up.

Members of huddles rally around the opinions of their leader, particularly when the leader is their boss.

The quality of decisions is raised or lowered by the qualifications of the group.

• Look back to the exercise you completed on Day 11. How did Huddling affect the decision you were trying to make? Did you experience any of the Huddle Rot described above? Watch out for the problems that are common in huddles.

- Think back on a solo decision you made that didn't turn out well. Chances are you fell prey to one of the problems with solo decisions mentioned above. For each list, write down the opposite statement of each pitfall and study it. Then, the next time you make a decision on your own, or with a huddle, consult this list before determining your ultimate decision.

## DAY FIFTEEN

We've talked so much about what to do when making decisions, it's time to concentrate on what not to do. When making decisions, acting too quickly can be an obstacle to confident decision making.

- Think of a decision where timing is a factor. This might be a decision involving limited offers, stock-market deals, or anything else where the outcome could produce a change for the better or for the worse. Taking no longer than three minutes, write down what you feel would be the best decision to make, based on the information as you see it.

- Now go back over your decision. Often when we make decisions under time constraints, they aren't good decisions. It's important that you eliminate or ignore time constraints forced on you. It's also important to make a decision only when you're calm and relaxed. Try to get as much information as possible about a decision, ask for expert opinions, and make sure you're not so enthusiastic about the expected result that you can't remain objective.

• After you have invested more time following the above advice, try making a new decision about the same problem. Is there a difference between this decision and your old one? When you run across decisions involving limited time factors, you might want to remember a few of these techniques.

## DAY SIXTEEN

Another obstacle in confident decision making is acting too slowly. What would happen if you knocked over a glass full of wine and let it sit there, without wiping it up? The next day, the liquid might have hardened or become sticky. Maybe in a couple of days it might have stained the counter so badly that when you do wipe it up, it will leave a mark. Sometimes when we are faced with a problem, we take so long to make up our minds that it can create more trouble than when we started. Acting too slowly is another barrier to good decision making.

• Below are six reasons we avoid acting on a decision within a feasible time period. With which reasons can you identify most? Write them down on a separate piece of paper.

Defensive avoidance or a tendency to avoid problems

A "Don't fix it unless it's broke" attitude that stops you from taking new risks

An obsession with Huddling that stops you from reaching a final consensus

Gathering too much information so that you delay even more

Wasting time trying to predict the future

Fear of failure without a realistic look at the worst that might happen

- Now think of a decision you have been putting off. Have you been using some of these reasons to keep yourself from finding an answer? Give yourself until the end of the day to come up with the best decision possible. When it comes time, examine the outcome of your decision. Did you find more problems caused by the decision you made, or was making the decision your biggest problem?

- Give yourself a deadline every time you find you are stuck making a decision. If you can't make a decision within the deadline you've established, take out the piece of paper on which you wrote down some of these six reasons and review them. Then try making your decision again.

## DAY SEVENTEEN

Take the following quiz:

1. I make decisions based on what I see, not what I feel.                                          ___T ___F

2. It's better to make a decision quickly, without waiting to find out how others feel about it.     ___T ___F

3. I agree with the motto "Strike while the iron's hot."      ___T ___F

4. I generally rely on my instinct to understand a problem.      ___T ___F

5. I become enthusiastic about ideas quickly.      ___T ___F

6. I like action and tend to lose interest quickly if something isn't moving along at a good pace.      ___T ___F

7. When making decisions, I prefer to trust my feelings, even when they don't agree with the facts.      ___T ___F

8. I like to take other people's feelings into consideration before making a decision.      ___T ___F

9. I don't like to rock the boat.      ___T ___F

10. Feelings are not important in decision making, facts are what matter most.      ___T ___F

11. It's important to analyze everything very carefully before rushing into any conclusions.      ___T ___F

12. I prefer not to take unnecessary risks.      ___T ___F

Now match your answers to the personality type described below.

*If you answered mostly "True" for questions 1–3*, then you might best be described as a Bull. Bulls tend to rely on conscious thought rather than instinct. They prefer to go by what they see, rather than how they are feeling. They are very action-oriented.

*If you answered mostly "True" for questions 4–6*, then you might best be described as an Eagle. Eagles have a strong instinct and like to follow it. They also tend to be action-oriented but have terrible follow-through.

*If you answered mostly "True" for questions 7–9*, then you might best be described as a Bee. Bees like to make decisions based on preconceived beliefs. They are comfortable with having a consensus and very slow to act.

*If you answered mostly "True" for questions 10–12*, then you might best be described as a Bloodhound. Bloodhounds like to rely almost totally on facts. They would rather analyze something forever than come up with a decision about it.

## DAY EIGHTEEN

Now that you have determined your decision-making style, it is important to become more attuned to the decision-making styles of others. Familiarity with all these styles will help you to apply them in situations where persuasiveness and strategy play an important role. See if you can match the following profiles to their personality styles.

- Jack is late for the sales meeting. When he gets there, it takes him a while to set up his notes. He pulls out a calculator, and forms three piles of information. From where you stand, a couple of seats away, you can tell he has numerous charts from which to draw facts and figures for the meeting. Somehow you are going to have to convince him that the latest report from your assistant shows his approach is all wrong. What type of decision-making style might Jack use, and how will you best convince him?

- At the same meeting, Sara arrives a little late. She is just in time to hear the tail end of your presentation, and boy, is she excited. She seems to think you've hit the exact solution for the problems your department has been having. She volunteers right away to help you implement your plan. What type of style does Sara have, and what should you watch out for when accepting her help?

- Barbara has listened to all the facts presented by both you and Jack. She poses questions to both of you, and it seems as though she could go either way. She is very interested in Sara's reaction and the feelings of a few others at the meeting, but when you ask for a final vote, she won't make a commitment. What's the best way to handle her uncertainty, and how would you characterize her style?

- Tom is ready to leave, even before the vote is cast. He has everything he needs to know and is convinced his decision is the right one. Unfortunately, it's the wrong one for you. You keep trying to gently guide him back to some of the points you've made while at the same time trying to figure out his objections. He is getting extremely impatient, however, and you've very nearly lost him. What's the best way to bring this type of decision maker around to your point of view?

## DAY NINETEEN

Because of their characteristics, certain styles complement each other, while other styles clash. While Bulls and Bloodhounds tend to be more logical in their decision-making approaches, Bees and Eagles would rather rely on intuitive and creative thought. So, Bulls and Bees conflict, as do Bloodhounds and Eagles.

- Is your decision-making style intuitive and creative or logical and fact-oriented? Review a decision you have already made today. What would happen if you used the opposite decision-making technique that you used to reach this decision? For example, if you found yourself brainstorming earlier today, next time try the report-card method, and vice versa. The more you stretch your decision-making ability, the more flexible you will become in making decisions. Soon you will be able to match your decision-making techniques to the type of decision with which you are working, not the decision-making style with which you are most comfortable.

- Go back to Day 2 and notice the adjectives you used to describe your personality. How well do these adjectives correlate to your decision-making style? If your style and personality are fairly consistent, you'll probably find that Bulls tend to be Pragmatic, Eagles are Extroverts, bloodhounds are Analytical, and Bees are Amiable. Write down the names of three acquaintances and their personality styles. Next see if their decision-making styles correspond accordingly.

## DAY TWENTY

While you may not be able to tell Confident Decision Makers just by looking at them, there are characteristics common to great decision makers. To see if you possess these traits, answer the following questions.

---

*1. When faced with a situation where I won't know the result, I:*

    a. Panic. I like everything to be in black-and-white.
    b. Shrug and do the best I can with the information I have.

*2. When faced with a decision that might not be a popular one, I:*

    a. Will decide against it. After all, if everyone's saying it's not right, I must be wrong.
    b. Stick to my guns. I don't need other people's approval to make decisions.

*3. When making a decision that will affect a large group of people, and some of them are against the decision, it's more important to:*

    a. Ignore the naysayers and create an illusion of power. People should know not to question your judgment.
    b. Gain the support of everyone in the group before going ahead with a decision.

*4. You've decided to go ahead with a deal, and you've received the approval of company management. The day before the deal goes through, you see a potential snag that might cost the company money. What do you do?*

    a. Continue with the deal and hope for the best; after all you already have everyone's support.

    b. Be prepared to abort, cut your losses, and admit your mistake.

*5. Your marketing report on a new product says the success of the product is guaranteed. However, your staff disagrees. Which information should you consider?*

    a. Stick to the facts. People will always have their opinions.

    b. Listen to both hard and soft input and don't act until you can reach some consensus of the two.

---

    If you've answered "b" to many of the above questions, congratulations, you're well on your way to possessing the traits of a great decision maker. If you've answered "a," review Chapter Twelve and see why your choices might backfire.

## DAY TWENTY-ONE

Turn back to Day 1 and look at the decision that you wrote down. Now look at the steps you took to make your decision. What might you do differently now that you have followed this 21-Day Plan? Answer the questions below:

a. What kind of decision were you trying to make?

b.  Did you blueprint your decision well?

c.  Does it require a creative technique or a logical one?

d.  Is this a decision with a certain outcome, or is the result uncertain?

e.  How many people should be involved in making this decision? Would it benefit from a group huddle?

f.  Are there any barriers that might keep you from making the right decision?

g.  How might your decision-making style affect the decision you make?

h.  Did you take into account the nine personality traits that might help you to make a great decision?

- Compare the decision you make today with the decision you made on Day 1. Was this decision any different from the one you made previously? How do you feel about the decision you are making now?

Confident Decision Making is an attainable goal that simply requires practice. If you continue to use the techniques I have outlined here and throughout this book, you will be on your way to making the right decisions and feeling good about the decisions you make. And remember, there is no magic involved in making good decisions. The magic you create comes from the positive effects of your decisions on your life and on the lives of others.